TREATING ADULT CHILDREN OF ALCOHOLICS:

A DEVELOPMENTAL PERSPECTIVE

STEPHANIE BROWN

Merritt Peralta Institute
Oakland, California

JOHN WILEY & SONS, INC.
New York • Chichester • Brisbane • Toronto
Singapore • Weinheim

This publication is designed to provide accurate and
authoritative information in regard to the subject
matter covered. It is sold with the understanding that
the publisher is not engaged in rendering legal, accounting,
or other professional service. If legal advice or other
expert assistance is required, the services of a competent
professional person should be sought.

ISBN 0-471-85300-3 (cloth)
ISBN 0-471-15559-4 (paper)

Printed in the United States of America

10 9 8 7 6 5 4 3 2 1

For Makenzie, Randy, and Stephanie
The Next Generation

Preface

This is a book about adult children of alcoholics. It is a book about theory and practice, written primarily for clinicians, for all professionals who treat children of alcoholics (COAs) and adult children of alcoholics (ACAs) in counseling or psychotherapy. It is a book for other professionals—primary care physicians, pediatricians, nurses, educators, and employers—who are constantly in close contact with COAs and ACAs but may not know it or may not know what to do about it if they do. Importantly, this is also a book for these same professionals at a more personal level: many are themselves adult children of alcoholics.

This book is first and foremost about theory and practice for therapists. The theory is an integrated one, combining knowledge about alcoholism, family environment, and systems theory with child development and cognitive and dynamic theories. Much of this theory development has application for professionals other than therapists.

Is this a book for the nonprofessional, the interested reader, the adult children of alcoholics, or those individuals deeply affected by the alcoholism of another? Yes. The clinical examples, the "voices" of the adult children of alcoholics that fill this book to illustrate theory development, transcend professional language and concept and thus speak clearly to all.

While this book will be useful for both professional and lay audiences, guidelines are necessary at the outset to make the most of this material. Ironically, the only "how to" in this book is how to read it.

GUIDELINES

First, the material is complex. The reader follows through a process of theory development that requires the individual to

simultaneously hold several major theoretical frames at the
same time and to integrate multiple variables within these
frames. Stressed repeatedly are the critical importance of integrating a systems, environmental view with theories of individual development. The relationship is by no means simple.

Repetition is used to manage the complexity and to integrate
the multiplicity of variables throughout the text. Core theories
and major themes are repeated many times to integrate a new
variable or expand the theory after integrating new material. A
particular variable, such as denial, may be important across do-
mains and thus reappears as a major factor. Denial is central to
understanding the environment (Chapters 1, 2 and 3), it is central
to defensive adjustment (Chapter 4), and it is central to attachment and identity formation (Chapters 5 and 6).

The reader might also think of the task of theory development
as one of holding simultaneously and integrating macro and micro
points of view—the system, the individuals interacting within the
system, the individual alone, and the integration of both.

It is my hope to provide in this book a framework for understanding the ACA as an individual. I hope to add to a well-
established descriptive base, building a broad and complex
theory of alcohol as the central organizing principle, governing
family and individual development.

The theory and the wide range of clinical examples are not
inclusive nor exhaustive. Rather, they are a frame from which to
better comprehend differences and tailor treatment accordingly.
Which aspects of this theory best fit this patient?

The children of alcoholics are not all the same. They are as
varied in their experiences and their personal development as
their numbers. For example, the level of denial varies greatly in
alcoholic homes and affects development accordingly. Variance
in the child's age at onset, one alcoholic parent or two, siblings,
how many, the presence or absence of a stable adult—perhaps a
reliable nonalcoholic parent, a savvy grandparent, neighbor or
teacher who understood reality and the child knew it. Or there
was no one. There are many intervening variables that have a
profound impact and it is exceedingly important to grasp what
they are for *this* particular individual.

In this book, I hope to provide a theoretical link between
the descriptive and the dynamic—the critical significance of
combining a focus on shared experience and similarities with a

thorough understanding of individual differences—familial and developmental. The process of recovery includes both.

In an earlier book (Brown, 1985), I developed a theory of alcoholism that integrates behavioral, cognitive, and dynamic modalities of psychotherapy and combines AA, with its emphasis on support, identification, and shared experiences, with more traditional dynamic psychotherapy. I will be urging the same expanded framework in working with ACAs and endorsing the use of AA, Al-Anon for ACAs, Alateen, and Al-Atot—the autonomous arms of AA for families of alcoholics—and the non-affiliated ACA 12-step support groups.

I will be referring to the dynamic model of alcoholism and various aspects of that theory within the context of the present book and will review it in Chapter 7 in relation to the process of recovery for ACAs. It will be helpful if the reader is familiar with the first text, but not essential.

I also assume that the reader is familiar with the nature of the 12-step self-help programs, particularly Alcoholics Anonymous (AA) and Al-Anon. I propose the same triadic therapeutic partnership in working with ACAs that I outlined for the alcoholic, even though we do not yet have a history of individuals participating in Al-Anon for ACAs and concurrent psychotherapy to examine the relationship in depth. That work lies ahead. We do have 10 years of clinical history however on which the current work is built.

HISTORY OF THEORY AND CLINICAL DEVELOPMENT

The integrated theory developed in this book has emerged over the course of more than 15 years of research and clinical work with children of alcoholics, primarily adolescents and adults. I (Brown, 1974) worked with teenage daughters of male alcoholics (one group with sober fathers and another with drinking fathers) and a control group with no parental alcoholism to determine whether there were differences in personality development. The subjects were members of Alateen groups in the San Francisco Bay Area. This self-help group had recognized the difficulties children face and the need for an organization designed to meet their primary needs, not second to those of the alcoholic.

In 1978 we started our first group for adult children of alcoholics at the Stanford Alcohol Clinic (now the Stanford Alcohol and Drug Treatment Center), recognizing that specialized services, independent of the alcoholic, were also necessary for adults. I had seen many alcoholics in treatment who were also the children of alcoholics but they had no forum to examine the latter experience though they desperately needed to do so.

We started our treatment program in a climate of professional reluctance and even outright denial. What would it mean for professionals to label children of alcoholics as a separate population? To acknowledge that children are adversely, even profoundly, affected by parental behavior and beliefs as they relate to alcohol? And what would it say about our current theory and practice?

Once accepted and developed by the media, the idea has found wide acceptance within the alcohol and broader chemical dependency fields. The traditional mental health field was slower to accept the idea of children of alcoholics as a separate treatment population although many practitioners responded to this new information with a sense of relief and excitement, similar to their patients. As one therapist recently stated: "Things make so much more sense when you label parental alcoholism as a critical factor in a child's development."

Ten years ago the idea was still novel or even radical. It took eight months to form a first group of four members—all women. Within a short time, this group was full (8) and we added more groups. We rarely were without a waiting list and regularly saw several hundred ACA patients a month in group and individual therapy.

Following a research and clinical practice established in working with alcoholic patients (Yalom, Brown, & Bloch, 1975), I prepare a detailed written summary of every group meeting. The summary is a single spaced, three- to four-page content and process account of each meeting from the therapist's point of view. Dictated after the therapy group, it is then mailed to group members. The therapeutic benefits of the summary are many (Yalom et al., 1975) as patients overwhelmingly find it useful. It is invaluable as a therapeutic record and research tool as well. We have the benefit of 10 years of long-term group work, hundreds of detailed clinical summaries, following not only the process and progress of the groups over time, but individuals as well. It is through careful content and process evaluation of the summaries and work with individuals that the key theories in this book were developed.

The long-term framework is particularly important to theory development and to the kind of clinical practice that follows. A long-term framework allows the therapist to integrate an environmental focus with developmental theory and to trace over time the major themes related to both and their impact on the course of treatment. Throughout this book, I will use clinical examples of individuals in long-term individual and group psychotherapy, self-identified as adult children of alcoholics, to illustrate theory development and practice and to make the abstract more concrete. In essence, how does what we hear and see relate to theory? And practice?

Following theory development, the focus is on the clinical material, outlining major themes and issues that emerge and characterize the long-term ACA group in the process of recovery. Coming full circle, it is these very themes and issues that formed the base for the theory development that comes first.

Acknowledgments

During the time I was writing this book, I frequently found myself thinking about my acknowledgments: who to thank and how to thank in a way that would really communicate the depth of my gratitude. It is clear to me now that thinking about the acknowledgments so often functioned as a beacon, a sign of hope, and a "transitional object"—still in my imagination, but very real—something I could hold onto to get me through what was often a difficult and painful task. On several occasions, as I sought refuge in imagining the acknowledgments, I went to other books to see if authors ever said what a struggle it had been to write the work. Nobody said it quite like I felt it.

Now finished, it seems to me that my deep gratitude to others would ring hollow if I did not say directly that it was extremely difficult for me to write this book; that I have shared many of the experiences reported by others within these chapters; and that I have been greatly helped by my patients throughout the years of my work as a therapist. While writing this book, I sometimes felt as if I were but a week ahead of my patients in certain struggles and there were other occasions when I knew for sure that I was more than a week behind. To all my "patients" through the years, I give my thanks.

Along the same line, I also thank Dr. William Fry who has helped me rewrite my "story." I am grateful to him for many years of consultation with me and others at the Stanford Alcohol and Drug Treatment Center.

Many individuals, groups, and organizations have been tremendously supportive of me, my ideas, and my work in the field of alcoholism. This book was supported directly through generous gifts from the Christian deGuigne Foundation and Rudolph Driscoll. Quite simply, I could not have written it without their help. My deepest gratitude and appreciation to both.

Thanks also to the Institute for Research on Women and Gender at Stanford for the honor of working on this project as an Affiliated Scholar.

Thomas and Katherine Pike, mentors and friends, supported the birth and growth of the alcohol clinic at Stanford and have provided solid and certain personal support to me. I remain deeply indebted and grateful to both.

Thanks also to the J.M. Foundation for past support of the clinic's training efforts, Mary Pike, Fluor Foundation, the Kaiser Family Foundation, the Exxon Education Foundation, and National Institute of Alcohol Abuse and Alcoholism. Thanks to the many individuals who provided consultation by serving on the Stanford Alcohol Clinic's Advisory Board in the early years of the clinic's development. And deep gratitude to Anne Miner and Carole Price for a "mission impossible."

Many individuals have shared in the development of theory and practice of adult children of alcoholics. We have literally "grown up" together as the field moves through its own infancy and developmental stages.

Dr. Tim Cermak and I started our first long-term therapy group for ACAs in the fall of 1978. We both knew it was a good idea, that there were adults who grew up in an alcoholic family who needed psychotherapeutic help. We had an inkling of what was ahead, but no idea we were part of a rising tide which would reach flood proportions virtually overnight.

Dr. Claudia Black was also wading into the water at the same time. I am deeply grateful for her pioneering spirit, clear message, and her friendship.

Many others were becoming interested in the area at the same time around the country. With a generous, cooperative spirit and a wish not to be a voice alone, these individuals formed the National Association for Children of Alcoholics in 1982. That organization, along with the Children of Alcoholics Foundation in New York, has legitimized and served the needs of millions of children of alcoholics.

I was enriched by colleagues and friends in the Stanford program. Dr. Susan Beletsis and Dr. Vicky Johnson were important collaborators in clinical theory development and research design. Dr. Robert Matano and Dr. Beth Gorney were tremendously supportive as were all the trainees.

The development of our long-term treatment program for ACAs was aided by community professionals who provided supervision and consultation to trainees and staff. Thanks especially to

Joan Fisch and Drs. John Beletsis, Richard Corelli, Robert Harris, Reggie Kriss, Alan Sherman, Alan Sklar, and William Weber.

Special, deep thanks, personal and professional, to my husband, Dr. Robert Harris. It was a marathon discussion with him that opened up the notion of "defensive maneuvers" which provided a critical missing link in my theoretical formulations.

Many thanks to my friends, Chris McDonald and Rudy Driscoll, and to my good friends and colleagues at O'Connor Hospital in Campbell, California and Kids Are Special in San Jose for personally and professionally enriching consultative affiliations. Special thanks to my new colleagues at Merritt Peralta Institute for a warm welcome and a stimulating research environment.

Deep thanks to my secretaries for their commitment, interest and never-ending support—Bea Mitchell for her excellent typing and Diana Kennedy for running things so well on so many fronts. Thanks to Jim Mahood for a strong friendship established many years ago in my early writing and to Butch Colyear, for his professional visual rendering of the dynamic model of alcoholism in my first book and the family diagrams in this text. Thanks to Larry Lovaglia, Joyce Schmid, and Dr. Marshall Kane for reading the manuscript in draft form. And thanks to Katy Butler for her enormously helpful editorial critique of the working draft.

For their support throughout the preparation and production of this book, I thank my editor Herb Reich and his assistant, Judith Overton.

Finally, my deepest thanks to my mother, my husband Bob, and our daughter Makenzie for valuing this project and my work as much as I do.

S.B.

Contents

Attachment.

TREATING ADULT CHILDREN OF ALCOHOLICS

Introduction

"I was born and raised in the family of alcohol. And that's what my life has been about."

The *family of alcohol*—that is what this book is about: specifically, children and adult children who have grown up in a family with one or two alcoholic parents.

Much has been written about these more than 28 million individuals since they finally gained legitimacy as a "group" in the late 1970s and 1980s. Early research focused on genetic transmission and psychopathology. More recent studies have explored family dynamics, with the recognition that all members of the family suffer consequences as a result of living with an alcoholic parent.

Much of the emphasis has been descriptive: What is it like in such a family? How do family members cope? What adaptations and adjustments do children make in order to survive? We are beginning to know the painful realities of what it really was and is like for countless children—the arbitrary, unpredictable, inconsistent environment, the sudden shifts in behavior and meaning, the arguments, violence, incest, the unavailability of parents as parents; the constant tone of terror, parents out of control.

The early work of description focused heavily on establishing similarities: What experiences did these children share in their families and what do they share now as adults? The focus on establishing a common portrait has been beneficial in building the legitimacy of the children of alcoholics as a separate population with specialized treatment needs. It also has been helpful politically to emphasize needs of children of alcoholics as a special interest group.

1

The focus on similarities is a vital first step in the process of recovery. Adult children of alcoholics (ACA) are no longer alone. The sharing of experiences and the acquisition of the label ACA provide a powerful base from which treatment and recovery begin.

This focus on description, shared experience, and problems in common is reflected in an emphasis on classification and categorization—roles, styles, patterns of behavior that describe a particular defensive adjustment or coping style.

The focus on description and classification established the legitimacy of the alcoholic family as a traumatic environment. The reality of parental alcoholism and the consequences of the family's accommodations and adaptations to it constitute for most a chronically stressful, chaotic, and emotionally disturbing environment. The impact of living in such an environment contributes to a first level of consequence or pathology emerging in childhood or at critical periods in adult development.

Individuals who have grown up in the traumatic environment of parental alcoholism often exhibit the signs of post-traumatic stress disorder, anxiety disorder, and depression. These problems stem from the reality of the traumatic environment—living with uncertain, unpredictable, inconsistent, and incompetent parents—and from a failure of the major defensive strategies, particularly in adulthood.

Thus we have a legitimate treatment population described in detail as defensively oriented and suffering from the long-range consequences of living with chronic trauma. This is a critically important base.

There is a tendency to stop with description, to assume that recognition of common patterns—those that established the group's legitimacy—is the same thing as effective treatment. This assumption misses entirely an indepth understanding of how the shared experiences affect children beyond the defensive level. How are basic developmental tasks affected? What happens in the process of attachment between a child and a chronic alcoholic mother? Father? What is the impact of the family's emphasis on denial? How is cognitive development affected? Social and affective development? And most important, how can we make use of our knowledge of similarities as a base and build a theory that will begin to include important individual differences?

This book is a first move in that direction. There is a push to establish a diagnostic category for the children of alcoholics based on the traumatic environment and the commonalities of the codependent response (Cermak, 1984, 1986). While beneficial in establishing legitimacy, improving diagnosis and promoting greater awareness, such a category may also prove restrictive by ultimately muting significant differences. The tendency is then to lump together all children of alcoholics into one diagnostic category and make them fit, ignoring differences that might determine a more individualized therapeutic approach. After the initial process of identification based on shared experiences has begun, the more individualized approach is absolutely necessary.

This view also results in expectations by patients and therapists alike that significant deep changes in behavior, affect, and interpersonal relationships automatically follow increased awareness. There is great disappointment when this does not occur.

We need to build a theory that incorporates a second level: assessment of the nature and quality of relationships within the family and the opportunities for accomplishing the normal tasks of individual intrapsychic and interpersonal development that existed within the context of the traumatic environment. There are many significant differences between individual ACAs on this dimension. It may also be this dimension which will ultimately provide the key to understanding the very different degrees and kinds of adjustment and pathology that ACAs, within and between families, demonstrate.

We need a much more sophisticated theory, one that goes beyond the break in denial; beyond establishing legitimacy. We need a theory that starts with the break in denial about parental alcoholism instead of ending with it. It is this break in denial which begins a process of recovery that will involve a major uncovering, indepth reconstruction of one's life and core identity and an equally indepth process of construction of a new identity based on acknowledgement of having grown up with an alcoholic parent.

In this book, the base of shared experience—what it was like in the home with an alcoholic parent(s) (an environmental and systems point of view)—is linked with developmental theory. How are the major tasks of normal development affected or impaired by living with an alcoholic parent? What are the consequences for young children? For adults? What is the process of recovery? Treatment? How can we merge the base of shared experience with the recognition of critical individual differences in order to tailor treatment more effectively? This is a diverse approach, looking at the children of alcoholics from several traditional theoretical points of view to establish an integrated developmental framework.

The integrated model proposed is predominantly cognitive and developmental, bound together by a core thread of alcohol as the central organizing principle in the family. As alcoholism progresses, the alcoholic and the family develop a thinking disorder (Brown, 1985) that explains increasing drinking and denies it at the same time. This disorder includes rationalization and denial, primitive cognitive defense mechanisms, and a distorted logic that reverses cause and effect ("I drink because I have problems" rather than "The problems are the result of my drinking.") and consistently distorts reality.

The contradiction that fuses alcohol as the central organizing principle in the family and yet denies that reality forms the core for understanding childhood and adult development: the strong emphasis on defensive adaptation within the family, developmental difficulties that result, and the process of recovery that begins with the break in denial.

Thus alcohol is also the central organizing principle of this book. An integrated theory merges a family-environmental point of view (with a central focus on alcohol) with theories of child development. This merger produces a core theory: the reality of parental alcoholism and its denial (the organizing principle) structures the development of the child in the family system both intrapsychically and interpersonally.

I have been very much influenced in theory development by the current trend toward integrating cognitive and dynamic models of development. Central to my thinking is an integration of the work of cognitive-dynamic theorists Guidano and Liotti (1983), Rosen (1985), and Beck (1985) with the attachment and developmental theories of Bowlby (1980, 1985).

I've also borrowed from the cognitive and social learning theorists (Mahoney, 1977; Bandura, 1985) to emphasize the critical significance of the interaction between the environment, or the system, and the individual, utilizing Mahoney's concept of "reciprocal determinism" and Bandura's theory of "triadic reciprocality." Cognitive and social learning theories are also highly relevant to issues of identity formation, including imitation and identification, both part of modeling.

It is not possible to comprehend the development of children of alcoholics from a single theoretical perspective, but it is possible to develop a model that incorporates knowledge of the family or environment and individual development within that system and the interaction between the two. It is that model of inter-action that is proposed in this book. It is grounded in the follow-ing core theory which is repeated throughout the text:

Attachment—early and ongoing—is based on denial of percep-tion which results in denial of affect which together result in devel-opmental arrests or difficulties. The core beliefs and patterns of behavior formed to sustain attachment and denial within the fam-ily then structure subsequent development of the self including cognitive, affective and social development.

Part One focuses on the environment and, in essence, consti-tutes the first "track." In Chapter 1, the literature is reviewed, outlining the historical development of this newly recognized re-search and treatment population. In Chapter 2, the focus is on the family environment, describing "what it is like" and how the real-ity of parental alcoholism and its denial constitute a traumatic environment. A broad description of the ideal family highlights what goes wrong in the family with an alcoholic parent(s). In Chapter 3, the environmental point of view is extended to examine codependence, the response of an individual to the dominance of another within a pathological system. The systems point of view builds the case that the alcoholic family establishes an equilibrium or homeostasis around the core pathology of parental alcoholism. The system and the individuals within it accommodate to find a point of balance that both denies the presence of alcoholism and insures its maintenance at the same time.

In Chapter 3, the base of knowledge and methodology estab-lished for children of the handicapped is used to outline the multiple variables involved and to shape the limits of the present work.

Part Two examines the impact of parental alcoholism on the individual by integrating the second "track." Chapter 4 outlines the consequences of the traumatic environment, briefly describing the elements of post-traumatic stress syndrome, anxiety disorder, and depression. Chapter 4 also provides the bridge from the envi-ronmental emphasis to the individual, examining the defensive adaptations developed in the service of survival in the alcoholic home. These defensive adjustments characterize the family as a whole and relationships within. The theory builds that the neces-sity for defensive adaptation overrides or significantly colors the tasks of individual development. In this chapter, the major defensive adaptations are outlined using clinical examples to illustrate their defensive and structural functions. In the course of long-term treatment, defensive function appears immediately in the beginning group while the structural function is not challenged or recognized until the advanced level of the group's work. Thus the defensive adaptations which were adaptive for the child, often now constitute the core of the individual's problems in interpersonal relationships and the only sense of self at the same time. The defensive maneuvers developed to cope with the traumatic environment structure the process of recovery, manifested as central themes throughout the course of treatment.

Chapter 5 outlines the impact of parental alcoholism and its denial on attachment, a developmental issue emerging over the course of long-term group treatment. Within the framework of attachment, role reversal is examined and the impact on the child of accommodating to a narcissistic or egocentric parent, including identification with pathological defenses. Clinical material from the group is used to illustrate themes and process that arise in relation to attachment and role reversal.

Chapter 6 examines the impact of parental alcoholism on identity formation, another issue that is present as an underlying core throughout treatment. The significance of denial and the dominance of other defenses are illustrated in relation to developmental disturbances within a cognitive-dynamic theoretical frame.

The focus is on the cognitive theories of Piaget, as interpreted by Greenspan (1979) and more recently Rosen (1985) and Guidano and Liotti (1983), outlining how attachments in an alcoholic family are formed around the denial of alcoholism, with acceptance of whatever family story or beliefs are necessary to maintain it.

The need for attachment and the emphasis on denial lead to disturbances in the development of the child's "personal identity" (Guidano & Liotti, 1983), that is, the core of the self. This book emphasizes the serious developmental problems children and adults encounter at all levels, but especially the cognitive process of identity formation, including the familial transmission of alcoholism from one generation to another.

Alcohol, the organizing principle that links attachment, denial, and identity formation also provides the central focus for understanding severe problems with separation and the establishment of a mature, autonomous, adult identity. Our adult patients from 18 to 70 and above have experienced serious failures at one or more stages of development. All remain emotionally attached to their first families and enter treatment with a variety of problems related to the failure to differentiate and separate.

After developing a framework for understanding developmental difficulties, a model of recovery that is also predominantly cognitive and developmental is outlined. With the break in denial and acquisition of the label ACA, individuals begin a process of recovery that centers on a transformation in identity. This process involves a parallel reconstruction of the past and construction of a new personal identity based on acknowledgment of the realities of parental alcoholism—what really happened. The process of recovery is a process of new knowledge construction, including a revision of core beliefs about the self and the family leading to ultimate differentiation and emotional separation from parents and the family of origin.

The process of recovery does not take place in a vacuum. The central processes of reconstruction and new construction occur within the framework of a new attachment: to a therapist, a therapy group, an Al-Anon group for ACAs, or to the principles of Al-Anon. The new emotional attachment and the identity as an ACA provide the structure from which recovery occurs. It involves a breakdown in defenses, regression within the therapeutic context to repair developmental failures, cognitive and affective reconstruction of the past and the development of a new personal identity with new belief schemas. The essence of the process of recovery is captured by the title of the last chapter. Incorporating the realities of parental alcoholism provides a second chance for "growing up, growing out, and coming home."

PART ONE

The Alcoholic Family

What is it like for a child growing up in a family dominated by the alcoholism of a parent? In the first part, we will closely examine this question, outlining the critical significance of alcohol as a central organizing principle governing family development.

Chapter 1 sets the stage for this exploration and the theory development that follows in Part Two and Part Three as well. The first chapter outlines the "state of the field" of children of alcoholics. What has been written and how has the field developed from a research perspective? What are the parameters of knowledge and present thinking?

A review of the literature captures the significance already accorded to the family environment, including the impact of that environment on the individuals within. Research over the last 40 years, particularly the last 10 to 15, delineates the complex task that lies ahead: integrating multiple variables and multiple tracks with an emphasis on interaction, including genetics, biology, physiology, neurology, family systems theory, developmental theory, cognitive and social learning theory, prevention and treatment.

Chapter 2 starts with theory, outlining a rationale for elevating the significance of the family environment as a core variable affecting a child's development. What goes on in the family, what doesn't go on in the family, what it feels like at home—the tone, the atmosphere—all have an impact on the child's development.

In this chapter, the "ideal" family is briefly described contrasting the deviations and pathological adjustments characteristic of the alcoholic family. Most significant to the alcoholic family is the centrality of denial. The alcoholic family is organized around the dominance of the parent's drinking and the nature of the family's responses to it—behaviorally, cognitively, and dynamically. The alcoholic family becomes organized and stabilized around a "normalcy" that includes denial of parental alcoholism and behaviors and thinking that maintain it at the same time. Chapter 2 further describes the characteristics of the environment that result from this double bind.

Chapter 3 continues exploration of the family environment, now focusing on interactions, patterns, and adaptations necessary to maintain family homeostasis. Codependence is defined broadly as a reactive stance in relation to the dominance of another and then applied to the alcoholic family: What is it like for a codependent parent or codependent child? Next, the problematic issue of research is broached: How to look at this population—children of alcoholics—characterized by multiple and even infinite variability? There is no single theory or single line of inquiry that will neatly tie it all together. Fortunately, however, there is an example to follow. Research variables and key findings already established are outlined for the children of the handicapped, noting significant similarities and differences.

Next core variables necessary to the study of children of alcoholics are outlined: time of onset, severity of parental alcoholism and which parent is alcoholic. Finally, emphasizing again the importance of interaction, pattern, and variability, a tool of assessment—the family diagram—is introduced. This tool enables the clinician and patient to better comprehend the family dynamics and the particular adjustments and consequences that result for individuals within. This instrument is also useful in charting changes over time.

Chapter 1

The Children of Alcoholics

The children of alcoholics, COAs; the adult children of alcoholics, ACAs or ACOAs—according to recent estimates (Children of Alcoholics Foundation, 1985) this group of children and adults who share the experience of having grown up with an alcoholic parent numbers 28 million. Many of these individuals suffer a variety of problems related to the alcoholism of a parent that was never labeled as such including school phobia, learning disabilities, attentional disorder, depression, anxiety, and mood disturbance.

It is only within the last 10 years that COAs and ACAs have been recognized as a distinct population requiring intervention and treatment specifically for the problems they developed as a result of living with an alcoholic parent. It is only within the last 10 years that COAs and ACAs have been accorded legitimacy as a treatment population, separate from the alcoholic.

This book is founded on the acceptance of children of alcoholics, young and adult, as a primary population with legitimate treatment needs separate from those of the alcoholic parent.

This chapter reviews the literature about children of alcoholics, outlining the scope of knowledge and theory development to date. While there is a strong research base extending back at least 40 years, the academic focus has been overshadowed by the popular press. People who couldn't name or recognize the source of their suffering could identify with clear, simple, and poignant descriptions of family life in which parental alcoholism was acknowledged.

The down side of this media popularization is over simplification. We do not have another cookbook problem with an "answer" waiting to be applied with magical results. We have, instead, a good beginning; a good description that forms the base for indepth theory development and theory integration.

FOCUS ON THE ALCOHOLIC

Ten to twenty years ago the field of alcoholism dealt only with the drinking alcoholic. Extensive research existed in many areas—his (or her) personality traits (Jones, 1968), the etiology of the disease (Lisansky, 1960), and methods of treatment (Catanazaro, 1968). In studies of alcoholism it was the drinking alcoholic, and the male alcoholic in particular, who received the primary and almost exclusive attention.

Studies of the alcoholic continue but research now includes women alcoholics in addition to men (Sandmeier, 1980) and studies of abstinence as well (Brown, 1985).

ALCOHOLISM AS A FAMILY DISEASE

The singular focus on the alcoholic was altered with the work of Jackson (1954) and others (MacDonald, 1956; Fox, 1962; Futterman, 1953; Jacob, Favorine, Meisel & Anderson, 1978) who began to examine personality traits and the role of the wife who had been thought to perpetuate or reinforce the active alcoholism of her mate. Jackson (1954) outlined stages in a developmental disease process of alcoholism for the spouse and family of the alcoholic.

These beginning studies drew attention to the problem of alcoholism as a *family disease* though the term was not yet used. Fox (1962) suggested that "every member in such a family is affected by it—emotionally, spiritually and in most cases economically, socially and often physically" (p. 72).

Following Jackson's work, the concept of "family disease" or "alcoholic family" was born with the focus of research not primarily on the alcoholic, but on the interactions, adjustments, and development of the family with an alcoholic member. Still, the children of alcoholics were not the focus of primary attention.

Recognition of the children of alcoholics was slow to come. For the most part, academia and social services echoed Hunter's (1963) discovery that wives seeking help in dealing with an alcoholic mate resisted discussion of the children.

Baker (1945) in alluding to the existence of disturbances among the children pointed to the neglect of children's problems: "the child's problem often has to be subordinated to the primary situation" (p. 434). The primary situation was always the focus on the alcoholic.

Cork (1969) is credited with finally raising public and professional awareness to a point that children of alcoholics could no longer be ignored. Her book *The Forgotten Children* is viewed as the starting point of what has become not only a major new focal point of research and treatment, but a national social movement.

The idea finally took hold when adults were included. In the late 1970s, *Newsweek* (1979) reported on the early research of Brown and Black with both describing and labeling adult children of alcoholics as a new, unrecognized, legitimate population. Since then, popular press interest and self-help groups associated with or modeled after Al-Anon have overwhelmed the capacity of academia to formulate theory. "Catching up" with theory development is one of the main reasons for this book.

From that point, it's been like "a prairie fire." The National Association for Children of Alcoholics was formed in 1983 and the Children of Alcoholics Foundation was started to support research and public awareness. Numerous articles and books have been published and conferences for lay and professional audiences abound.

Like many social movements, the sudden recognition, widespread interest, and emotional intensity have been powerful and helpful for many children and adults. However, there continues to be a lack of a solid clinical research and theoretical foundation on which to base important decisions for intervention, education, prevention, and treatment.

It is a primary purpose of this book to establish clinical theory and its application to practice. The groundwork for that theory development lies in a review of the research to date.

REVIEW OF THE LITERATURE

The first published study of children of alcoholics was in 1945 (Roe), but it was not until the decades of the 1950s and 1960s that citations appeared routinely, thus establishing the children of alcoholics as a legitimate treatment population. Still, the studies were relatively few. The early research focused on genetic transmission and psychopathology. With increased recognition, there was also a more complex literature including familial transmission (genetic and social-psychological), family interaction patterns, role adaptation, psychopathology and disturbances in young children of alcoholics (COAs) and adult children of alcoholics (ACAs), prevention, and treatment.

Transmission

Familial transmission, the mechanisms by which parental alcoholism is passed on to children, began with genetic research. The first major studies originated in Scandinavia. A team of researchers at Washington University in St. Louis (Goodwin, Schulsinger, Hermansen, Guse & Winokur, 1973) and the University of California (Shuckitt) joined the Scandinavians in genetic research. Through twin, adoption, and half-sibling studies, Shuckitt, Goodwin, and Winokur (1972), Goodwin (1971, 1979), Goodwin et al., (1973), and Goodwin, Schulsinger, Knop, Mednick, and Guze (1977) established convincing evidence for the presence of a genetic factor in the intergenerational transmission of alcoholism.

Related to genetic research are studies focusing on genetically influenced characteristics related to alcoholism. These include biological markers, neurophysiological and biochemical factors as summarized by Russell, Henderson, and Blume (1985) in their review of the literature. This direction reflected the possibility that there are different types of alcoholism with different biochemical determinants, patterns of inheritance, and clinical manifestations.

Although genetic research always has been a primary focus, more recent studies reflect a recognition of the complexity of the disease, and the likelihood of multiple causal factors, especially the interaction between genetics, environment, social, psychological, and cultural factors. The incidence and transmission of psychiatric problems is an example.

Winokur et al. (1970) established a strong correlation between alcoholism in families and affective disorder. Winokur, Cadoret, Dorzab et al. (1971) also found a 15.5 percent chance of depression and a 15.1 percent chance of alcoholism in first-degree relatives of alcoholics. In addition, male alcoholics frequently had female relatives with a depressive disorder (Winokur, Reich, Rimmer & Pitts, 1970). These researchers and others (Sandmeier, 1980; Beckman, 1979) also examined the different manifestations of alcoholism in males and females. Kaufman (1986) summarized the differences. Women's drinking patterns and behavior emphasized hiding much more than men. Drinking by women was also related to problems all women encounter in society, such as lack of social power and pressure to suppress parts of themselves that do not conform to sex-role stereotypes.

Women alcoholics had a higher incidence of depression and anxiety and a higher incidence of familial alcoholism and depression (Kaufman, 1985). Winokur and Clayton (1968) found a 25 to 50 percent incidence of alcoholism in the fathers of female alcoholics and a 12 percent incidence in mothers and siblings. Alcoholic fathers were more likely to physically or sexually abuse their children, whereas mothers more often abused through neglect. Sandmeier (1980) noted that children of alcoholic mothers tended to be cold, distrustful, rigid, and reserved as well as submissive and dependent like their mothers and to have learning difficulties and school problems. While important, such clear-cut distinctions are not supported by our clinical data.

The interaction between genetics and environment has been explored recently by Cloninger (1981, 1983). Continuing this emphasis, Goodwin (1984) proposed a new, separate category of "familial alcoholism" which underscored the now recognized differences in the development and clinical presentation of alcoholism when it runs in families.

Following this same line, Fawzy (1983) focused on the intergenerational use of substances, highlighting the significance of social learning and family environment theories of transmission. In studying families with psychiatric illness, Post (1962) suggested that interaction with a persistently ill parent, rather than heredity, seems to be the more likely mechanism of transmission.

Burk (1972), Wolin, Bennett, and Noonan (1979), and Wolin, Bennett, Noonan, and Teitelbaum (1980) examined modeling, cultural factors, and changes in family situations as significant in familial transmission.

Alcoholism does run in families as these studies demonstrate. In fact, the children of alcoholics are from four to six times more likely to become alcoholic than individuals who do not have an alcoholic parent (Goodwin, 1979; Cotton, 1979).

In the integrated theory proposed in this book, the central organizing principle of alcohol and its denial significantly affect development and transmission through social learning, modeling, and the psychological processes of imitation and identification.

Family Systems

Recognition of the need for a new category of "familial alcoholism" (Goodwin, 1984) and agreement that transmission is
multifactorial (Russell et al., 1985) also evolved from earlier
family systems theory and research. Steinglass (1981), Bowen
(1974), and Hindman (1976) examined interactional patterns
that may precede or result from alcoholism.

The pattern of drinking and its influence on family process
was emphasized by Wilson and Offord (1978) and others (Moos,
Finney & Gamble, 1982; Gorad, 1971; Orford, Oppenheimer,
Egert et al., 1976). Johnson (1984), continuing the interest in
pattern, examined differences between alcoholic parent-child
and nonalcoholic parent-child interactions. She and Steinglass
underscored the critical significance of including a developmental perspective in research formulations. It is now agreed
(Kaufman, 1986) that there is no single family system.

Rutter (1966) emphasized the importance of interaction in his
review of the literature on illness in parents and their children.
Morris (1958) suggested that "the psychiatric illness of one member inevitably presents a distinct social problem, in that the balance of interpersonal relationships is disturbed."

Ackerman also stressed the importance of pattern and interaction (1956 a, b; 1958); he emphasized the need for a "psychosocial
diagnosis of the family," noting that psychiatric illness is rarely an
isolated event in family life. "The sick behaviors of these family
members are often closely woven and mutually reinforcing."
(Ackerman, 1958)

Pollack (1952) extended the significance of interaction, noting
that emotional disturbances of children were frequently created
by "emotional disturbances" in those "close by." Further, the social environment of an individual is a combination of the intrapsychic problems of others. (Rutter, 1966, p. 11)

Examination of interaction and pattern is therefore extremely
important in understanding differences among children who
have grown up with an alcoholic parent. It also emphasizes the
significance of including a focus on the environment—what it
was like in the family—in developing theory and treatment. A
clinical history of the COA or ACA must include *both* a portrait
of the family and the environment of childhood and a more individualized developmental or intrapsychic history as well. The
two are not separate. It is essential to include both in theory

formulation. A focus on alcohol as the organizing principle—in the family and in the child's subsequent development, intrapsychically and interpersonally—provides the connecting link.

Problems in Childhood

The Swedes, pioneers in genetic research, were also the first to look at psychopathology and emotional problems in young children concomitant with parental alcoholism (Nylander, 1960). Fox (1962) described children as distrustful with a tendency to hide behind a defensive facade. Children were noted to experience authority conflicts and unfulfilled dependency needs (Fairchild, 1964), to be intensely defiant, aggressive and high in anxiety (Parnitzke & Prussing, 1966), and to be low in self-concept (Bosma, 1975).

Haberman (1966) found the occurrence of temper tantrums, fighting with peers, and trouble in school to be more frequent among children of alcoholics than children of nonalcoholics.

Chafetz, Blane, and Hill (1971) noted the greater frequency of difficulties which they classified as disruptions to growth and development in the children of alcoholics. These included serious illness or accident, school problems, difficulties involved with the police or courts and the greater likelihood of early separation from their parents. These authors suggested that the children of alcoholics suffer deleterious social consequences more than health consequences: that family disruption impedes becoming a socialized adult. We have confirmed the significance of this finding in our clinical work. Throughout this book, the difficulties that children have in translating their experiences in the alcoholic family to the outside world are highlighted.

In an early study, Hawkins (1950) found a high incidence of anxiety and ambivalence toward the father, reactions of hostility, aggression, and neurotic traits.

Nylander (1953) found a higher rate of physical symptoms without organic basis, mental insufficiency and anxiety neurosis, and depression than in children of non-alcoholic fathers. A significantly greater percentage of the children of alcoholic fathers were considered to be problem children by their teachers.

In another sample, Nylander found a greater incidence of physical symptomatology in girls from alcoholic families and a higher occurrence of inhibition of development. Projective tests revealed prevailing tones of depression and anxiety. Forty-four percent of this sample were diagnosed as neurotic and 26 percent as suffering from environmental damage. Once again, early researchers linked the significance of the environment to serious consequences.

Kearney and Taylor (1969) treated 20 emotionally disturbed children of alcoholics in a psychiatric clinic. They found that seven had experienced the loss of a parent through death or divorce, five had attempted suicide, eight had been institutionalized, eight were school dropouts and nine had had legal difficulties. They added further that only seven improved with therapy.

Bosma (1972) described the children of alcoholics as "victims in a hidden tragedy" (p. 34). He suggested that male children of alcoholics become assertive, rebellious, and hostile. Daughters become self-defeating, pessimistic, withdrawn, and fluctuating in their moods.

Fine, Yudin, Holmes, and Heinemann (1976) noted that children of alcoholics have a greater likelihood of behavioral disorders and difficulties containing or regulating their excitement and moods. In addition, they noted significant disturbances in use of the senses, emotional disturbance, and social aggression. Children of alcoholics are less likely to maintain attention, less responsive to environmental stimuli, anxious, fearful, socially isolated, and preoccupied with inner thoughts.

Whitfield (1980) noted that other serious problems are likely to occur at a higher incidence for children of alcoholics than the general population. These included hyperactivity (Cantwell, 1972), enuresis (Sloboda, 1974), fetal alcohol syndrome (Rosett et al., 1966) and child abuse (Hindman, 1977; Mayer & Black, 1977; Seixas, 1979; and Ellwood, 1980). Depression, suicide, behavioral, and school problems were also related to having an alcoholic parent (Wegscheider, 1978).

Most of the studies focusing on children of alcoholics have been concerned with the issue of personality traits in relation to a predisposition to alcoholism. They have been concerned with traits to the extent that they may be predictive of later alcoholism, or to reinforce the notion of a specific personality pattern common to and also predating the onset of alcoholism.

An exception was the work of Aronson and Gilbert (1963) who investigated the presence of personality variables commonly associated with alcoholism in the preadolescent sons of male alcoholics. The characteristics of "dependency" and "evasion of unpleasantness" were highly significant, with acquisitiveness, inappropriate emotional expression, and self-dissatisfaction also pronounced. Contrary to what the others expected, sons of alcoholics were rated as less personable than their peers and more likely to express overt and directed aggression. The authors concluded that the preadolescent sons of male alcoholics exhibit significant negative differences in personality characteristics in relation to their peers.

In investigating personality variables believed to be influenced by parental alcoholism, Kammeier (1971) found a lack of differences in problems of maladjustment between the children of alcoholics and those of nonalcoholics. However, ninth- and tenth-grade daughters of alcoholics did show evidence of more distress in the areas of emotional stability, family relationships, social relationships, conformity, mood, and leadership. Kammeier suggested that if the girls related closely to their fathers, their conflicts may have been tied to the "inability of some alcoholics to form positive relationships, to care about people, and to give of themselves to others" (p. 371).

The early literature emphasizing family disruption suggested strongly that the children in an alcoholic family live in an unhealthy and abnormal environment which is likely to affect their personality development. It is this early emphasis and subsequent confirmation in our clinical work that lays the groundwork for the necessity of including a focus on the environment in the development of an integrated theory.

The introduction of studies on role broadened the research perspective to include examination of coping and adjustment. Black (1981) and Wegscheider (1981) developed classification systems describing coping styles in alcoholic families. Black identified three key roles and their behavioral presentation—the responsible child, the placater, and the adjuster. Wegscheider described four—the family hero, the scapegoat, the mascot, and the lost child. Both classification systems were quickly adopted by the public and formed the core of early media coverage (*Mademoiselle, Parents, Los Angeles Times*) and the structure for the sharing of experiences and identification in early lay conferences. Both were also translated into schemas for treatment.

These classifications according to role remain extremely useful in providing a general description and thus a framework for *beginning* exploration of one's childhood adaptations to parental alcoholism. However, many ACAs have been disappointed that these classifications do not also provide the prescription for change. These frameworks do not provide a dynamic theory of development that will enable clinicians to determine individual differences and tailor long-term psychodynamic treatment accordingly. The integrated theory developed in this book should begin to fill this gap.

The introduction of role theory had another major impact as it dramatically altered the primary research emphasis on genetics and psychopathology. The range of consequences now included much more than the "problem" or the "disturbed" child. Black and Wegscheider had focused on maladaptive role patterns but they, along with Nardi, (1981) and El-Guebaly and Offord (1979) also recognized the importance of the "competent" child who, rather than developing apparent psychopathology as a result of the environment, exhibits characteristics of a "model" child instead. Niven (1984) called this group the "invulnerables." This child is unlikely to enter either the mental health or the juvenile justice systems and, therefore, will not be identified as having difficulties related to parental alcoholism until adulthood, if at all.

There is now a wide body of literature that describes the problems and variety of consequences that children suffer as the result of parental alcoholism. With established recognition, there is also a growing emphasis on education of teachers and health personnel (Triplett & Arneson, 1978; Morehouse, 1979) to improve and increase intervention, diagnosis and treatment for the school age population.

Adult Children of Alcoholics

While young children of alcoholics have been recognized as a research and treatment population for at least 30 years, the concept of adult children of alcoholics is newer (*Newsweek,* 1979). In a few years, recognition of adult children of alcoholics as a research and treatment population has grown from an idea to a national social movement. There is now widespread agreement that adults who grew up with an alcoholic parent(s) (ACAs) do suffer consequences and do have legitimate treatment needs of their own (Beletsis & Brown, 1981; Black, 1981; and Cermak & Brown, 1982).

In our long-term clinical research and treatment program for ACAs at Stanford, we found (Brown & Beletsis, 1986) that ACAs report serious emotional difficulties in their adult lives which they relate to their childhood family environment and particularly to the alcoholism of one or both parents.

Cermak and Brown (1982) defined several key issues emerging in the course of group therapy including an excessive emphasis on internal and interpersonal control, hypervigilance, difficulties with trust, excessive feelings of responsibility, and problems with intimacy.

There are studies of the process of recovery for ACAs (Gravitz & Bowden, 1984) and several efforts to define the consequences of parental alcoholism as a syndrome (Cermak, 1984) of codependency. Following this line of reasoning, there is also a move to define children of alcoholics as a separate DSM diagnostic category (Cermak, 1984).

Cermak (1984) has likened the after effects of growing up with an alcoholic parent(s) to Post-Traumatic Stress Disorder with chronic symptoms of acute anxiety, nightmares, and sleep disturbance similar to those experienced by war veterans or children of the holocaust (Wilson, 1985). This is an important line of research that adds a useful theoretical framework to our current knowledge. However, it is not exhaustive and should not be viewed as such. The range of symptoms and disorders crosses many diagnostic categories including depression and anxiety disorder which are explored later in this text. We need to establish an indepth theory that integrates our growing body of knowledge about the childhood environment and experiences of living with an alcoholic parent with established theories of child development.

The Family Environment

As already stressed, the environment in the alcoholic family is a critical factor affecting children's development and later adult difficulties. Wilson and Orford (1978) identified the "family atmosphere" as a central theme in children's understanding of parental alcoholism. It is this atmosphere or environment that provides the base of shared experience which facilitates rapid bonding in ACA groups. It is most often the similarities which are accented in the bonding process. There are few children or adult children who do not have a painful Christmas or holiday memory of disappointment, fear, terror, or harm. The family environment is a vital part of theory development which is explored in Chapter 2.

Much of the early literature on the children of alcoholics focused on a description of the alcoholic as a father (the alcoholic was believed to be the male) and the family climate in which the child was raised. Though descriptive in nature, these studies formed the background for the suggestion of problems.

Jackson (1954) suggested that as a whole:

Family members are influenced by the cultural definition of alcoholism as evidence of weakness, inadequacy, or sinfulness; by the lack of cultural prescription for the roles of family members, and by cultural values of family solidarity, sanctity and self-sufficiency. (p. 571)

She suggested that, in adapting to these roles, the family goes through stages which include denial of the problem, social isolation, and behaviors which are geared to relieve tension rather than control drinking. She suggested in general terms that "disturbances of children are more marked at this latter stage" (p. 572). In a later study, Jackson (1962) characterized the family as feeling guilty, ashamed, inadequate, and above all isolated from social support (p. 483).

Newell (1950) and Fox (1962) also accented themes of family disruption. Newell focused on the effects of behavior inconsistency, suggesting that in periods of sobriety the alcoholic father:

Inspires the natural love of his offspring, who build therefrom an ideal father image of omnipotence and loving kindness. The disillusionment of the drunken episode is shattering to the frail superego structure of the child who is subjected to alternating experiences of exalted hopes and blighting disappointments. (p. 91)

Newell characterized the child in such an inconsistent family situation as the "hungry, experimental animal which is tempted with food and frustrated by barriers" (p. 92). An adult group patient confirms this description:

Janice feels "icky" and embarrassed. She fears her vulnerability will be dangled in front of her and used against her manipulatively.

Newell suggested further that the child presents a "bewildering array of ambivalences, inconsistencies, antagonisms, and touching overtures of affection" (p. 29).

Fox (1962) suggested that inconsistency makes it difficult for the child to develop consistent standards of behavior, and that the emotional warmth and support needed for the development of a sense of self-worth are seriously lacking. Fox concluded by noting that if the child can step outside of the family, he or she is likely to become delinquent. But the child who is frightened of the outside world "feels hopelessly trapped in the hostile, growth-inhibiting isolation of a battling family" (p. 90). The child comes to believe that the drinking bouts or fights between the parents are his or her fault. The youngster may develop feelings of frustration and guilt, with neurosis often the result.

Bacon (1945) further stressed family disruption with the thesis that alcoholism is incompatible with marriage. He suggested that:

> Alcoholism makes close interpersonal relationships more diffi-cult, increases suspicions, provides a safe retreat from reality and allows inmaturity, cynicism, aggressiveness, egoism and self pity fuller play. (p. 229)

He suggested that becoming a father is upsetting and fearful to the alcoholic because he is used to playing the emotional role of little boy. Perceiving dimly that he does not want the child, he may be anxious about its safety and comfort.

Jackson (1962) suggested that roles are often distorted in an alcoholic family with the father assuming the role of naughty child. As a result, both boys and girls may have problems in identification.

Fox (1963) noted that girls may identify their fathers with other males, developing fear, distrust, and hatred for members of the opposite sex.

The notion that family members play an important part in the alcoholic's difficulties was stressed by Lemert (1960) who sug-gested resentment of the children from birth, and Jackson (1962) who suggested that fatherhood tends to intensify the alcoholic's problems. Jackson found that among alcoholics, parenthood is "one of the life events associated with a sudden and marked increase in the number of alcoholic behaviors . . . " (p. 491).

Fox (1962) suggested that battles over discipline of the chil-dren are almost always present in the alcoholic family with the child suffering confusion regarding what is expected of him or her. Children may be used as pawns, played back and forth by the mother or father, or they may receive the misdirected anger or over-indulgence of a frustrated parent.

McCord and McCord (1960) summed up a picture of the alcoholic as a father by saying:

> They are unstable members of their families as well as their communities. They perform roles as fathers in a passive or dictatorial manner; they are prone to express frustration through conflict with wives, rejection of sons, and the imposition of a radically punitive discipline on their children. (p. 129)

They suggested that if a child's needs are erratically satisfied and frustrated, they will increase in intensity, becoming the most powerful motivating force in the child's life.

Finally, Blane (1968), in discussing the tendency of the children of alcoholics to become alcoholics themselves, characterized the family situation as one of:

> Family tensions, strife and bitterness; threats of corporal abuse and punishment are the lot of children in a family with an alcoholic member. Chances for these youngsters to become emotionally or socially deviant are high. (p. 157)

With great variation, family life of the children of alcoholics may be described as chaotic and isolated with an abundance of inconsistency. With less variation it may be described as abnormal, with the presence of emotional turmoil a constant factor (Baker, 1945).

As this review illustrates, early research targeted a focus on the environment as critical in understanding the variety of problems children experience as a result of living with an alcoholic parent.

Prevention and Treatment

The final area of research is the least well-developed although there is little disagreement about the need for preventive intervention and treatment services for children of alcoholics. But the problem remains: there is a lack of theoretical research and clinical knowledge from which to base program development and "prevention" strategies. O'Gorman (1981) targets fetal alcohol syndrome, child abuse and neglect, hyperactivity, mental health problems, and alcohol abuse and alcoholism as the critical problems for prevention research to address.

Brown (1985), Russell et al. (1985) and others have emphasized the importance of viewing the family as a whole and individual members as viable candidates for treatment independent of the alcoholic. However, acceptance of this point of view theoretically and in the provision of service is just occurring.

It is also difficult to obtain service even if it is available because of obstacles for both providers and patients. Parental consent for treatment is required for young children. Parents may deny that their children have difficulties or interfere with treatment once started (Morehouse, 1984). In recovering families, there remains a good deal of denial: that children knew about the drinking or that there were any problems if they did.

Niven (1984) and others recognized the difficulties of getting children into treatment and helping them once there when parents are not in treatment and continue to deny any difficulties with alcohol. Niven stresses the need to focus on techniques that will break the family's denial and move them all into treatment.

Morehouse (1984) outlines a framework for intervention with adolescent children of alcoholics. She and others (DeCicco, Davis, Hogan, MacLean & Orenstein, 1984) echo Niven's understanding of the difficulties of targeting young people for treatment that openly labels parental alcoholism when it has not been labeled by the family. To date, children of alcoholics who are in intensive treatment have parents who are also in treatment.

With this overview of research, the groundwork is laid for outlining the integrative theory of development that forms the core of this book. The first piece is a focus on "family environment."

Chapter 2

The Alcoholic Family
Environment

FOUNDATIONS FOR THEORY DEVELOPMENT: INTRODUCTION

Although recognition of the concept "children of alcoholics" as a research and treatment population is relatively recent, there is a wide body of literature and research from other disciplines to provide a strong foundation for theory development. The key question is how to choose from and organize this range of knowledge in a manner that will provide an integrated theory with coherence, clarity, and depth. How can we merge different theoretical points of view in a way that accents and incorporates a multitude of variables without hopelessly muddying the water?

First, by recognizing that we are not dealing with a single-dimension research or treatment population that can be easily reduced and quantified. We are not looking for answers, but rather guidelines and frameworks. This recognition comes from our long-term clinical work with adults who identify themselves as children of alcoholics. This theory emerges from practice: Our patients tell us we must find a way to include the significance of the family environment—quite simply, what it was like—and an understanding of pattern and interaction within that environment and the impact of *both* on intrapsychic, interpersonal, social, cognitive, and affective development.

Why do clinicians and researchers resist acknowledging the multidimensional nature of this and other problems and ignore or avoid the significance of interaction and mutuality? One reason is that such complexity interferes with predictability, standardization, and generalization. The proposed model deepens the complexity and the knowledge base, including knowledge of the variables, but lessens predictability, at least at this early stage.

Therapists must be able to include multiple variables and to make sense of the impact and meaning of parental alcoholism for *this* individual. Only then can we tailor treatment to really fit the individual. As Kagan (1984) notes: "the effects of most experiences are not fixed but depend on the child's interpretation. The interpretation will vary with the child's cognitive maturity, expectations, beliefs and momentary feeling state" (p. 240).

In support of the need for individual interpretation Kagan (1984) further states: "it is the child's personal interpretation of the experience, not the event recorded by the camera or observer that is the essential basis for formulation of and change in beliefs, wishes and actions" (p. 241).

THEORETICAL RATIONALE FOR THE "FAMILY ENVIRONMENT"

The literature (Beletsis & Brown, 1981; Cork, 1969; Black, 1981; Seixas, 1979) describes the alcoholic family environment as one of chaos, inconsistency, unpredictability, unclear roles, arbitrariness, changing limits, arguments, repetitious and illogical thinking, and perhaps violence and incest. The family is dominated by the presence of alcoholism and its denial. The alcoholism becomes a major family secret, most often denied inside the family and certainly denied outside. This secret becomes a governing principle around which the family organizes—its adaptations, coping strategies, and the shared beliefs that maintain the structure and hold the family members together.

This global portrait emphasizes the centrality of the secret and the resulting disorder and disruption and underscores the need for a family or family systems point of view. What is the impact of an unstable environment, of a "family atmosphere" characterized by tension, hostility, and fear? How does the family—as a system—respond to the development of alcoholism in a parent?

There are several areas of research that provide a clear rationale for asking these questions and for stressing the importance of the environment. Krystal (1978) suggests that the history of psychoanalysis can be viewed as an attempt to reconcile seemingly opposite theoretical points of view in understanding individual development and psychopathology: the "unbearable situation" versus "unacceptable impulses." Krystal writes about the impact of trauma on affective development, emphasizing the "unbearable situation"—the danger or trauma experienced in the environment as the core for later psychological disturbance.

Hong (1978) suggests that to understand adaptational processes, one must "consider two sets of variables: one is the individual's internal needs and the other is his environment" (p. 71). Hong adds that the individual's needs vary according to constitution and developmental stage.

Lidz (1973) writes about the relationship between schizophrenia and family settings, emphasizing the significance of "dual endowment."

Unless we understand that each infant is born with a dual endowment, a genetic inheritance and a cultural heritage, we can never correctly understand his development and how it can become confused. (p. 18)

Lidz stresses the interaction between genetics and environment repeatedly noting that the family is the mediator:

The family is a necessary derivative of his biological make-up because it is the basic social system that mediates between the child's genetic and cultural endowments, provides for his biological needs while teaching societal techniques, stands between the individual and society and offers a shelter within society and against the remainder of society. (p. 18)

He adds:

Any attempt to study the child's personality development or maldevelopment as an autonomous process independent of the family matrix distorts as much as it simplifies; it is bound to error, for such abstractions can be made only by eliminating the essential factors in the process. (p. 18)

Thurman (1985), in his studies of children of handicapped parents, provides a strong case for including environmental factors in theory development. Thurman emphasizes the need to focus on studies of ecological systems and their development to enhance our understanding of human-environmental relationships. He believes we need to shift away from delineating developmental patterns within the individual, moving toward the ecological system as the unit of study instead.

Thurman suggests that the presence of a handicapped parent is of special concern in understanding the family because the family represents the initial point of social involvement: "the family provides the basic social network for most infants and young children." Thurman emphasizes the importance of understanding the nature of the environment, the nature of the individual and the interactions of both with each other. According to Thurman, we have "overlooked the fact that there is a mutuality of effect between individuals and environment." He also emphasizes the need to examine the system at different points in time.

Sameroff (1975), Sameroff and Chandler (1975), and Bronfenbrenner (1977) are unequivocal in their view of the significance of the environment: "the context of development is an essential ingredient in understanding the course of development itself" (Thurman, p. 118).

Family systems theorists have long appreciated the interactional model. Glass (1985) relates the impact of parental disability on children to a disequilibrium or disruption in family homeostasis. Steinglass (1980, 1981a, 1981b) and others (Wolin et al., 1980) already have examined family homeostasis as a critical variable in understanding not only the impact of parental alcoholism, but differences between families with an alcoholic parent.

There is little doubt (Bosma, 1972; Cermak, 1984) that the child in an alcoholic family is the victim of an ongoing trauma. Kaufman (1986) summarizes:

> Alcoholism is a major stress on individual members and the total family in many ways. Alcohol is a direct economic drain on family resources, and it threatens job security. Drinking behavior may interrupt normal family tasks, cause conflict and demand adaptive responses from family members who do not know how to respond appropriately. In brief, alcoholism creates a series of escalating crises in family structure and function which may bring the family system to a catastrophic state.

The particular family circumstances define the nature and extent of the trauma; the underlying constant is the need by all family members to adjust their lives and development to cope with or survive the realities of alcoholism. The literature on trauma and its impact on children provides an important reference point of view.

Often families adjust to the alcoholism of a parent, establishing a new equilibrium. Acute traumatic episodes involving a crisis may punctuate longer periods of chronic stress which characterize the "everyday" family atmosphere. Families may stabilize and live with acute trauma and disequilibrium for years (or lifetimes). This state of chronic tension or chronic trauma becomes the norm. The families adapt to the "in-law who has moved in to stay" (the intrusion of alcoholism) and adjust accordingly.

With this emphasis on chronicity and "disability," it is useful to examine the research on children of the handicapped. What is it like for children to grow up with a handicapped parent? Fortunately, there is a good beginning in this field of research (Thurman, 1985) from which to draw parallels and to note differences as well.

The recognition that many children of alcoholics are also high achievers and "model" children, the "invulnerables" (Niven, 1984) provides yet another reference base. This one is critical. There is a tendency now to look for "positive" (Niven, 1984) outcome—what are the "benefits" of growing up with an alcoholic parent? While many people may indeed come to view their experiences as positive, the automatic assumption by others that high achievement, for example, is positive is value laden and misses the defensive implications.

Our clinical experience and the literature on roles tell us that many children develop adaptive coping mechanisms and defenses that serve them well as children. In this sense, they are certainly positive. However, these same "positives" become maladaptive and restrictive for the adult. The high achiever is fueled by compulsion—the individual cannot change or broaden focus—the model child feels controlled and driven by the need to please. These "positive" outcomes are all the adult has to draw upon. This individual frequently has no sense of stable, autonomous identity, no initiative stemming internally from a cohesive sense of self, and little social or interpersonal knowledge of, or capacity for, intimate relationships.

Throughout the process of therapy, we see that this "positive" outcome was in the service of defense. And the overriding necessity for defense *precluded* many important tasks of normal development that *do* provide the base for "positive" outcome, that is developmentally complete, or more fully so.

With this many theories taken into account, the reader may note that living with an alcoholic parent is *not* the same as the Holocaust, Vietnam, or living with a disabled parent. Although this is certainly true, there are important parallels. As the children of alcoholics movement grows, we hear from many individuals who are not the children of alcoholics about their need to be included.

> My mother was periodically depressed and psychotic throughout my childhood. We lived through her craziness and never once spoke about it. I really identify with children of alcoholics and need a group for myself too.

> What's so special about you children of alcoholics? What about chronic illness? My father had a heart condition. We lived in constant fear of his collapse. We had to be constantly aware of his comfort, never tire him or cause him irritation, lest we precipitate a heart attack. And we didn't talk about it.

With all the interest in children of alcoholics, some suggest facetiously that we need a group for "children of parents." These criticisms illustrate the danger of over generalization or exclusion and underscore the importance of including the environment in theory formulation. It may be that children share defensive traits and deficits as a result of growing up with a secret, along with the presence of chronic or acute tension and trauma, *in addition to* the differentiating specifics of alcoholism. We need to draw parallels to and determine the criteria for understanding differences: What do children of the handicapped, children of divorce, children of alcoholics share in common and what are the differences? What is the impact of trauma or a secret, maintained by denial? Once again, how can we best understand what it was like for *this* individual and what is necessary and appropriate now?

A brief look at theories about the family sets the stage for understanding the relationship of the family environment in an alcoholic home to developmental difficulties and childhood and adult disturbances. This simple description of the "ideal" family provides a structure and reference point to comprehend the significance of the deviations in the alcoholic family.

THE IDEAL FAMILY

Theorists from many fields—psychology, sociology, anthropology—write about the significance of the family to individual development. Kagan (1984) states succinctly that the family is the unit to which "loyalty is given and identity derived. . . . The fate of each person rests with the vitality, reputation and success of the kinship group. The concept of self is dependent on the resources, status and socially perceived qualities of the family group" (p. 242).

Kagan emphasizes the core significance of the parents and the family to every aspect of the child's development. At the basic level, he notes that "attachment to the caregiver creates in the child a special receptivity to being socialized by that individual. The child accepts the family's standards and establishes harmonious relationships" (p. 253). An insecure, faulty or pathological attachment may result in serious disturbances and certainly puts the child at risk. Children develop standards of behavior from parents. They need a parent to inform them what behaviors are proper and improper. If the parents' behavior or their standards for the children are inconsistent, the child will *not* develop standards. Kagan notes further that the arbitrary, harsh, and nonfunctional exercise of firm control has negative consequences for the child's behavior.

In outlining the ideal, Kagan provides a core definition of identification:

> Parents are the role models with whom the child identifies; parents should display behavior the child classifies as good, for a five year old who perceives parents as nurturant, just and virtuous and identifies with them, will come to regard him or herself as possessing those desirable qualities. (p. 265)

He adds that five-year-olds must believe they are valued in order to grow up valuing themselves. Lidz (1973) also describes the importance of the family in human adaptation and integration. He suggests that the family must foster and direct the child's development by carrying out interrelated functions: (1) the parental nurturant function; (2) the influence of the dynamic family organization; (3) the family as a social system; and (4) the transmission of the instrumental techniques of culture, particularly its system of meaning and logic.

The nurturant function involves fulfilling not only the child's physical needs but also his or her emotional needs for love, affection, and a sense of security. Lidz notes that the quality and nature of the parental nurturance will influence emotional development—vulnerability to frustration, anger, aggressivity, anxiety, hopelessness or helplessness the child experiences under various conditions.

Lidz defines the dynamic family organization as the necessity and strategies for maintaining boundaries between generations and adherence to gender-linked roles. Lidz states simply that "conflicts and role distortions in these areas will interfere with the proper channeling of the child's drives, energies and role learning."

Like others, Lidz defines the family as the first social system from which the child grows and acquires familiarity with the basic social roles of society. "Family behavior teaches the child the family's value system, role definitions, and patterns of interrelating with one another far more than what he is taught, or even what is consciously appreciated, by the parents."

Finally, Lidz defines the family as the agent of transmission of language and symbol, necessary for social adaptation and cooperative interactions with others.

Lidz examines schizophrenic disorder as a "deficiency disease" (Lidz & Fleck, 1965), a deficiency in the family's capacity to nurture, structure, enculture, and socialize a developing child (p. 22).

How clear and straightforward these descriptions are, though, of course, no individual or family meets the ideal. However, children with an alcoholic parent(s) often fall far short of receiving the necessary positive foundation at every level. Throughout this book, we will return to these guidelines as Lidz did with schizophrenia and Thurman with the handicapped: What is the impact on key tasks of development for children with an alcoholic parent?

Following this brief description of the "normal" family, we may look at the alcoholic family. As outlined in Chapter 1, the alcoholic family is one in which one or both parents suffer from alcoholism.

ALCOHOL: THE CENTRAL ORGANIZING PRINCIPLE

In developing the concept of alcohol as the organizing principle for the alcoholic (Brown, 1985), I outlined the development of a behavioral and thinking disorder. The primary focus becomes alcohol and the drinking behavior while the primary cognitive focus is the denial of that behavior. The defenses of denial and rationalization are necessary to maintain the alcoholic's belief in self-control. The drinking behavior and its denial becomes the central organizing principle for the alcoholic.

The preoccupation with not being alcoholic and a focus on alcohol grow, dominating the individual's life. The availability of alcohol, opportunities to drink, and the success of denial are the main criteria for decision making. Relationships and activities not related to alcohol, such as hobbies or association with nondrinking friends, are relinquished to accommodate increasing drinking activities with drinking friends.

> Subtle though it may be, the individual's life gradually becomes dominated by alcohol. This change in style of life may be characterized as a turn toward alcohol; alcohol begins to serve as the central organizing principle in life. This turn is the point at which the individual ceases to choose alcohol freely and begins to need it. The need for alcohol becomes the central focus (most often unconscious) and, in effect, the organizer of the individual's behavior and thinking. The need to include more and more alcohol in one's life without disturbing the central belief in self control becomes the dominant and incompatible focus of daily life. (Brown, 1985, p. 77)

Steinglass (1980) and Brown (1985) refer to the "alcoholic family," that is, a family in which alcohol is the organizing principle. Each person in the family develops the same behavioral and thinking disorder as the alcoholic: They are controlled by the reality of alcoholism and they must deny that reality at the same time. To preserve this inherent contradiction, all family members must adapt their thinking and behavior to fit the family's "story," that is, the explanations that have been constructed to allow the drinking behavior to be maintained and denied at the same time. This "story" becomes the family's point of view. It includes core beliefs which family members share and which provide a sense of unity and cohesion, often *against* an outside world perceived as hostile or unsafe.

The strength of the organizing principle is also illustrated in family rules. As one of our patients explains (Beletsis & Brown, 1981):

> There were two rules in our family: the first was "there is no alcoholism" and the second "don't talk about it."

Alcohol is special to the alcoholic, like a secret partner. It is an intruder to others in the family who must make major adaptations and accommodations in their personal relationships within the family and outside (Brown, 1985). To understand fully the centrality and organizing function of alcohol, one might envision a scene in which all family members are seated around a dining table with a large bottle of alcohol at the center. The constant presence of alcohol functions as a filter, coloring all family interactions, perceptions and affect. Think of this bottle as an in-law who has moved in to stay. Other authors have referred to this intruder as the elephant (Typpo & Hastings, 1984) in the living room. The presence of an in-law changes family interactions, roles, and even perceptions about events. Yet families may deny the presence of this permanent visitor, ignore it, or attempt to go around it. Nevertheless, the impact is very real and significant. The image of the bottle on the table is just the same. It is a constant, real presence which influences every aspect of individual and family life. Kaufman (1986) and Wolin et al. (1980) stress the importance of differences in pattern and family systems, suggesting that not all families deny parental alcoholism or organize around its centrality. Kaufman (1986) suggests that there is considerable disengagement from the alcoholic and the alcoholism as both progress. Although this is certainly true and verified by a wide diversity of clinical reports, appropriate or positive disengagement is, in fact, infrequent. While parental alcoholism may not be denied, and family members do find ways to go around it, parental alcoholism is still a major organizing principle within the family.

The alcoholic's "turn toward alcohol" may be subtle and prolonged, or precipitous, jolting the individual and others who are close. Either way, as the alcoholic's need for alcohol grows, members of the family "turn toward alcohol" as well, making adaptations in their perceptions and logic to preserve the family's belief in the alcoholic's ability to control his or her drinking. Or, they shift the focus of control to themselves, believing in *their* ability to control the alcoholic's drinking. Thus family members develop the same distorted thinking as the alcoholic—a logic that reverses or skews cause and effect.

Members of AA refer to this logic as "alcoholic thinking," a system of core beliefs, especially the illusion of control, that is maintained through denial and rationalization. This logic maintains that alcohol is a means to cope with something else that is identified as the major problem. This notion—that there is a problem and it is something other than alcohol—is central to the core belief system of the alcoholic and family. It is a problem that ties and holds them together.

> We learned early on that Dad needed his martinis at night to unwind after a hard day at the office. His boss was the target of many an angry, bitter dinner hour as we all attacked this cause of our family's unhappiness.

Often the major "problem" is identified as someone else within the family. Instead of banding together against an outside problem, the family now splits internally as more and more members take the blame. Often it is the spouse.

> My husband always told me if I were a better wife, more loving, sexually responsive and less demanding, he wouldn't need to drink so much. I spent years trying to be that better wife but his drinking didn't change.

Often the source of blame ends up being the children. The alcoholic always needs a target to explain the drinking and the partner, the "codependent" (Wegscheider, 1981), needs one to explain his or her frustration and feelings of guilt and failure in being able to control the alcoholic.

> Mom reminded us, not always nicely, that we were the cause of the family's strife. If we didn't fight so much or if we got better grades, she wouldn't feel so upset all the time. I grew up knowing one thing for certain: I would cause some problem today though I couldn't necessarily determine how, what, or why.

The preservation of the drinking privilege and the denial of any difficulties with alcohol require a scapegoat. Often everyone in the family (including the alcoholic) feels responsible and guilty for not being able to solve the problem (the one that is labeled or the drinking that is not) or change the situation. Each individual tries harder to figure out what he or she can do—be a better wife, get better grades—to no avail. Nothing changes. The seeds for severe problems are sewn as a consequence of this perpetual cognitive double bind: What is most visible and obvious must be denied *and* explained as something else.

DENIAL: AN EMPHASIS ON DEFENSE

As noted earlier, there is in most alcoholic families a major secret—alcohol. The secret and its preservation become the central focus around which the family organizes (Steinglass, 1980; Brown, 1985, 1986). Denial is the defensive cornerstone that maintains the secret and secures alcohol as the unacknowledged central organizing principle in the family.

The level of denial varies considerably from one family to another. Assessment of variance is extremely important in understanding consequences and adaptations that children make. It is also important in understanding transmission. Wolin and Bennet (Williams, 1984) suggest that familial avoidance or denial of parental alcoholism increases the risk of passing alcohol problems on to the next generation.

For some families the presence or reality of alcoholism is "nonexistent." Although there may be hints of concern about a parent's drinking (perhaps father has begun to count mother's drinks after dinner), the idea that alcohol itself may be a problem is an unexplored possibility. The belief that alcohol is a solution to another problem is tightly maintained.

> It's incredible to me now. My parents drank themselves to oblivion every night yet at no time ever did anyone suggest that anything was wrong! No wonder I was frightened.

> I have just realized that my mother is an alcoholic. I am 35 years old. I have an older brother 38 and a sister 41. We lived with my mother's alcoholism for as long as I can remember and we never once talked about it. I told my brother and sister I was joining a group for ACAs and they were dumbfounded, then furious. It wasn't true! What was I saying about the family by joining such a group?

In some families the presence of alcohol is acknowledged, but not the realities of alcoholism. The alcoholic and the family deny the centrality of alcohol and any problems or consequences. There may be underlying concern but it is masked.

> My father always had a drink in his hand or within reach. Now that I think about it, it was kind of like his security blanket. We never thought much about it, although I remember being upset because his drinking came before a hello kiss from me.

Other families recognize and acknowledge the presence of alcohol and incorporate its centrality into the family's beliefs.

Everybody in my family drank. That's who we were! Alcohol was a part of our heritage, passed on from one generation to the next. As kids, we couldn't wait to join the grown ups. Uncles, aunts, everybody had such a good time drinking together.

Not surprisingly, this adult is a recovering alcoholic who struggled with the sense that alcoholism was "normal" in his family and that he has abandoned a prized membership in a drinking clan by choosing abstinence.

Other families may glorify alcohol less but still incorporate its necessity and regular use.

We belong to a lively social group—lots of gourmet dinners, wine tasting, tail gate parties and Sunday brunches. Drinking is always a part of these activities.

True, but not quite. Drinking for this couple is actually the main event, illustrated from the child's point of view.

My parents were constantly on the go or entertaining in our home. And they were always drinking. As the years passed, they socialized less. They said it was too much trouble to go out or be with friends. Socialization now interfered with their drinking.

Rarely is alcohol acknowledged by all family members to be the main problem and the cause of other difficulties. A seat-mate on a recent flight was immediately responsive to hearing that I had just come from a conference on children of alcoholics. As I said the words "children of alcoholics" she raised her hand. Then she easily reported the following:

I was overwhelmed by it. My father's alcoholism was the scandal of the town and the center of our existence. His alcoholism organized all our lives. We didn't deny it. We were constantly dealing with it. When I left home and got some distance, I could see that there were lots of other problems in the family that none of us ever recognized because everything was overshadowed by the focus on his drinking.

Out of the home for a long time, with parents now dead, she explained that she had undergone years of psychotherapy to deal with the consequences of her childhood family life. She wondered whether many children of alcoholics have trouble with intimate relationships, do they marry late or with great fear, and do they necessarily become alcoholic? I was amazed at her knowledge and wondered if she had read a lot about children of alcoholics.

No, I didn't know there was anything published.

As alcoholism progresses and encompasses more of the family's life, the need for denial increases. Children are faced very early with the need to join the denial process or experience a continuing challenge to their own perceptions. The latter is almost impossible for children to sustain.

I can remember pleading with my mother to do something about Dad's drinking. She became angry with *me* saying I was selfish after all he'd done for me. After trying to get her help a few times with this result, I gave up trying.

I was terrified of driving with my parents. Both of them drove around drunk all the time. Once I refused to get into the car, telling my Dad he was drunk and I wasn't going anywhere with him. He hit me and shoved me in the car. My mother cried and told me never to criticize my father's drinking again. Look what I had done! I'd really upset him now. How could I spoil such a nice family outing?

The strength of the denial prevails and the family becomes increasingly isolated and defensive. The reality of alcoholism and the pressure to maintain denial necessitate withdrawal from friends and community activities. There may be frequent moves and job changes which intensify the sense of isolation.

My father's alcoholism shaped our entire lives. He was so erratic and crazy, we were constantly coping. We tried to maintain an image of respectability but he always blew it with some dumb or obnoxious drunken episode. Then he'd wake us up in the middle of the night, we'd grab a few things and move *again*. We were always "getting a fresh start."

The need for coping and the necessity of denial lead to a predominance of defensive strategies. The threat of discovery of the family's secret and the threat of disaster resulting from the alcoholism are constants.

In the drinking, denying family, it is impossible to accurately assess personality and developmental strengths and weaknesses. The defensive posture, necessary for survival, is all encompassing. It is unfortunately the defensive posture that becomes the "role" children adapt and frequently the only sense of self that develops. Thus the core of treatment for the ACA is often the unraveling of the defensive posture—the false self—and the building, often seemingly from scratch, of a new real self, based on acknowledging and reconstructing the reality of parental alcoholism. (Part III focuses on this reconstruction process.)

Lidz (1973) has examined perception in relation to communication in families with a schizophrenic child. He wonders whether children "because of their parents' difficulties in communication or because of the peculiarities of the meaning and reasoning used within the family, develop confused meanings that distort perception of experience and perhaps impede efforts at problem solving" (p. 63). He speculates that children's means of relating are impaired and they may have trouble acquiring useful expectancies. Because of the peculiarity in language and logic, do children grow up learning that the meanings of words can be changed to defend against emotional turmoil? Most importantly, he asks whether language remains a "high road to fantasy" escape rather than an instrumental tool.

In describing schizophrenic language distortions, Lidz suggests that parents unwittingly force children to distort perception, meanings and reasoning. He describes a "folie en famille," the sharing and taking for granted of an aberrant or delusional concept that pervades the family's relationships (p. 63).

Denial requires significant distortions in perception and logic, similar to what Lidz describes in the schizophrenic family. The impact is serious and pervasive. Denial of the obvious is the chief mechanism of defense in the alcoholic family.

Lidz further defines the concept of the double bind in family communication, delineated originally by Bateson and Jackson (1956). A child cannot escape from an impossible situation of conflicting demands because of his or her dependency upon and need for the parent or parents imposing the demands. The bind may be established verbally or nonverbally and also through denial of the obvious, if it threatens the parents' self-image.

The Impact of Denial

Since the beginning of our clinical work, we have noted the importance of perceptual problems (Cermak & Brown, 1982). Adults reported in the initial interviews and demonstrated in the intensive group setting difficulties trusting their own view of reality. Quickly and frequently our patients made the connecting link: their own perceptions conflicted with the view of reality presented by their parents. They had to join in denial and accept the family's core beliefs and attitudes or risk betraying the family. They learned to view the family experience and the world outside the family through the filter of denial. They learned not to test reality, not to take action, because it would not be congruent with the parents' reality.

A television movie about the children of alcoholics (*Shattered Spirits,* Greenwald, 1986) brought back painful feelings of living with an alcoholic father for one group member as he thought about the impact of his father's denial.

> Dan was amazed at how angry he felt at his own father for the arbitrary, erratic outbursts of anger and manipulation. Dan also feels upset with himself for "buying into" the distorted reasoning. Dan feels tremendously affected by living with someone who was so out of control and who so dominated the way the family behaved and explained reality. He has had to struggle hard as an adult to understand what is real for him.

Another member identified with the strong denial exercised by all family members in the movie. She related this to her current experiences with her mother.

> Margo would very much like her mother to be more open and honest about her feelings and about the reality of their lives. Margo remains frustrated because her mother continues to exercise a tremendous amount of denial which Margo must accept and adapt to. Her mother's need to deny means that Margo does not have permission to feel her own feelings about the realities she now *does* recognize. It is a betrayal, or a disloyalty, to go beyond one's mother in feeling and in recognition of reality.

> Margo, Pen and Sara now acknowledged the almost intangible "tie" they feel to their mothers: to choose a different way, to see things differently, to feel more than mother, is to lose the relationship with her.

Then Pen wondered whether Margo really ever had one anyway. Margo realized that she didn't, but recognizes there is still the wish for something.

In a beginning group, members repeatedly reflected on the impact of denial. Sally still has to maintain the family's charade with an elderly aunt and uncle who frequently reminisce about the wonderful times shared by all at family reunions. In the group, Sally clutches her chair and notes:

> I am bursting with the need to say how it really was.

For many weeks Sally was preoccupied with the subject of denial and her need to break it.

> Sally noted that three of the women had on the same kind of shoes last week. This observation led members to question what it must have been like to be able to notice so much growing up but not to be able to see it at the same time.

Group members then spoke about the importance of having at least one adult who knew how things really were. That one person served a tremendously important function in anchoring the child to a reality different from the parents' version, though it still could not be acknowledged. The impact is, nevertheless, of major proportions. Adults in treatment often reveal a profound attachment to that one person who did know. In many cases, the attachment to that individual and that view of reality provides the key to understanding improved coping or significantly better developmental adjustment than would be expected based on the family history and patterns of attachment to parents alone. A patient illustrates:

> Jerry presented a family history characterized by serious parental abuse and neglect. His mother was a severe alcoholic, frequently violent or passed out in her bed. His father also drank, ignored the children, physically abused his mother and traveled frequently. Jerry remembers lying awake at night, terrified, figuring out ways to escape the attention of both parents.

> In relating this history, Jerry brightens as he notes his major method of escape. He used to spend hours after school with a favorite teacher who took a special interest in him early-on. That teacher encouraged his academic pursuits, clearly communicating

affection and approval contrary to Jerry's sense of himself as a "pain in the ass." As Jerry talks about this teacher, he smiles:

> Mr. Johnson *knew* how it was. He knew my parents were alcoholics and I needed help even though we never talked about it.

The subject of "appearances" is also related to denial, perception and "point of view."

> Following attendance at a conference on children of alcoholics, the therapist reported that a mother of a patient in the group had introduced herself to the therapist and thanked her for the work she had done with her daughter in the ACA group. Group members reacted strongly. Would there now be "sides"? Would the therapist abandon them for the parent's point of view? Would the therapist stop believing the patient's view of reality? Would the therapist be fooled?

> Several patients were alarmed and angry as the therapist registered her impression of the mother as sincere in her appreciation of the help her daughter had received. They urged the therapist not to be "taken in" by the "two faced" con artist parent. Several spoke about how wonderful and loved their parents were in the community or professionally. But that was the "face." They weren't so wonderful at home.

It is extremely difficult or impossible for patients who are beginning treatment and just breaking denial "publicly" to appreciate in-depth the complexities of the alcoholic parent and that, indeed, the individual *was* awful at home and not awful outside. It is all or none for a long time. The parent who was supposed to be "good" is now "bad." To entertain a mix is impossible cognitively and emotionally. Therefore, a therapist's positive view of an interaction with a parent is enormously threatening to the newfound sense of safety, based on a break in denial and a different point of view. In essence, patients say to the therapist: "Please don't change your mind about what it was really like for me."

THE CLINICIAN'S VIEW: TARGETING ALCOHOL AS THE CENTRAL ORGANIZING PRINCIPLE IN THE FACE OF PERSISTENT DENIAL

While knowledgeable and sensitive clinicians may recognize the realities of parental alcoholism and drug abuse, it is another

matter to incorporate that recognition into diagnosis and treatment planning and still quite another to identify alcohol as the
central organizing principle in the family and therefore central
to understanding the child's or adult's problems. The following
clinical vignettes illustrate the course of treatment for two children identified in the evaluation as having an alcoholic parent.
These case presentations were prepared by Dr. Mary deLuca, a
child psychiatrist, as an introduction to Grand Rounds about
the children of alcoholics.

Tommy, a seven year old Caucasian boy, was referred for school
placement and psychotherapy after having been hospitalized for
two months on a children's ward where he underwent individual
and family psychotherapy and treatment with antidepressants
for his depressed mood, suicidal ideation, aggressive behavior towards peers and authority, cruelty to animals, encopresis, and
learning difficulties. These symptoms had been present for three
to four years. His family situation was, as expected, chaotic and
included multiple serial relationships on the part of both parents
and a previous marriage by the mother. Both parents had extensive
family histories of psychopathology and alcohol and drug abuse
and the mother had been sexually abused by a paternal grandfather. Both parents acknowledged abusing alcohol themselves
and the mother had also periodically abused marijuana, cocaine
and amphetamines (including during her unplanned and unwanted pregnancy with Tommy). However, history and details of
the substance abuse were minimized in the records from Tommy's
hospitalization. They both also insisted that they had stopped
using all substances when Tommy went into the hospital and did
not see themselves as alcoholic or drug-dependent. Both held responsible occupational positions and reportedly functioned ade-
quately on the job.

Tommy and his family were seen in treatment for only three
months. He initially presented as a sullen, hesitant, slow to trust,
husky boy who, nonetheless, exhibited a positive response to attention from an adult figure and made attempts to relate and
interact. He was quite spontaneous in play sessions and repeatedly displayed scenes of parental inadequacy, role reversal, external as well as intrapsychic chaos, and responses to this alternating
between denial, helplessness, and fantasied grandiosity. During
an early session, he made a series of drawings of his sister and him
driving a racing car while his parents observed from the sidelines,
sitting in a much smaller, less powerful car. Play with a doll house
repeatedly displayed both parents either asleep, up all night in the

shower, stumbling, falling over, watching TV, or otherwise oblivious and unavailable while the children (who had "special powers") organized and ran the home, made household repairs, prepared meals for themselves, and successfully fought off intruders who wanted to invade and take possession of the house. Three "brothers" also watched as a "step daughter" and "step father" retreated to a closet for mysterious activities and then observed helplessly as the "step father" forced the girl into the chimney and gleefully watched her burn. This was followed by a flurry of generalized violence and chaos as the brothers flew about the house destroying everything in sight. On other occasions, Tommy would portray the children as rearranging the house, setting up "secret quarters" in the basement, and banishing the parents to the children's room, locking the doors and preventing them from going anywhere.

In his real life, Tommy was dealing with continual parental conflict, a sense of helplessness in being able to control his father's erratic work schedule or mother's frequent business trips, a loss of his previous therapist and uncertainty about continuing with the present one. Due to school district refusal to fund school placement in combination with financial difficulties and a rather long commute, the family elected to change therapists. Of particular interest, however, is the fact that the transfer was initiated at a time when both parents were confronted about resuming alcohol use (which they insisted they had under control).

*   *   *   *   *   *

The second case involves David, a 16 year old Caucasian boy, from a middle class family who was acutely hospitalized for an impulsive suicide attempt (a fairly deep laceration of his wrist with a knife) after a family argument in which both mother and step father were again drinking after previously promising to go to an AA meeting. David's parents had divorced when he was eight years old. Prior to that time, his natural father was a constant drinker and away from home frequently on business and the mother was alternately over involved or neglectful of David. There had been repeated moves and changes in schools, and loss of friends. Subsequently, David lived alternately with both parents, his father still drinking and frequently expressing suicidal ideation. His mother remarried and both the step father and she began drinking heavily, with marital turmoil and episodic physical violence being characteristic. Although David had made previous suicide attempts, they were usually ignored, other than one which resulted in a few therapy sessions terminated by his father.

In therapy, David was initially overly polite, deferential, articulate and pseudo mature. However, he had a great deal of difficulty with negative affect (depression, anxiety and especially anger) and defended against feelings by using denial, avoidance, splitting, somatization, and excessive and inappropriate humor. He revealed recurrent feelings (often experienced through the transference) of not being cared for or listened to, and communicated a profound need for nurturance, approval and acceptance, a fear of erratic behavior or abandonment/rejection by the therapist, and a rage at parental figures for the role reversal he experienced. He also dealt with sexual identity concerns, poor school performance (despite above average intelligence), low self esteem, and fears of being crazy or out of control. (Indeed, he did become disorganized and overwhelmed by intense affect.) Most recently, David's own experiments with alcohol and drugs had come up as an issue.

Individual and family treatment continued with ambivalence about out of home placement on discharge so he was temporarily placed with family friends. David was rehospitalized after returning home and shortly after his parents terminated family therapy. (Out of home placement had still not been accepted even though family conflicts and alcoholism remained problems.)

The second hospitalization was spurred by another family argument in which parental drinking was involved and David pulled a knife on his step father and threw a table through a window. After much ambivalence and resistance, David and his parents agreed that out of home placement was the only option and a court hearing was scheduled.

These case examples illustrate several major difficulties. With so much chaos and so many presenting complaints, it is hard to target parental alcoholism and drug abuse as the central issue. The therapist illustrated the outcome in the first case when she tried to do so: the boy was withdrawn from treatment.

With such a chaotic and disturbed history, how is it possible to formulate and understand developmental difficulties?

The starting point is the diagnosis of parental alcoholism. If parental behavior and the environment do not change, it is extremely difficult for the child to change. If the parents reject the diagnosis of alcoholism, it is also difficult for the child to accept it, though he will hear the therapist's acknowledgment of reality. Doctor deLuca described two different styles of adjustment or coping, a sullen, angry 7-year-old and a polite, pseudo mature 16-year-old. She described a presenting portrait directly related to the atmosphere, environment and interpersonal adjustment within an alcoholic family. The theory and the clinical examples in this book illustrate how to think about the reality of parental alcoholism and drug abuse and the denial of that reality as the central organizing principle in the family. Dynamics—individual and familial—may be quite differently understood from this perspective. Also illustrated repeatedly is the ability of adults when they accept the label "adult child of an alcoholic," to talk about a reality they could not see or speak about as children.

A FOCUS ON THE ENVIRONMENT: WHAT IS IT LIKE?

Earlier, the alcoholic family environment was described globally as chaotic, unpredictable, inconsistent, with arbitrary, repetitious and illogical thinking, and not infrequently, violence and incest. This is a family that is out of control with no means to regain it. The alcoholic is number one in the family, setting the shifting rules and tone to which everyone else must adjust and respond. The child's needs, feelings, and behavior are always secondary to those of the alcoholic and often regulated by the needs of the drinker. Added to the organizing function of alcohol and its denial is the need for a focus on control.

Control

The centrality of alcoholism and its denial is supported by a strong belief in control. The thinking disorder for the alcoholic (Brown, 1985) emphasizes the significance of two beliefs:

1. I am not alcoholic.
2. I can control my drinking.

These beliefs form the core of the individual's identity and structure interpretations of self and others in the environment. The individual's perceptions and beliefs about the world *must* fit these two beliefs. Incoming data that challenges them must be either altered to fit, ignored, or denied.

These beliefs are also central to the identity of the alcoholic family, that is, the family's "story" when denial is intact. There is no alcoholism and no lack of control. The chaos, inconsistency, and unpredictability are denied, incorporated into the family's sense of normality, or attributed to some other problem.

In the face of strong and continuing denial, the struggle to control a situation that cannot be controlled is the overriding reality. As the woman on the plane stated:

> We were constantly coping with it.

We have accumulated much clinical evidence to support the hypothesis that the parents' unsuccessful struggle for control over alcohol becomes internalized by the child (Beletsis & Brown, 1981). Children believe they can cope with conflict and chaos by controlling themselves and others.

Children often assume major responsibilities in the family, learning early how to cope with rapidly changing situations. They are adept at shifting roles from child to parent and often are engaged in attempts to "manage" the actions of others.

> I knew I could get what I wanted with the proper timing. Mom was most remorseful and receptive in the late morning before she started sipping sherry through the afternoon. She said yes to almost anything at 11:00 while the same request would get an angry no at 3:00.

As a child, the individual achieved a sense of control by figuring out the importance of timing. As an adult, she reports feeling guilty because she "manages" and manipulates other people so well. She cannot see the flaw in her belief in her control of others though group members repeatedly point it out: her "management" was always a *response* to someone else's control, or lack of it. Underneath her belief in control were painful feelings of desperation, helplessness and deep need, never alleviated and therefore covered and ultimately denied in the interest of survival. A patient illustrates the consequences of her successful denial.

> Sue describes deep painful feelings in a rational, matter of fact way and the group responds to her at that level, offering advice. Then she is disappointed; she is not getting what she wants. Sue then explores her need to look good, to be in control and to "manage" the reactions of others.

Group work demonstrates how this "management" is carried further. Individuals believe they can gain a measure of control and therefore safety in their interpersonal relationships by "managing" the ways in which others see them. It is a strong but faulty defense that maintains that individuals have the power and ability to determine how others will interpret and, therefore, respond to them. Recognition that this belief in control of the perceptions of others is false is often met with anxiety or panic, experienced and possibly expressed as a sudden vulnerability and lack of safety. It takes a long time to uncover this side of the management issue. Recognition of the quality of "magical thinking" embedded in this belief is also fiercely resisted. In the advanced group, relinquishment of this belief also uncovers feelings of utter helplessness, desperation, and need.

Chaos

The family "atmosphere" has been identified as a central theme in children's understanding of parental alcoholism (Wilson & Orford, 1978). Chaos is one of the most prominent features of this atmosphere. We have noted elsewhere (Beletsis & Brown, 1981; Brown, 1986) that it may be overt or covert, an important distinction. Not all or even most alcoholic families *look* upset, disheveled, disorganized, or out of control, though certainly this is true for some. Defensive adaptations and efforts at coping often successfully mask the underlying chaotic reality. This reality reflects the overriding dominance the alcoholic exercises over the family and the ever-present sense of impending doom: things are or soon will be out of control. A group patient illustrates.

> Ted's cousin was impressed with the stability of Ted's family because there were book shelves and books all around. He imagined that Ted enjoyed stimulating intellectual discussions over dinner. As the group howled with this story, Ted said bitterly that the intellectual discussions got as far as his father's screaming for the dictionary because somebody had used a word improperly.

This recollection introduced a discussion of "appearances."

> Sally remembered the ironing board, always up in her living room. If mother could do the ironing, things must be under control.

> As she thinks about this, Sally laughs ironically. She struggles constantly to alter her negative view of the world. She lives through terrible disasters everyday so she doesn't have to be on guard against them.

The potential for instability is a constant as daily routines may be upset at anytime. Families often adjust to the sense of chaos and it ironically becomes predictable. As a patient explained:

> The chaos was the only thing I knew for sure. I always could rely on the unexpected and the knowledge I'd have to quickly adjust—turn my attention to the crisis at hand and get into gear. I always grew up "on guard." It was the only way to survive.

After a few difficult weeks in group, a new patient reflected on his entry:

> Hank expects a hostile environment and therefore was on guard as he entered group. He sees fierce animals in the group or simply walking down the street. He always makes a quick assessment of the environment: he must be careful not to be trapped by someone so he would make a mistake, break a rule or humiliate himself. His general attitude is to approach everyone with suspicion and the expectation he will be betrayed.

Mike also recalls the unpredictability, but describes a different reaction.

> Mike remembers how distressing his mother's unpredictability was to him. He felt constantly on guard and shielded from her violence and rage. Mike recalls insulating himself emotionally and physically; now he does not feel or even remember much of his life. He can recall in detail the houses he lived in but not what happened inside of them. Mike realizes there are huge, unknown, unexplainable parts of himself that need to be filled in.

Being "on guard" hypervigilant in response to unpredictability & chaos.

Being "on guard" carries over and is a way of life for many. It is described as a constant watchfulness, a hypervigilant stance, and a defensive attitude of mistrust toward others. In attempting to understand the origins of this chronic anxiety, adults frequently recall an environment characterized by constant uncertainty, unpredictability, and arbitrary parental behavior and logic. It was in reality impossible to guess what was coming next, or to "manage" anything, much less the behavior of others.

> Joyce describes her father's cruelty and love for her: she could never predict how he would be or what behavior from her would

elicit an angry, cruel response. Pleasing men is important. But she is always certain she will fail and it will be her fault. It must have been her fault that she got beaten up on certain occasions and not on others.

Other group members recall the chaos, lack of control and violence as well:

Jack describes having no control over his parents as a child—his mother beat him often in an uncontrolled manner. She would be violent and abusive, then guilty and ingratiating as she needed to hear from him that he loved her.

Hank and Bonnie were also victims of uncertainty and unpredictable violence. They could not predict which parent would lose control. Hank would work with his father building something when suddenly his father was hammering him. He lived with a constant sense of fear and uncertainty.

And finally:

Mike is amazed that Paul can claim group time or feels he deserves it. Mike had no strong feelings or reactions. He grew up detached from all emotions, maintaining a guarded stance to survive. Mother was unpredictable. There was no carry over in rules or expectations.

Sally nodded: she calls this the "children of alcoholics shuffle."

Inconsistency and Unpredictability

Inconsistency in parental behavior and logic is a chronic interference in establishing stability and predictability. Children cannot feel secure and free to turn their attention to their own internal development when the rules and roles in the family are constantly changing. Children especially will have difficulty establishing standards of behavior when parents model arbitrary and inconsistent behaviors and values themselves (Kagan, 1984).

Inconsistency also may be evident in changing standards of authority and limit setting. A behavior considered funny today will be harshly punished tomorrow. A permission granted today will be rescinded or forgotten tomorrow. Kagan (1984) notes that the harsh and arbitrary exercise of firm control results in very negative consequences.

I'll never forget the anger and humiliation I felt as a teenager. On Tuesday, I asked my Dad for permission to use the car for a date on Saturday. He said, "sure." Saturday came and I was ready to go. He'd been drinking all day and lashed out at me: "Who did I think I was expecting to get the car? I was ungrateful and unhelpful and I wasn't going anywhere."

The inconsistency is also evident in changing explanations for behavior and events. Today's explanation is contradicted, edited or forgotten tomorrow. Distortions or contradictions in logic are necessary to support denial and rationalization. In addition, the effects of alcohol interfere with logical, clear thinking and certainly with memory. Many children and adults report their frustration at hearing the same story repeatedly from a drinking parent who has no idea she has told it before. They also refer to a "haze" or confusion that often characterizes the family atmosphere.

There was a tendency towards being "numb" about feeling—what goes on, what people say and recognizing what they saw. Tony used to operate in a "haze." Mike was always numb and still is. Bonnie is sure her sense of confusion and "haziness" about her family and her interactions with others is due to the chronic haze of their drinking.

The inconsistency and confusion in logic also have an impact on perception, as noted earlier. Children come to believe that they do not see things accurately. As adults, they recall being told by a parent that what they saw—the drunken parent—was not what they saw (Brown & Beletsis, 1986).

Sandra's mother informed her that her parents were not arguing and fighting late into the night as Sandra perceived, but rather were having "discussions."

Inconsistency affects children interpersonally as well. They cannot learn to predict the interpersonal consequences of their behavior because of the changing rules and logic (Cermak & Brown, 1982). As a result, they suffer a constant feeling of fear, uncertainty, and deep distrust.

Roles

Many authorities have noted the inconsistency evidenced in unclear or changing parental roles (Hanson & Estes, 1977; Black, 1981; Wegscheider, 1981; Kaufman & Pattison, 1981; Brown, 1985). The pattern of the drinking behavior—stable or erratic—will affect role assignment and stability. One parent, the non-alcoholic, if there is one, may regularly assume the roles and responsibilities of both father and mother with the alcoholic incapacitated and excluded from the family's routine function. The alcoholic may become another child, taken care of, cleaned up after, and not consulted in decision making.

Inconsistency may be minimal in such a home although the non functional, childlike parent creates confusion for children and later difficulties in identification because of a lack of appropriate modeling (Jackson, 1962). Parents may change roles according to the drinking behavior of the alcoholic. Some alcoholics drink "periodically" or in a "binge" pattern, alternating with periods of sobriety and stable functioning. These families adjust to the alternating patterns with all members ready to switch roles when the alcoholic begins to drink.

> When Dan's father began to drink, his mother exhibited a sense of vigilance and wariness, as if she would need to take control or make it safe for the children. In the group, Dan perceives the female therapist in the same way. She is on the lookout for someone to be out of control. That person is Dan: he equates his own internal feelings with being out of control and, therefore, drunk like his father.

Parents may take turns with one assuming responsibility while the other one drinks and vice versa. Both parents offer confusing and erratic models for their children as well as unpredictable emotional availability. The consequences of the lack of any consistent, stable parental figure are severe.

Frequently a child substitutes for one or both parents, assuming major responsibility for managing the home, caring for younger children or an incapacitated parent. Sometimes this substitution is part of a cross-generational coalition or triangulation (Kaufman, 1986) with a nonalcoholic parent.

> Shirley remembers helping her mother feel better by being a good girl. Shirley was always "on duty," cheerful and available to take

charge of her younger brother and sister. She now muses that her career choice as a helping professional allowed her to carry over her sense of responsibility and intense involvement with others. She never considered she might work in a field that would not demand such intense involvement and over responsibility.

Most adults in treatment share a conscious sense of having missed childhood. Some of them yearn for a fantasied sense of closeness, achieved through a secure relationship with a parent. They speak of an inner freedom and spontaneity, imagined and longed for—the kind of freedom a child ought to experience in a safe and stable family—the kind of freedom described by Kagan (1984) and Lidz (1973) as part of the ideal or "normal" family. Such freedom is impossible in an atmosphere of tension, unpredictability, and inconsistency, with lack of safety a constant concern. Such freedom is also short circuited by the necessity for too early responsibilities for others. A patient in an advanced group frequently experienced this sense of longing and missed opportunity. When a new therapist joined the group, she reflected on her reaction:

> I don't have any great expectations for you. I imagine you'll just sit there. I would like to be able to hope that you would be openly supportive and nurturing, excited about my discoveries. I would love to feel the freedom of a child blossoming with a delighted parent cheering me on. Can you imagine what this would be like for a child?

Many adults are aware of their longing to be cared for because they have consciously tried to provide for their own children what they did not receive themselves. As they see their children "blossom," the pain of what they missed is awakened.

> As a child I swore I'd "be there" for my kids so they'd never have to experience the loneliness and the fear I lived with constantly. I often look at them and feel intense envy for what they've gotten from me that I missed getting from my parents.

The longing for what was missed is a constant, sometimes expressed directly as the above examples illustrate or indirectly. Christmas frequently evokes painful memories and discussion in the group about what it was like.

Members recalled not having a father or a family for Christmas because they were always drunk. Brad said, "it was pretty hard to be a kid." Christmas simply added more chaos. Brad's father was always saying he might not be with them next Christmas or even the next event which was terribly distressing to Brad.

> Kate recalls how needy she felt all the time. But as Christmas rolls around, she feels a deep sadness that she missed having any parent at all who could have taken care of her so she could have had feelings herself.

If parents are sober, will they take a drink at the holidays?

> Carl never enjoyed Christmas. His father was sober on and off and there was often a disaster around his drinking. Carl tried to withdraw and to blend into the wall. Christmas was a sure sign that his father would begin to drink. Embarrassing and painful situations would follow.

Tension

The atmosphere in the alcoholic family, regardless of outward signs of disturbance, is chronically tense. As the dissonance increases between the realities of alcoholism and its denial and the pressures of inconsistency build, the defensive posture tightens. Because family members "know" they are sharing a "secret," the fear of discovery looms large within the family and outside. The fear of discovery requires an enemy. That potential source of harm then becomes the recipient for projected feelings of hostility. Children learn that the family must stick together and that the world outside is a hostile one, not to be trusted.

Within the family, there may be constant tension with periodic outbursts of anger, rage, or violence (Jacob, Dunn & Leonard, 1981). Black notes (1986) that ACAs report that their fear of parental arguing outweighed their concern about the drinking.

Shame

In characterizing the family atmosphere, many adults recall intense feelings of humiliation and shame. Often they were painfully and publicly embarrassed or ridiculed by a drunk or hostile parent. Jack recalls a sense of constant humiliation in public places:

I hoped people would know I wasn't like those two.

Adults often recall a need to fade into the woodwork as children to minimize humiliation or abuse. Being visible was dangerous; not only did they run the risk of being held responsible for causing the parent to drink, but they were the likely target for everyone's hostility.

Dan's father was often angry and cruel, suddenly critical and attacking toward Dan. Dan remembers feeling awful as a child. In his adult life, he has spent considerable time and effort checking out with others just how bad he really is.

Adults frequently experience deep feelings of shame as a constant and will go to great lengths to avoid awakening them. In the group setting, Nancy recognizes that this chronic sense of shame is not hers, but rather belongs to her parents. As a child she experienced the shame and humiliation they should have been feeling but did not because of their denial and their drunken state.

Nancy experienced fear and emotional constriction before each group meeting. During the week she thought a lot about what occurred in group but as she drove to the meeting, she grew "foggy" and confused. Finally, she realized that she expected the therapist to do or say something ridiculous, illogical or hostile. She would then be embarrassed on the therapist's behalf and ashamed for the therapist's loss of control.

Nancy's experience triggered memories for others who recalled painful feelings of humiliation and shame in the past and present.

Lisa said she identified with the humiliation her parents should have been feeling but were not because they were so clouded with alcohol. She filled in enormous gaps in feeling that her parents weren't experiencing. As a result, she was also thought of as over emotional and "hysterical" a good deal of the time.

Brent became visibly agitated and upset as several members began discussing their feelings and sexual attraction toward one another. In a burst of anger, he left the room. Returning the next week, he reported intense feelings of shame and explored the relationship of what had occurred in group to this childhood experience.

> I had to continually watch my mother and father behave erratically and unpredictably. I felt I had to control them or be forced to watch them embarrass me. It's very difficult for me to spend time each week in group listening to people reveal themselves to a degree I can't control and in a way that makes me feel disoriented when I leave.

With repeated experiences of anxiety and shame in the group, Brent explored further several months later:

> Is everyone in a group of ACAs a little bit weird? I always felt such shame and embarrassment at the stigma of being the child of an alcoholic father.

This discussion of shame and the other core themes of control, chaos, inconsistency and unpredictability, roles, and tension emphasize the realities of family life and establish the validity of the alcoholic family as a traumatic environment. In Chapter 3, we will look more closely at the patterns of interaction required to maintain relationships, adjust to the realities of the family and sometimes, quite literally, to survive.

Chapter 3

Interactions, Patterns, and Adaptations

Like the alcoholic, the family becomes organized around the denial of alcoholism and the maintenance of the drinking behavior. The emphasis on denial and the defensive postures and adaptations necessary to maintain it becomes all encompassing. With few exceptions, those close to the alcoholic may be characterized as "reactors," establishing patterns of adjustment, relationships, roles, and self-identities in response to the dictates of the alcoholic, the parents' defensive strategies, and the requirements of the environment. In most alcoholic families, there is a central primary reality—parental alcoholism—to which all members must respond.

Given this singular emphasis on reaction and response, how can we systematically examine the impact of parental alcoholism on the family as a whole and individuals within it in a way that maximally includes differences as well as similarities?

In this chapter, we will first focus on the individuals within the family, outlining the "syndrome" of codependence. The literature on children of disabled and handicapped parents provides a framework for assessing the many variables that must be included in examining the impact of parental alcoholism on the family and individuals within. It also provides a rich model for comparison.

Before examining the family as a system, the similarities and differences from the handicap model will be examined.

There is no single portrait or formula for assessment. Rather, this exploration of individuals within the family and the family as a whole emphasizes the complexities and multitude of variables that must be considered. It also emphasizes the importance of including *both* an individual and an interpersonal point of view.

58

CODEPENDENCE

In its broadest sense, codependence describes individuals who organize their lives—decision making, perceptions, beliefs, values—around someone or something else. In relation to alcohol, codependence describes the individual (adult or child) who has become submissive to or controlled by alcohol as the central organizing principle in the family and/or the dominance of the alcoholic. The issue of dominance is a critical variable in recent research on patterns of interaction (Gorad, 1971; Paolino & McCrady, 1979; and Chiles, Strauss, & Benjamin, 1980).

In describing the family system of alcoholism, early researchers (Jackson, 1954) outlined the process of developing codependence, the stages in the reactive behavior of the spouse (usually the wife) in response to the alcoholism of her husband. More recently, Kaufman (1986) outlined stages in the development of coalcoholism. As noted in Chapter 1 (MacDonald, 1956), the onset of alcoholism in the male was thought to be a response to a disturbed wife who entered the marital partnership with a strong need for a dysfunctional husband. This belief— that the wife was to blame for her husband's alcoholism—has been discarded. The current view emphasizes the belief that pathology does not necessarily predate nor cause the onset of alcoholism. Rather, alcoholism disrupts the homeostasis and produces a reactive pathological adjustment in all members of the family (Vaillant, 1982).

This reaction, first labeled coalcoholism, is now called more broadly codependence (Wegscheider, 1981). Many studies (Schaffer & Tyler, 1979; Gorman & Rooney, 1979) now exist. While codependents are most often thought to be the nonalcoholic partner or child, the alcoholic also can be a codependent to someone else's alcoholism. For example, *both* parents may be alcoholics and, therefore, both codependents as well. Alternatively, the ACA may be a codependent in relation to the alcoholic parent and an alcoholic him or herself.

Importantly, dependence and codependence are part of all human development and not inherently negative or dysfunctional. Much development centers on the working out of a balance between autonomous development of the self, dependence on, and interdependence with others. But in alcoholic families, both dependence and codependence can be very destructive: they describe dysfunctional reliance on or submission to a substance (the dependent person) or a person (the codependent).

Alcoholic dependence and codependence imply a lack of, loss of, or submersion of a sense of an independent autonomous self, the self that permits an individual to regulate closeness and distance and develop strong interdependent relationships with others (Miller, 1981; Miller, 1984).

Individuals caught in a dysfunctional codependent position experience a loss of self as a major accommodation. Quite simply, people who spend their days reacting to another rather than following their own inner voice, will lose, or never develop, a sense of independent self. Instead, a false sense of self develops—one tied to the needs or dictates of the dependent person, and thus not easily recognized nor relinquished.

Often the false sense of self is based on role reversal and a feeling of responsibility.

> I exist and I am important because I take care of my mother.
> If I didn't watch out for her everyday, she would die.

The deep sense of responsibility and submission of self to the perceived needs and dictates of another forestalls recognition by the codependent person of object loss: both the loss of self in service to another and the reality that the dependent person is not and has not been emotionally available.

The codependent partner or child often experiences deep fears of object loss. Individuals respond to the fear by increasing codependent behaviors and defenses, perpetuating a vicious pathological cycle. The cycle is maintained by the dichotomous all-or-none cognitive frame characteristic of the reactive defensive position. The all-or-none view and the loss of self required in the codependent position underscore one of the most significant themes in the treatment of the ACA. How is it possible to have relationships, or be involved with people, without submitting to or experiencing a painful loss of self? For most ACAs early in treatment it is all or none:

> I can't have a relationship without controlling it or losing myself. Neither way is satisfying.

In the interpersonal and interactional long-term group, these issues are often demonstrated early as members attempt to form attachments with one another and create a working group. The issue of control arises immediately.

Because of the central organizing principle of alcohol and the dysfunctional dependent relationships, all family members are constantly struggling for control over something or someone else or, more frequently, the illusion of control.

Implicit in these concerns of dependence and codependence is the centrality of the issue of control. At the core, the alcoholic family—as individuals and as a whole—is chronically out of control, or seems to be. As one ACA individual put it:

> I was always on guard, always ready for the next crisis or disaster, the next drunken binge. Now the only time I feel "off duty" is when I'm alone.

The categories of dependence and codependence reflect the all-or-none dichotomous and rigid adaptations available to individuals in terms of role assumption, modeling, behavioral imitation, identity formation, and identification. Someone is dominant and winning and someone is submissive and losing. Children often get caught between the two, unconsciously frightened and rejecting the destructive models available. Individuals perceive self and other in strict all-or-none terms which preclude the ability to experience "shades of grey" or partnerships based on negotiation and compromise. The all-or-none frame pits the individual *against* others who will be damaging. The codependent adaptation required of the children—the reactive posture, responsive to the centrality of someone else's maladaptive control or dominance—precludes functional family development or healthy autonomous individual maturation. A group member illustrates:

> There is a sharp noticeable shift in the group when Barry says he is alcoholic. He is suddenly seen as more active, powerful, or instrumental in being able to "manipulate" the group or guide its direction. Members realize that they suddenly become "reactors," constantly watchful lest they be manipulated or intruded upon.

> Then Barry speaks of himself as a child with an alcoholic father who was out of control inside and outside the home. His father did bizarre, crazy things and embarrassed Barry tremendously.

> The group shifts again, relaxing as Barry talks about himself as a child. Dan says he can identify with Barry and relax as Barry speaks about himself as a child with an out-of-control father. Dan

becomes wary and threatened as soon as Barry shifts to describing himself as an alcoholic. Dan described the pain, fear, and uncertainty he experienced living with his father and with his drinking. Dan spent his childhood having to respond to the out-of-control direction of his father.

Children and adults struggle unconsciously with the all-or-none choices characterizing relationships in their families—who am I?

> I am either alcoholic and powerful like my father or passive, weak. and depressed—a victim like my mother. There is nothing in between.

The all-or-none perspective underscores the most important clinical themes and individual issues ACAs bring to treatment, which will be examined in detail later. Within the family system, you are either in control or you are not and paradoxically it is usually the alcoholic who is "in control."

> I do much better with a smaller group. When there are more than five, suddenly it feels like my family and I can't keep track of or control everything that's going on. Then I feel overwhelmed and frightened.

Reflecting the reactive posture, ACAs are chronically preoccupied with issues of control—am I or will I soon be out of control—who is in control now? Am I being controlled by someone else?

> Life is a constant struggle for a sense of control or the anticipation of losing it.

Another individual, in group for over four years, now recognized internally and within the transference in the group his strong identification with his father's loss of control and his neediness.

> I feel the constant tension of holding myself together so I don't act it out. You know, lose control.

CODEPENDENCE: WHAT IS IT LIKE?
THE PARENT

What is codependence—the response to alcoholism—in the broadest, descriptive sense? With the onset of alcoholism and the need to deny it, the partner begins to adjust his or her life to the thinking and behavior of the alcoholic in an attempt to gain a sense of control and stability. It is a behavioral and thinking disorder, just like alcoholism (Brown, 1985). The behavior of the alcoholic becomes an obsession for the codependent who begins to be preoccupied about the welfare of the alcoholic.

The partner also adjusts her view of self and the world to fit the distorted logic of the alcoholic. She and the family may hear that her nagging and overcontrol are the real problem. He would not have to drink if it weren't for her. So she tries harder to alter her behavior and her thinking in an effort to please him and solve the drinking problem. To no avail. Her self-esteem plummets. She denies for a long time that she feels helpless, depressed, and victimized because she believes it is her own fault.

To counter the sense of self-blame, she bolsters her denial. She may don an outward pose of superiority and pride that defensively announces "there is nothing wrong here." She begins to feel more shame and increasing isolation as her unconscious recognition of the reality of alcoholism deepens. She becomes more obsessed with the need to control her spouse, to protect him and maintain denial at the same time. This futile struggle for control of the other results in chronic tension, anxiety, depression, and underlying resentment and rage. She worries when he drinks and when he does not. Will he come home, lose his job, get killed on the highway? Kill someone else? She denies that she worries. As her "codependent" obsession and preoccupation take over, she has less time, direct attention or unencumbered emotional availability for her children. The alcoholism is now a bigger worry and it is central to everyone.

Because of the obsession with alcohol, both parents may be irresponsible, chronically or periodically. The codependent may assume more and more responsibility for protecting the alcoholic from his or her excesses and less responsible for anything else. In many families, the codependent becomes more responsible superficially, assuming the role and duties of the other. This individual may provide adequate parental care. But it is the rare family in which the issue of alcohol does not interfere significantly at some point. The processes of denial and protection simply require too much emotional and physical energy.

For example, the issue of alcohol may serve as a hostile weapon between the parents. The alcoholic drinks "at" the other and the codependent responds through the children, overprotecting them from a deep sense of guilt or perhaps expressing misplaced anger and hurt directly at the children:

> My mother would alternately lavish us with praise and attention and sudden outbursts of attack and rage.

The parents may become more and more preoccupied with their own relationship and its central focus on alcohol.

> At the first meeting of a new group, several members recalled the preoccupation and focus on the parents' problems as a major difficulty for them as children. "There was no room for me."

The initial emphasis on denial leads to underlying anger and constant fear. At first, the codependent will attempt to control the situation through nagging, lectures, or extraction of promises from the alcoholic. Next, the codependent will take action—hiding liquor, withholding money, or engaging in power struggles around the issue of drinking. By now, the family is characterized by intense conflict and a constant focus on who is going to control whom. Any open or realistic communication is declined. Instead, communication centers on attempts of family members to control one another.

CODEPENDENCE: WHAT IS IT LIKE? THE CHILD'S PERSPECTIVE

Children in alcoholic families do not feel (for the most part) the primary attachment or primary parental care coming from their parents. Their response may be similar to that of a codependent parent or they may, in fact, substitute for a parent, as a partner to the alcoholic or parent to siblings. Wegscheider (1981) and Black (1981) outlined a great diversity of codependent or defensive responses in their definitions of role adaptation. Most adults report feeling responsible for the alcoholic and for making the family well. And children, like the codependent parent, often are blamed for the family's problems.

> If you kids wouldn't fight so much, your mother wouldn't have to drink.

Or they assume blame themselves:

> I always knew deeply that I caused it. Therefore, I could fix
> it too.

Children learn not to care, not to have needs, and when they do, to take care of them themselves, regardless of age.

Both parents present confusing models of behavior because of the predominance of denial. Children recognize lies and alibis and are befuddled at the disparity in what they see and what they are permitted to see and acknowledge as real.

It is difficult to emulate either parent but children do so unconsciously. The nonalcoholic may be seen as strong and dependable but a martyr without any joy. The alcoholic is commonly seen as weak, full of needs, yet perhaps carefree and loving as well.

Because so much of the family's effort is invested in the defensive process of denial, members of the family and outsiders may interpret the absence of overt uproar and difficulty as a measure of happiness and stability. No interventions occur. Any potential change is interpreted as a threat to the quasi-stability of the moment (Steinglass, 1980). At any given time, the mood of the alcoholic governs the family environment and interactions. The codependent's relationship to the children is governed by the way that individual feels toward the alcoholic at any particular time. It can range from overprotective to rejecting of the children.

Given the codependent attachment and sense of self tied to the "other," separation from the alcoholic family is extremely difficult to achieve. Even those who have left their families physically, or whose parents have died, often remain too closely tied to the family emotionally (Brown & Beletsis, 1986). To leave is to give up hope, to abandon the family, or to be abandoned. Staying emotionally attached is a way of maintaining an important role in the family and a way of maintaining the family denial. For some, staying attached means becoming alcoholic. For others it means keeping the role of the rescuer, always being available in emergencies, continuing the responsible role taken in childhood. For many, the concern and involvement become a preoccupation even when they are not actively involved with the family. For all, the failure to separate becomes a major barrier to forming healthy primary attachments to their own families and causes great difficulty with intimate involvement in other significant relationships. It is as though the unfinished business in the first family precludes the perception of self as separate and available.

Adult children of alcoholics often find themselves replicating their relationship with the alcoholic parent by choosing a dependent or alcoholic mate. Some avoid close relationships altogether, finding themselves more and more isolated and less and less able to trust. Those who marry and have children frequently feel that their main commitment is still to their parents. They feel frightened of needing to depend on another person and often inadequate as parents.

Some are so preoccupied with their families immediately after leaving home, they are unable to concentrate as students, unable to be committed to career training or first jobs. To focus on themselves is to run the risk that a calamity will occur in their family and they will not have done all that they could to avoid it. Such children feel abandoned and are constantly frightened about the loss of one or both of these parents.

With this description of codependence in global terms, we now look more closely at differentiating variables, first outlining methodological considerations of research on children of the handicapped as a framework. We then incorporate both the global description of codependence and the variables for assessment into a family systems perspective.

CHILDREN OF THE HANDICAPPED: METHODOLOGICAL CONSIDERATIONS OF AN ANALOGOUS MODEL

The importance of the environment and the need for careful assessment of individual differences is clear. The literature and research on children of alcoholics are just beginning to reflect an appreciation of differences and critical variables necessary in assessment.

A review of the literature on children of the handicapped provides an excellent model and direction for research on children of alcoholics in the future. The children of the handicapped have been identified as a research and clinical population much longer and therefore provide a more sophisticated and developed base.

Thurman (1985) provides the best example for integrating environmental and individual theoretical points of view, so central to the theoretical development in this book. He and others have outlined the impact of emotional and physical disability on the family as a whole and on individuals within. Thurman stresses the need to examine the nature of the environment, the inhabitants, and the interactions of both with each other. He also emphasizes the necessity of examining the system at different points in time.

In the same volume, Coates, Vietze, and Gray, (1985) examine methodological issues, outlining the range and complexity of variables to be included in research or assessment. They emphasize the importance of assessing the impact of these variables on development and in determining the child's and the family's view—What beliefs do they hold about the disability? What meanings do they attribute to it, to the family and to themselves? This is a critical factor in assessing the impact of parental alcoholism on children. What sense do they make of it?

Coates notes the importance of including socioeconomic status, ethnicity, social-cultural orientation, and religious preference as background variables. Ablon (1980) has stressed the same factors in studying alcoholism.

In examining the family as a functioning unit, Coates et al. include family size, structure, number of siblings, spacing, presence of extended family, marital status of parents, rural, urban, or suburban residence. The latter are useful in providing an index of social support, community attitude, and availability of treatment. In determining the child's status, they include sex, age, developmental level, and birth order.

Much of the literature on children of alcoholics assumes that parental alcoholism produces the same result in children. There is an emphasis on categories and classification. The authors in the Thurman volume stress the importance of interaction and process. The family with parental disability is a changing system and therefore needs to be assessed at different points in time. Hethrington (1979) notes that children of different ages are affected differently by stressful environmental events. Parents are also affected differently by factors such as type of disability and outcome, chronicity, and severity.

These studies emphasize the significance of the environment and the multiple variables interacting within the system. Sameroff and Seifer (1983) demonstrate that severity and chronicity of parental disturbance (mental illness) are better predictors of outcome than the specific psychiatric diagnosis. This finding has great significance in studying the children of alcoholics. It underscores the need to carefully examine individual differences and variance in the experience of living with parental alcoholism.

The Impact of Parental Disability on the Family

Thurman et al. (1985) describe a global portrait with many similarities to widely accepted descriptions of the alcoholic family (see Chapter 2) (Jackson, 1954; Wegscheider, 1981; Black, 1981; Ablon, 1976). The researchers examine parental disability, emphasizing the importance of understanding patterns of interaction (Kornblum & Anderson, 1985), the impact of crisis, the increasing centrality and dominance of the needs of the disabled individual, and the resulting emphasis on reaction and adjustment required from others in the family. Kornblum and Anderson (1985) outline key features of the impact on the husband-wife relationship with the onset of diabetes. They note an increase in uncontrolled moodiness and irritability similar to the erratic, unpredictable mood swings of the alcoholic. Because the increasing needs of the diabetic conflict with the needs of other family members, they state clearly that there is great need for spouses to understand and accommodate or get divorced. The onset of the illness and its progression require a response and major adjustments from all family members.

The same circumstances exist for the alcoholic partnership with one major exception: Alcoholism is most often denied and, therefore, healthy or open accommodation cannot be made to cope with the acknowledged reality.

Parental disability may also be denied or the impact minimized. Kornblum and Anderson (1985) note that parents frequently believe their children are not affected. In fact, they add, children experience fears of abandonment or death and a grave concern that the same disability will happen to them. They quote McCollum (1981):

> Children of ill parents struggle with worrisome questions: what is wrong with Mommy, Daddy? Will she get worse, could it happen to me too? Is it my fault? Young children construct their own theories to account for illness; they frequently believe that it is the consequences of their own "bad" words, thoughts or deeds. Older children, though often more realistic, struggle with feelings of sadness, guilt, helplessness, fear or resentment when a parent is ill. (p. 107)

Kornblum and Anderson note further that kids feel responsible for the parents' well being. They must deal with the fact that they may inherit the disease and with the reality that the parent *is* different. This is particularly difficult in adolescence as the maturing child tries to integrate multiple identities and a sense of compatibility with the "normal" world outside.

Children respond to and adapt to the alcoholism of a parent in very different ways. Children within the same family may respond differently and the same child may exhibit varying responses related to interactional patterns between parents, child and other (Wilson & Orford, 1978; Brown, 1986).

Brown (1982) and others focus on the multiple factors that affect a child's reaction including the relationship with the alcoholic parent independent of drinking behavior, the child's age at onset, the child's resources outside the family, the child's innate constitutional makeup and endowment, and the availability of and interaction with the non-alcoholic parent, if there is one. These variables must be included in clinical assessment or research.

This review of important research variables in studying children of the handicapped and disabled lays the groundwork for assessing the alcoholic family system as a whole.

FAMILY SYSTEMS THEORY

Family and systems theorists (Bowen, 1974; Watzlavick, Weakland & Fisch, 1974; Satir, 1964) have provided frameworks to understand the kinds of responses and interactional patterns individuals within families develop to maintain homeostasis (Steinglass, 1980a, 1980b) or equilibrium, the point of balance around which the family functions.

Family homeostasis is a point of balance, not a judgment of health or well being. Many disturbed and unhealthy families achieve a stable balance by incorporating problems, faulty beliefs, roles, and defenses into the family's internal sense of equilibrium. The alcoholic family, with its focus on alcoholism and dependent and codependent adaptations, is a prime example. Homeostasis is the "norm" for the family, the state in which all members recognize, intuitively if not consciously, that roles, patterns, perceptions, and beliefs are congruent and everyone is operating accordingly. That is, everyone agrees on what is true.

Disequilibrium or disharmony occur in a system whose primary sense of balance has been disrupted. Minor or major events or changes within a family require accommodation by the system in order to restore the former level of homeostasis or to achieve a new one. Piaget (1970) and others (Watzlavick et al., 1974) describe the normal or natural flow of systems development in terms of the on-going interactive processes of assimilation and accommodation. With the former, the system incorporates changes into the stable family system without altering its core. With the latter, the system itself must alter in order to incorporate the changes.

Glass (1985) outlines stages in the family's response to the onset of parental disability (similar to Jackson's in relation to alcoholism) including shock, denial, mourning, depression, and despair. The family then moves into a period of trial and error, adapting and accommodating to the disruption caused by the disability. Eventually the family moves toward renewal of routines, including new role patterns, stability, recovery, and reorganization.

There is great variability in response due to variations in the amount of disruption, physical and emotional cost, time, and effort needed to reach homeostasis again and the level of function finally achieved. Glass notes that the onset of disability has an impact on the lifestyle of children and parents and interferes with the physical and emotional routines of daily living and the plans and expectations of all family members. The disability and the disruption present a challenge to the family's value system, role patterns, and communication networks that cannot be solved by customary methods.

The impact causes acute and often continuing stress in the present with ripple effects in all areas of life. Glass suggests that these multiple and significant changes in response to the disability cause feelings of loneliness, abandonment, anger, guilt, depression, despair, and sometimes panic in parents and children.

Glass notes further that adults are more likely to have the cognitive abilities to deal appropriately with crisis within the framework of their established value systems and life patterns. Children, however, have not developed cognitive and coping skills to understand the causality and contingency relationships surrounding the onset of the disability and will have a much more difficult time making sense of the disruption (p. 46). These cognitive factors are especially relevant to children of alcoholics. They are affected by the same age-related developmental capacities *and* the requirements of the alcoholic system to maintain denial and explain the reality of parental alcoholism as something else. Children cannot make sense of the disruption caused by parental alcoholism without massive distortion or accommodation. Another study of disability, De la Mata, Gringras, and Wittkower (1960), showed that adolescents reacted to the disruption of the family unit while younger children were more upset by the unrest and prevalent mood in the home.

Glass concluded that adjustment is a process not a state—the effectively functioning family solves the problem, achieving a new stable and healthy homeostasis while the ineffectively functioning family does not.

Earlier studies on disability in parents noted differences between children in tuberculosis families and children of mentally ill parents (Ekdahl, Rice & Schmidt, 1962). Most important, children of the mentally ill were often involved in the symptomotology of the parent's illness. For example, a father destroyed a child's toys; in another, children were abused physically and sexually, and in another, children were confused and frightened by a parent's strange stories.

There are many parallels for the alcoholic family. The systems theories of homeostasis and equilibrium are important to understanding adjustment of the family to the disruption of parental alcoholism. The disability model offers many parallels but falls short around the issue of denial. In fact, the alcohol literature is probably more developed around the issue of denial than is the study of disability. Most commonly, the alcoholic family does not "recover" from a disability—parental alcoholism—that is *labeled.* Rather, it accommodates and adjusts to a new level of homeostasis that incorporates denial. While the family is changing, under great stress and perhaps in crisis, they are also denying that anything is wrong.

If denial is not entirely successful, the family may recognize problems but label them as something other than alcohol, for example, a nagging wife, job pressures, marital difficulties. The family then achieves its new homeostasis around *another* problem, identified as central rather than alcohol.

The "other" problem may be a child who, through illness or delinquent behavior, takes the focus off the parents. The family may gear up to solve the "other" problem but all efforts must fail. If the "other" problem were solved, parental alcoholism would then be more visible as a central problem.

The centrality of denial and the need to maintain it results in a negative, highly dysfunctional homeostasis. No one can deal with feelings of anxiety, loss, depression, guilt, or fear of parental abandonment because the problem cannot be labeled.

Wolin et al. (1979) have looked closely at the family's style of incorporating parental alcoholism and its denial into the family culture, particularly in terms of observance of rituals, such as birthdays and holidays. They note that the degree of incorporation has a great impact on current and subsequent adjustment of the family. The degree to which the family can maintain its structure, moving *around* the alcoholic, is the significant variable in healthier adjustment.

In the alcoholic family, what may have started as a crisis, or as a slow almost indiscernible process, often becomes the *norm*. For the most part, this is not a stable family that incorporates a "disability"—in this case parental alcoholism—and maintains its structure. Rather, the need for denial and the maintenance of behaviors that support it require massive accommodations that alter the structure of the family.

The accommodations required to maintain denial and preserve the drinking as a behavioral and thinking disorder for all members of the family have been described (Brown, 1985). The behavioral and thinking disorder becomes the norm—the new structure that incorporates abnormality and pathology.

Socialization

The *norm* is a critical variable in socialization of a child; it is the child's view of the world outside the family and his or her adaptation to it. Literature on the handicapped accents this point as well (Thurman et al., 1985). Lewis and Fering (1979) note that the family represents the initial point of social involvement: "the family provides the basic social network for most infants and young children." Newbrough (1985) reports on the importance of considering the handicapped parents' view of themselves within the family and the culture. How am I different, deviant, or marginal? How do family members view the parents and themselves in relation to the culture?

Newbrough and others researching the handicapped emphasize

positive as well as negative outcomes in socialization. Newbrough views the handicapped family positively as bi-cultural, possessing a wide range of social and cognitive skills that enable them to participate in many community and social arenas. Hofmeister (1985) suggests that living with parental handicap instills a greater tolerance for deviance and difficulties in others. He also notes that children with a disabled parent learn lessons about sensitivity to others and familial interdependence.

In comparing the impact of parental alcoholism, denial once again is the significant variable. In most alcoholic families, parental alcoholism is a secret, denied inside and outside the home. The family is struggling to appear normal. Individuals do not identify themselves or the family as deviant from the outside world. Therefore, there can be no acknowledged recognition of "bi-cultural" standing.

To support denial, the alcoholic and family struggle to appear "normal" to function as a family in the world outside the home, while projecting hostility on "outsiders" at the same time. The world outside becomes the enemy, the threat to the family's tenuous sense of security. There becomes an inside world of shared beliefs and an outside world from which the family increasingly retreats and isolates itself. Involvement with friends, community, church, and school poses a constant threat to the family's denial.

> I hated to go out to dinner or anywhere socially with my family. There was nothing wrong of course but I had to endure the shame of watching my father get drunk, tip over drinks, argue with everyone and often leave in a tirade. My father acted like he owned the world. Anybody who objected to his behavior or questioned him was the enemy.

The child in a family in which alcoholism is "normal" learns at some point during development that alcoholism is not normal for other families or the world outside (Brown, 1974). This realization may come suddenly, or gradually as the child begins in latency or preadolescence to engage with peers outside the home. Memories of shame, humiliation, and embarrassment characterize the growing awareness that "something is wrong with my family."

The need to appear "normal" has a tremendous impact on adjustment and later developmental difficulties. Our adult patients who have acknowledged parental alcoholism and labeled themselves ACAs as a result, challenge their "normality" as children

(Brown & Beletsis, 1986). When denial is broken, they acknowledge instead the terrible split they felt:

> There was something wrong with my family and I knew it. I was damaged goods. Growing up was awful, but my troubles *really* began when I left home. I now know I had no foundation to make it on my own or in the world outside. I learned an abnormal form of reality at home and it didn't carry over. Suddenly I knew I was trying to look normal when I had no idea of what that meant. I was supposed to be an adult but I felt like a child, frightened and helpless. I was sure I'd missed something that others had gotten.

This man speaks in retrospect, recalling the agony of his early twenties and his rapid dissent into his own alcoholism:

> I just drank. That was all I knew. I also realized quickly that something was terribly wrong. But I had no idea what. It was awful.

This man—born and raised in a family of alcohol—has yet to feel like a "normie." He finds comfort in the culture of AA where his sense of "craziness" is normal.

> I still feel out of sync in the world outside. It's like I'm always holding myself together so my bad breeding won't show. In AA, we let it show and it's fine.

The question of normality is critically important in another way. As noted earlier, there is much emphasis in the field of alcoholism (Niven, 1984; Brown, 1986) and the literature on the disabled to look for "positive" outcome. The authors in Thurman's excellent volume are almost unanimously defensive on behalf of the disabled, wary of "blame." Greer (1985) is particularly so. She reflects the long-standing attitude that is also held in the field of alcoholism that kids are not damaged or even affected by parental drinking (Hunter, 1963). There has been a need by researchers, clinicians, and family to minimize damage, accenting the belief that "kids are OK." Greer accents her belief that parents with handicaps mean well and, therefore, there can be no damage or problems, or none that can be recognized.

Hofmeister (1985) provides another example of the "skeptic," noting that one should not attempt to explain all children's behavior through the parents. He is wary of what he describes as a tendency of children to blame the parents' disability for all their own problems or to use the disability to explain their own adjustment.

While these are valid concerns, Greer and others miss the central fact that parental disability may be, and parental alcoholism most often is, the central organizing principle and children and adults in the family *have* to cope with it. The reality of parental alcoholism has an impact on development. Even when parents mean well, and most do, there is *still* the impact of alcoholism as the central organizing principle.

There is also a failure in this research to interpret the child's behavior according to its meaning to the child within the family context. Only then is it possible to understand that a "happy, active, normal" child *needs* to be so in terms of the family stability. The "normal" adjustment for many is a role, a defense, mastered in the service of appearing normal. This facade, or false self (Beletsis & Brown, 1981; Miller, 1984), is not an indicator of healthy development or coping but rather an impediment to normal development.

Our clinical evidence strongly suggests that children identify with family deviance and the conflicting need to look normal for the outside world. This split is a core feature of the pathology ACAs present on intake and through the course of treatment. Without clinical material, there is little evidence that the child or adult is in conflict or that significant developmental deficits exist underneath the defensive posture of adjustment because he or she seems to fit so well.

There is, thus, great danger in dividing research and treatment into crude, mutually exclusive categories—survivors or casualties, positive outcome or negative (Brown, 1986). Ironically, the same all-or-none categories and cognitive frame that are so characteristic and so problematic for the children of alcoholics also characterize the field of inquiry.

There is equal danger of denying service or legitimacy of problems to those recognized as survivors—those whose defensive adjustment fits well in a social context. Thus the model child, the high achiever, the hero, is driven to perpetuate these patterns while feeling empty, lost, lonely, and isolated with no idea why.

In examining the alcoholic family as a system and the members within it individually, it is necessary to look closely at the "norm" for the family. What is the point of balance at any given time and how is it achieved in a family with an alcoholic parent(s)? What is "normal" for this family? This distinction is critical in understanding the origins of maladaptive behavior patterns, defenses and beliefs, identity formation, transmission, and it is especially significant in understanding differences between individuals.

Like the literature on the disabled, key variables in examining the alcoholic family as a whole include time of onset within the family's development, degree of severity and determining which parent is alcoholic. These distinctions will have a major impact on assessing the "normal" equilibrium of the family, the impact of alcoholism on the family as a system and the individuals within it, and the course of recovery. If abstinence is achieved, is it a return to normal or a new state?

VARIABLES

There are multiple variables involved in studying children of alcoholics. Three emerge as vitally important in an initial assessment of "what it was like" for this particular individual: time of onset, severity, and which parent is alcoholic.

Time of Onset

Studies of parental disability accent time of onset as one significant factor in looking at the family system, while literature on children of alcoholics has been virtually silent on this question. According to Kornblum and Anderson (1985) "the time in the life cycle at which the disease occurred has important physical and psychological implications for parents and therefore, has an impact on relationships in the family" (p. 101).

The time of onset is important in determining whether parental alcoholism is an inherent part of the family's development or whether it has been experienced as a disruption, an intruder, beginning after the family has developed its primary sense of balance and core beliefs. Coates et al. (1985) refer to this distinction as congenital versus adventitious onset.

Has parental alcoholism always been present and, if so, to what degree? How has the family developed to include parental drinking as part of its "normal" functioning? Is the incorporation smooth, or is it dysfunctional, highly stressful, and problematic?

How is alcoholism incorporated into the family's identity, the family's "story," or core beliefs? Its rituals (Wolin et al., 1980)? And how is it explained? Ignored or denied? Is the onset slow or rapid, precipitated by a crisis?

The family and the individuals within it will have a very different sense of themselves if their view of "normality" includes an alcoholic parent in contrast to the family which experiences the onset of alcoholism as a disturbance, a disruption to an equilibrium that did not previously include parental alcoholism.

With alcoholism, what changes in homeostasis does the family experience? Is there recognition of disequilibrium? Of abnormality? Does the family experience a loss of balance, of normality? Has it been restored or must the family accommodate to a new level of equilibrium? Although parental alcoholism will likely be denied in either case, the differences in family adjustment and individual development are considerable. Two patients provide an illustration.

Toby and Allison listened to the new member outline her family history of alcoholism including the recent death of her father. Toby was visibly shaken, tearful and sad. Allison appeared unmoved. Their differences soon became clear.

Allison's father was an alcoholic for as long as she can remember. Her entire childhood was spent worrying about him. He was always at the emotional center of everything, draining everyone with no idea of the havoc he created. He died in a violent accident when she was 11.

Toby had quite a different experience. He recalled a warm, loving family before both of his parents became alcoholic when he was 13. Since then, he has experienced a constant underlying sense of expectation, hope and repeated disappointment. He had it all and suddenly it was gone. He could no longer rely on his parents to be parents to the children or to provide love and care. Suddenly their needs were overwhelming and they were gone emotionally.

Toby's parents stopped drinking periodically and he became excited thinking they would be available again and the family could return to normal. He was repeatedly overcome with disappointment when they resumed drinking. They are now both dead from alcoholism.

As the meeting progressed, Allison spoke with anger and determination: she had been used and was "closing the door" on her family.

There was no loss for her because she never had anything to begin with. Toby spoke sadly in contrast: he had a family and lost it. As a teenager and now as an adult, he wants desperately to find a new family, one he can belong to, warm and close like the one he lost.

Allison is bitter and angry. She believes strongly that she must take care of herself, that she can trust no one to help her or really put her needs first. Toby is sad and seriously depressed. He believes the perfect family is out there, if only he can find it.

Toby and Allison illustrate the impact of loss but of a very different nature in both family systems and developmental theory. Allison's "normal" experience was one of chaos, disruption, drunkeness, violence, and arguing. She and the other members of her family (two brothers and a non-alcoholic mother) were constantly coping with the erratic and unpredictable yet dominant behavior of her father. Allison recalls no sense of strength or protection coming from others in the family. They were not a unit, bonded together. Had they been, they might have developed a family culture separate from the alcoholic or one that could withstand disruptions from that individual. She might have experienced a semi-functional and supportive family structure and perhaps negotiated developmental tasks around her father's alcoholism (Wolin et al., 1980). Allison felt alone and isolated. Although there were four of them, they felt and operated as if they were alone in response to the behavior of her father.

Toby always thought of his family as a unit, a clan to which he proudly claimed membership. He was close to his siblings and extended family as well. Toby's experience of a close, bonded family was shattered as his parents withdrew into serious alcoholism. The children offered tenuous support for one another but all felt orphaned. As adults, each has become alcoholic, one after another. Toby wonders whether he must become an alcoholic, too, in order to find a family (Brown & Beletsis, 1986).

> Drinking validates my membership in my family. It's the one clear way to belong.

Toby's adult adjustment is quite different from Allison's. The cornerstones for healthy development were present. Toby's parents were emotionally available and positive attachments were developed. He was able to accomplish the major childhood tasks of development until they were interrupted at adolescence by his parents' alcoholism.

Severity

A second important variable in differentiating children with an alcoholic parent is severity of parental alcoholism, including degree and kinds of impairment. Just what *is* parental alcoholism for this individual and within this family? Assessment of severity is difficult and potentially problematic when comparisons are made. Indeed, many ACAs resist treatment because they believe "it wasn't so bad." Or, they hear others report experiences of violence or incest, and again wonder if they deserve treatment. They grew up with denial, parental arguing, and a stoic facade shared by all for the outside world.

Assessing severity is important in understanding the degree and kind of trauma present in the environment as well as the nature and quality of relationships available to the child. Which developmental tasks were accomplished with which accommodations and which were affected by or overshadowed by the dominance of parental alcoholism and its severity? How much of the child's life was devoted to coping with or actively dealing with the realities of parental alcoholism (for example, repeatedly experiencing the loss of a parent leaving home for a hospital or detox, divorce, or abandonment—the parent simply disappeared) and how much of the child's experience was passive, related to emotional neglect and deprivation? While the severity of parental alcoholism cannot be quantified, understanding both the physical and emotional consequences is essential. Both can be severe.

Which Parent Is Alcoholic?

Determining which parent is alcoholic is another critical variable in assessing the impact of parental alcoholism on children, both systematically and individually from a developmental perspective.

What is the impact on children if the father is alcoholic, if the mother is, or both? What are the differences? What is the impact on boys? Girls? Are there differences? We do not know the answers to these questions yet, although some studies of these variables do exist (Shuckitt, 1983; Shuckitt & Duby, 1982; Brown, 1974; Kammeir, 1971; Sandmeir, 1980).

ASSESSMENT: THE FAMILY DIAGRAM

We have recognized the importance of the environment and the central organizing principle of alcohol for many years. In attempting to formulate a framework for assessing variability in adaptation, pattern and response within individuals and between individuals, we developed a tool we called the "family diagram." We have utilized it clinically to develop an individualized family portrait.

In its simplest form, the diagram is a large circle representing the family as a whole, with smaller circles placed inside or outside the large family circle to designate the relationship of family members to each other and to alcohol. Either the patient and/or the therapist can develop the family diagram prior to or following clinical evaluation. Such a diagram provides a base for understanding the roles, alliances, and degree of denial operating within the family as well as accessibility of various family members to the world outside.

The diagrams may also be developed for different points in time to illustrate changes in the family system. For example, the therapist or the patient might draw a family diagram prior to the onset of alcoholism and another afterwards to illustrate shifts in relationship and the degree of centrality of alcohol and the alcoholic.

The family diagram is a framework for assessment. As such, its uses and interpretations are broad. Several examples follow to illustrate the variety of possible configurations and interpretations.

Figure 1 illustrates the centrality of alcohol—the hub around which the family is organized. In this diagram, the alcoholic is not identified. All family members come together through alcohol in the center. Several family members have access to one another on the periphery of the family circle, by-passing the central organizing principle of alcohol. This might represent a strong sibling relationship, for example, founded on a shared interest in sports or mutual support. Others in the family have no relationship to one another except through the core of alcohol. These individuals may feel isolated, but drawn together when a parent(s) is drinking or the family must actively deal with the consequences of someone's drinking.

In this example, each family member also has a tie to the outside world, although it is not clear what it is. Still, there is the suggestion from the arrows extending out that all individuals operate outside the family.

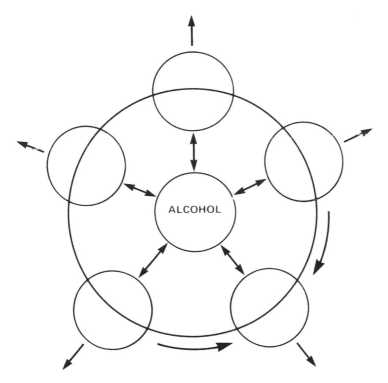

Figure 1.   Alcohol as the Central Organizing Principle of Family Development and Homeostasis

The patient or therapist might next label the individuals, including the alcoholic and further describe the meaning of the placements—the arrows in and those pointing out.

Figure 2 illustrates a family organized around alcohol but closed in from the world outside. Seeking more information, the therapist might learn that the kids in this family were instructed not to talk about home or develop close ties with "outsiders." As a patient explained:

> I was never permitted to talk with friends about my troubles at home. We had to keep it all within the family. When my father died, I wanted to tell a few friends from school but I just couldn't. He died drunk, so what could I say?

The patient added that everyone in the family is now an alcoholic, further reflecting the depiction of a closed family system.

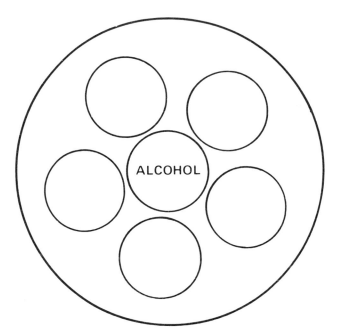

Figure 2. The Family Organized Around Alcohol and Closed from the Outside World

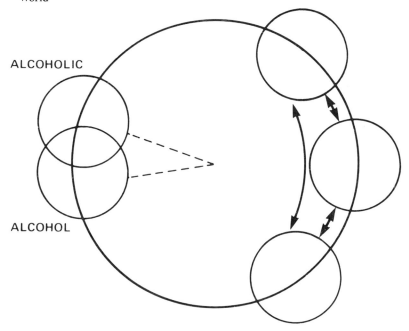

Figure 3. The Family that Bypasses Alcohol as a Central Organizing Principle

82

The next three diagrams illustrate other adaptations. Figure 3 suggests that the alcoholic and alcohol are isolated from other family members who bypass both to interact with one another. This family has no center. It is split and fragmented. The parent's alcoholism may be acknowledged or not, but family members have found a means to circumvent its centrality in their lives.

> Oh, yeah, my Dad was alcoholic. We just went around him.
> He wasn't nasty, just pathetic.

Later on, this woman expressed feelings of anger and deep sadness as she experienced the depths of what she had missed getting from such an ineffectual, absent father.

Figure 4 suggests that both parents are alcoholic and centered on alcohol with three children straddling involvement with the family and the world outside. Two of the kids have a close mutually protected relationship while the third feels isolated and cut off from everyone in the family. Further exploration might reveal that the adults provided little parenting because of their absorption in their drinking and their drinking relationship. The two

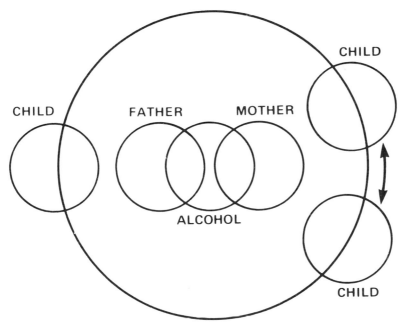

Figure 4. The Family Organized Around the Alcoholism of Both Parents

children provided care for one another with one actively assuming parental duties for the family. The isolated child felt neglected, helpless, and frightened.

Figure 5 illustrates yet another variation. The alcoholic, now recovering, is outside the family having left and divorced her mate while still drinking. The adult drawing this configuration recalls growing up with his mother gone and describes a mutually interactive system that also by-passed active interaction with the alcoholic or alcohol. Yet this same individual struggles with his sense of loss and the increasing responsibility he felt as a child after his mother left the house.

These diagrams are skeletons, to be elaborated on and explained by the individual. They provide a base and a structure from which to assess family organization and pattern. They also provide a base to move from the systems perspective to examination of individual development and the interaction between the two.

In the next part both are outlined; a theory is developed that merges the significance of the interaction between the family as a system organized around the centrality of alcoholism, defensive adaptations to the system and the development of individuals

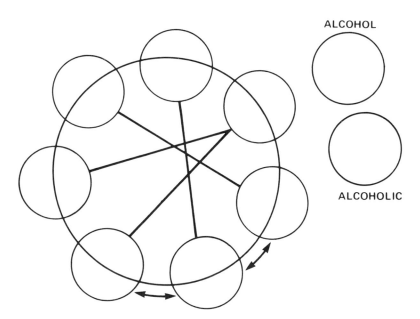

Figure 5.   The Family Without the Alcoholic

within. How and to what degree do the requirements of the system interact with and reciprocally determine the course of individual development? What is the link between the system and the individual? Are the requirements of the family system so strong and so pathological as to mute the centrality of the child's individual development? To what degree does the system take over, becoming the "object" of attachment? In assessing the impact of parental alcoholism on individual development, it is essential to determine to what degree the system, rather than the individuals within it, influences or structures individual development.

There are at least two levels of response or consequence to be considered at any point in evaluation or treatment. First, there is the impact of the environment—the family system with an equilibrium or homeostasis developed to conceal and cope with the pathology of parental drinking. What is the reality and how has the family dealt with or incorporated it? How has the family adapted as a system to include the alcoholism of the parent? We have examined these questions in Part One.

In the next section, we examine the degree to which the alcoholism becomes a central organizing factor in itself, structuring the maintenance of the system *and* interpersonal attachment and relationships within the family. To what degree has the pathological system overshadowed individual autonomy?

The systems focus in Part One included examination of role acquisition, patterns of behavior, and response. The individual focus in Part Two examines defensive adaptations and developmental tasks accomplished within the dominant system focus. What beliefs about the self and others are required to maintain the system? How do these beliefs structure the maintenance of the system and attachments within that system and how do they effect development of the self?

As we shift from a family systems perspective to a focus on individual development, it is essential to bear in mind the centrality of defense. To what degree is alcoholism and its denial so central and all encompassing as to dominate and influence all levels of individual development within the family? In moving to the next part, the emphasis on defense provides the bridge.

PART TWO

The Impact of Parental Alcoholism on Individual Development

The first part of this book examined the environment in an alcoholic family outlining "what it is like" from a systems and interpersonal framework. Alcoholism and the denial of alcoholism are the central organizing principles in the family, governing familial patterns of relationship and the family's view of itself and reality. I emphasized the overriding necessity for defensive adaptation with all family members in a predominantly reactive position, responsive to the dominance of the alcoholic and the organizing principle of alcohol.

The centrality of alcohol as an organizing principle and the predominance of defensive adjustment affect individual development as well. Like the family, the impact is complex, different for all individuals and dependent on a number of interacting variables. The connecting link and most important factor is the centrality of alcoholism.

In this section, the defensive adaptations and developmental issues that have emerged as central from our clinical data will be examined. These indicate strongly that the family environment—the system of parental alcoholism and the beliefs developed to maintain it—and the nature of attachments formed within the context of the family system both have a major impact on all aspects of individual development.

The move from an environmental systems point of view to a focus on individual development isn't clear cut. It involves recognition of reciprocal interaction and careful assessment of the degree to which the demands of the environment predominated. To what degree did the defenses or adaptations required to cope with the family environment overshadow or influence the normal tasks of development? The latter may have been entirely structured by the centrality of the parents' alcoholism and its denial. Alternatively parental alcoholism and the parents' defenses to cope with it may have been part of a larger whole with conflict-free and defensive-free areas of family life and individual relationship existing which facilitated "pockets" of healthier attachment and development. The family diagrams in Chapter 3 illustrated these various patterns.

In assessing the consequences of parental alcoholism on individual development, it is essential to consider the following variables:

1. To what degree was (or is) development influenced by or overshadowed by the individual's response to living in a chronically traumatic environment?

2. To what degree was the individual's development limited by the necessity for defensive adaptation? To what degree was development itself a manifestation of a coping response or defensive adjustment?

3. To what degree did the centrality of alcoholism and the defenses adapted to deal with it represent the path to or the bond of attachment?

4. To what degree did the centrality of alcoholism and its denial also represent the path or structure to identification and identity formation?

5. To what degree was autonomous development with mature separation-individuation impeded by the centrality of alcoholism and the demands of the system to maintain its denial?

Reflecting back to the family diagram, one asks the question repeatedly: Was there a relationship or core attachment that could operate independently of the system's demands or beliefs? Was the alcoholism of a parent so central an organizer as to preclude attachment or identity formation that could by-pass it?

In the first section, the problems inherent in attempting to develop or define a single theory or practice for such a large and diverse population were related to systems theory. The same problems apply as we shift focus to individual development. How can we pay appropriate attention to the centrality of alcohol or alcoholism without explaining everything and everyone on a single dimension from this new vantage point, especially since it provides the thread that pulls diverse variables and issues together?

One approach is to start with the centrality of alcohol as a base, a unifying theme across families but characterized by great variance as well. No single theory can explain the impact or consequence of parental alcoholism on child or adult development. Defensive strategies, childhood developmental tasks, and adult adaptations are all directly related to and woven around the central core of alcohol, but they are also dependent on the variables characterizing a particular parent or family and the nature of attachments between individuals. Time of onset, degree of severity, degree of denial, manifestation, responses and adaptations of others, and the centrality of other life issues or organizing factors are all determinants of consequences and adaptations.

As a starting point in looking at adult adjustment or adaptation, we must determine the degree to which alcohol or the denial of parental alcoholism was or is *the* central feature for this individual. Next we assess the degree or kind of influence. Did parental alcoholism affect all aspects of development or were there particular areas of a child's life or development that were free of the influence of alcoholism or could bypass it? In other words, to what degree was parental alcoholism *so* central and the defenses required to maintain the system so dominant as to preclude or strongly influence healthy attachments and development within the family and the course of individual development? This perspective—understanding the relationship between the system and the individuals in it, the relative dominance of each factor, and the reciprocal interactions—offers the key to understanding the wide range of consequences and patterns of development that ACAs experience. With these guidelines established, it is then possible to examine general issues and themes that emerge in the course of the long-term ACA therapy group that characterize or reflect the impact of parental alcoholism on individual development.

Our early clinical papers provided the groundwork and guidelines for the current task of integrating many variables, core issues, and theories. In our first group in 1978, we (Cermak & Brown, 1982) noted the most common themes emerging over the first eight months of therapy. This group had an overriding focus on issues of trust, control, perceptual denial and distortion, and feelings of responsibility. While general, these themes provided a beginning framework to link the experiences in the childhood environment with later difficulties in adult life. The centrality of denial and the early emphasis on perception also alerted us to the significance of cognitive theory. At that early stage, we could see the significance of the centrality of defenses to maintain the family system, but we could not yet see that the defenses had also become the core of the self for many. The emphasis on defense was so all encompassing as to constitute the structure for attachment and identity formation.

Next we went back to the childhood environment, examining the impact of parental alcoholism on the "normal" tasks of development using Erikson's developmental stages as a framework (Beletsis & Brown, 1981). Again, we illustrated how the environment and experiences or lack of experiences in childhood lead to severe problems in adulthood, expressed clinically in the long-term therapy group as major group themes or transference phenomena related to developmental issues including attachment and basic trust, autonomy and self control, mastery, identity formation, and separation individuation.

Finally, we took another look at themes and issues arising in a group, but over a much longer period of time (Brown & Beletsis, 1986). We identified key clinical themes characterizing the work of the beginning, middle, and advanced group. With the longer time frame, developmental issues of attachment, identity formation, and separation—individuation emerged more clearly. But so did the emphasis on defense and the centrality of alcoholism as an organizing principle.

Integrating these variables—the environment, the centrality of alcoholism, the defensive adaptations—and relating them to developmental issues is the task of this part.

In pulling the variables together, a central proposition, grounded in cognitive-dynamic theory, emerges.

> Attachment—early and on-going—is based on denial of perception which results in denial of affect which together result in developmental arrests or difficulties. The core beliefs and patterns of behavior formed to sustain attachment and denial within the family then structure subsequent development of the self including cognitive, affective and social development.

Thus alcohol and beliefs and symbols about alcohol are central to all aspects of development. Within the context of this core theory, one can assess the degree to which maintenance of the family system and the pathological relationships within it over-shadowed, influenced, or structured individual development.

ORIGINS OF THE CENTRALITY OF ALCOHOL AND THE IMPORTANCE OF COGNITIVE THEORY

In building a dynamic model of alcoholism and recovery (Brown, 1985), I emphasized cognitive theory, outlining the denial of alcoholism and the belief in control as co-organizers of the individual's and the family members' personal identities (Guidano and Liotti, 1983) and perceptions of others and the world. Cognitive theory is also a cornerstone in understanding children of alcoholics, particularly as a means to understand the relationship between denial, defensive adaptation, and developmental issues of attachment, identity formation, and perceptions about self and world. Cognitive-dynamic theory provides a crucial theoretical framework for understanding the impact of denial of one's perceptions and the structuring of one's attachments and identity on a base of false or distorted beliefs about the self and others (Bowlby, 1980, 1985).

Chapter 4 focuses on defensive adjustment, examining the direct impact of the child's environment on adult psychopathology, drawing parallels between theories of trauma, posttraumatic stress disorder, and anxiety disorder.

As noted in Chapter 3, development in an alcoholic family takes place in the context of "reaction to" rather than open exploration and self-initiative defined by Mahler (1975) and others as a necessary base for healthy development. In the alcoholic family, development occurs around the centrality of parental alcoholism *and* the reactive defensive adaptations required to deal with it.

Chapter 4 looks at these adaptations, key variables, or themes that reappear constantly as issues themselves, or as a background structure from which other themes or issues emerge or are examined. Depending on the context, these may be thought of as defensive maneuvers or character adaptations, acquired in the service of adjusting to parental alcoholism and now maintained as core dimensions of adult personality. As such, they may remain defensive in function and/or become problems in their own right. As a part of personality, they provide a structure for acquiring knowledge about the self and interpretations of self and other. These defensive maneuvers become the structure through which developmental tasks are experienced. Thus childhood and particularly adult concerns related to attachment, autonomy, identity formation, and separation-individuation are linked to or imbedded within these defenses or traits. The most important of these "defenses" are denial, an emphasis on control, all-or-none thinking and the assumption of responsibility for individuals and events outside one's control. Defensive adaptation may be the heart of what is visible interpersonally in the family and the core of what constitutes the sense of self. The degree to which these traits reflect the pathology of the system, and the degree to which they now represent the self as well, is the bridge that links the impact of the system to individual development.

Developmental issues also take place within this framework. Individuals experience a variety of parental "faces" depending on the parents' need for defense. To the degree that parents were dominated by their alcoholism and their need to deny it, so, too, were they geared to survival in the chaotic environment and also dominated by defenses. Thus, in many cases, it is the defenses that appear to constitute the core of the parental "self" and those defenses are pathological. Thus the defenses predominated and access to a "nondefended," nondenying parent was severely limited.

Many ACAs believe and experience that the whole of their parents' personality or sense of self consisted of their efforts to manage, deny, and cope with the alcoholism. Thus to identify is equal to destruction. For many, the process of treatment and recovery is a search for a stronger, healthier parental self that was covered by alcoholism and the pathology adapted to cope with it.

The move from a description of the environment to exploration of individual development within this environment must consider both levels. First, there is the reaction to the environment—to the trauma—which is characterized by symptoms of posttraumatic stress disorder, anxiety disorder, and depression. Next is the development of a dominance of defensive maneuvers first required to adjust to the need for denial and the requirements of a chaotic environment. The child, proceeding with the tasks of development, may identify with the parents' defenses, necessary to survive in the environment but which also come to constitute the self. Thus many ACAs feel dominated by a false self, constituting a facade of defensive adjustment required to cope. As one patient put it:

> All my energy went into surviving. There was no room for development separate from survival.

Dynamic themes of attachment and separation-individuation as outlined by Erikson (1963), Mahler, (1975), Blos (1962), and Miller (1981) are woven deeply throughout the long-term process of treatment. Problems in these areas are reflected in persistent group themes emphasizing the meaning and importance of belonging, the deep and often primitive need for nurturance along with an equally deep fear of such need and fears of abandonment (Brown and Beletsis, 1986). Problems and deficits in the basic tasks of attachment impair succeeding maturational processes so that the adolescent and adult tasks of identity formation and separation-individuation are seriously disrupted. Problems with separation from the family of origin are often noted as a critical factor in seeking treatment. The issue of parental alcoholism is a central feature of these themes as they emerge in group discussion and within the transference.

These clinical themes suggest that attachment, necessary for human development, is founded not only on nonverbal, early affective bonds, but also on the maintenance of the family's beliefs. Those beliefs—the family's "story"—are based on denial of alcoholism. As such, attachment has both affective and cognitive properties and includes the family's beliefs and explanations regarding alcohol.

Utilizing the frameworks of cognitive and developmental theorists, Chapters 5 and 6 examine the impact of parental alcoholism on the developmental tasks of attachment and identity formation as they characterize adult adaptation and as they arise in the group setting.

Chapter 4

Trauma and Defensive Adaptations

Recently there has been a push (Cermak, 1984) to classify children of alcoholics and adult children of alcoholics as a separate DSM clinical syndrome with identifiable and diagnosable characteristics, symptoms and patterns. Central to this trend is the move to view pathological consequences and adaptations of codependency as analogous to posttraumatic stress disorder (PTSD) (Cermak, 1984). Cermak lists the following symptoms of PTSD as relevant to ACAs:

1. A tendency to reexperience the trauma through obsessive thoughts about the family and compulsive reemergence of behaviors and feelings in response to symbolic equivalents of the trauma,

2. Psychic numbing, with a sense of isolation,

3. Hypervigilance (anxiety),

4. Survivor guilt (depression),

5. Intensification of symptoms by exposure to events that resemble the original trauma, such as withdrawal by others.

While useful in understanding similarities, and the reaction to real childhood trauma, this particular classification can miss much by reducing what is a childhood experience with great variance to an overly narrow classification.

This conception—the analogy to PTSD—is included as part of a larger spectrum of adaptation that also includes generalized anxiety disorder, panic disorder, phobias, and depression. The significance of these disorders also draws an important link for the emphasis on cognitive theory, that is, that cognitive defensive adaptations operate in the service of maintaining familial attachments.

EFFECTS OF TRAUMA

Krystal (1978) outlines the after effects of childhood trauma on adults, accenting a spectrum of cognitive and affective restrictions. He defines trauma as the "overwhelming of the normal self preservative functions in the face of inevitable danger. The recognition of the existence of unavoidable danger and the surrender to it mark the onset of the traumatic state" (p. 112).

Many think of trauma as a single event or episode outside of the "normal" pattern of events and relationships within the family. This category applies to natural disasters (Lindeman, 1944) such as fire, flood, or earthquake or a single episode of rape. In abusive and/or alcoholic families, the trauma is frequently chronic, the state of unpredictability, terror, and abuse the norm. Episodes of acute trauma—violence, incest, arguments, psychological and physical abandonment—may also occur within the chronic framework. Krystal (1978) notes problems with the term "trauma," accenting the differences between *acute* trauma or *strain* trauma, the more chronic state. Sandler (1967) also describes a state of "mounting vulnerability" stemming from the accumulation of potentially traumatic factors.

Khan (1963) speaks of psychological trauma and the after effects of the mother's failure to protect her child from a variety of adverse circumstances. Following these breeches of the mother as a "protective shield," Khan describes the cumulative trauma as "silent, unnoticed by all and visible only in retrospect" (p. 296).

It is important to understand both the "normal" chronically traumatic environment or life context (Reiker and Carmen, 1986) in the alcoholic home and particularly traumatic events that occur within this context as well. Krystal suggests that psychological trauma may predispose an individual to respond excessively and maladaptively to intense affects, manifested by a sense of being "dead" or by a variety of dissociative reactions from depersonalization to psychosis (p. 209). Reiker and Carmen (1986) describe the same process, accenting the use of repression, dissociation, and denial of the reality of the trauma.

Bowlby (1979) described "defensive exclusion," the ability of children to exclude, redefine, or distort information or events.

Bowlby suggests that the consequences of such distortion include chronic distrust of other people, inhibition of curiosity, distrust of their own senses, and a tendency to find everything unreal. (p. 405) A patient who grew up in an atmosphere of chronic tension with frequent violence and constant criticism describes his sense of both cognitive and affective awareness as an adult.

> I look at the world—people, events and feelings—through a filter. It's like a haze, a cheesecloth, that mutes the intensity of what's out there and what's coming in. I couldn't tolerate my feelings without this filter.

In defining a phenomenology of severe trauma, Krystal (1978) describes a paralyzed, overwhelmed state with immobilization, withdrawal, depersonalization, and disorganization, with the most common consequence a "mixture of depression and anxiety" (p. 291).

Krystal accents the fear of affect or "affect storm" as the central feature. The individual fears that any affect will be experienced as "flooding" and uncontrollable, leading to destruction or annihilation. Krystal distinguishes between a state of helpless surrender which results in a "closing off" of all affect, expression, and perception and a state of danger characterized by a hyperalert and hyperactive affective state. This is also the critical distinction between depression and anxiety (Beck, 1985). Our ACA patients range from the most extreme anhedonia—the absence of any affect or memories and a very limited cognitive range in adulthood—to severe chronic anxiety and depersonalization.

According to Krystal (1978), constriction and progressive blocking of mental functions follows affective blocking. Memory, imagination, association, and problem-solving abilities are all impaired.

Anxiety Disorder

Beck (1985) and other cognitive theorists emphasize the centrality of cognitive or information-processing theory in describing adult psychopathology, particularly anxiety and depression. Like Rosen, Beck stresses that disturbances in cognition lead to disturbances in feeling and behavior and vice versa: corrections in thinking result in improvement in feeling and behavior. This is important in the process of recovery: the break in denial and "making real the past" that follows, help alleviate the source of anxiety.

Beck suggests that anxiety symptoms are manifestations of survival mechanisms directed by cognitive processes and cognitive defenses: rationalization, denial, and projection. These are the major defenses utilized by the alcoholic parent and codependent parent to both deny and maintain the drinking behavior. Beck stresses that psychological disturbance occurs when there is a mismatch between the child's or adult's perception of the environment and the actual characteristics.

Krystal, Beck, and others (Guidano & Liotti, 1983) outline a theory of adult psychopathology based on a traumatic childhood environment or "life context" *and* the cognitive mechanisms utilized to cope with that reality. The disturbance is an expression not only of the reality of the trauma but of the distortions required to deny both the perception of reality and the affect congruent with it.

Adults experience and exhibit a very narrow and rigid cognitive equilibrium with accompanying affective exclusion, repression, or denial. Underlying severe problems in this balance are likely to be manifested in anxiety disorders characterized by a feeling of pervasive vulnerability and danger or depression.

Beck describes the key problems in anxiety as overactive, cognitive patterns relevant to danger that continually structure external and internal experiences as a sign of danger (p. 14). He adds that the anxious patient selectively attends to stimuli that indicate possible danger and becomes oblivious to stimuli that indicate no danger in a way that maintains and reinforces faulty thinking patterns.

Beck outlines the symptoms of "thinking disorder" in clinical anxiety, most of which characterize the "normal" state of the ACA. These "symptoms" may be labeled as presenting problems at intake or they operate as the cognitive structures that direct and limit perception and affect—the structures that must be challenged in the advanced phase of treatment.

In Beck's schema, attention, concentration, and vigilance are bound to concepts of danger or threat. The individual "uses up" cognitive capacities by constant scanning. Our ACA patients describe being "on duty," hypervigilant, and responsive to the threat of danger and to cues from others. For many, the hypervigilance is actively experienced as a search for signs of approval or disapproval from others. The codependent reactive stance reinforces the significance of the external environment and the dominance of others. A patient in an advanced group illustrates:

> Isn't it amazing how pervasive the threat of danger is? I know it's not real—there is no danger out there or in here (group), but I feel it nevertheless. It comes from within me and is always there.

Another patient describes her behavior in a new intimate relationship:

> I can't believe how I'm behaving. I want this relationship more than anything but I am pushing him away. I'm acting like I must be terrified but I don't feel it. I just feel awful about my rejecting behavior and the way I turn off—just literally freeze up emotionally—when things get too close or too good.

Beck describes the "alarm system" or "automatic thoughts," the loss of objectivity and voluntary control, stimulus generalization, and catastrophizing as additional symptoms. Our patients recognize the lack of objectivity as treatment progresses and experience "catastrophizing" within the transference:

> I am constantly on guard in this group. Life in here consists of waiting for the next disaster and then surviving it, just like outside.

Beck adds three more symptoms, all critically relevant to our clinical work with ACAs: selective abstraction and a loss of perspective, dichotomous thinking, and lack of habituation. With the center of control experienced outside the self and that center unpredictable, inconsistent, and likely damaging, the individual functions in a state of chronic vulnerability, the potentional of danger or harm a constant.

In the group setting, individuals select out cues, signs, and information that validate their sense of danger, reinforcing their deep belief of themselves as bad or unworthy (adapted to preserve the illusion of a good parent) and interpret this information within a dichotomous all-or-none frame. The circle is closed and self-perpetuating.

Beck notes the significance of rules to cognitive schemas, the patterns of thinking that orient an individual to a particular situation. With the all-or-none dichotomous frame, rules become critically important in assessing any situation and determining a response. In the beginning group, the search for rules is a major topic. The lack of rules is a serious problem for most patients whose anxiety mounts in direct proportion to the lack of structure. The search for rules or formulas continues as an enduring frame characterizing the advanced group as well.

> If I can just figure out what is required here I can behave accordingly and make the appropriate response.

This individual, after many years in the group, continued to believe that the key to understanding his interpersonal problems rested in his failure to "figure out" the "right" answer. Not unexpectedly, he and others complained of his cognitive and affective rigidity and lack of emotional spontaneity.

Beck emphasizes vulnerability as the core of anxiety disorders. He defines "vulnerability" as the person's perception that he or she is subject to internal or external danger over which control is lacking or is insufficient to provide a sense of safety (p. 68). In the vulnerability "mode," formal thinking is impaired and cognitive processing becomes dysfunctional. A sign of danger triggers the sense of vulnerability and the individual then processes incoming information in terms of weakness, rather than strength or confidence. To challenge or alter deep beliefs is equal to betraying the parent and losing the attachment.

The enduring nature of the anxiety disorder can be better comprehended when attachment behavior and dependency needs are considered. Understanding the relationship of attachment to cognitive dysfunction is also important in determining treatment modality. A strictly cognitive-behavioral approach may not be effective in altering core cognitive schemas because of the threat of the loss of attachment.

Beck emphasizes that the most effective antidote to anxiety is the availability of a caretaker, a person who is reassuring and with whom the individual feels safe. That person provides the security and/or cognitive corrections that enable the individual to emerge from cognitive and affective regression or disorganization characterizing the anxiety state to a higher level of function. In our long-term work with ACA patients, we often find that attachment to key parental figures is based on *maintaining* the cognitive distortions and therefore the vulnerability and anxiety.

Challenging or changing one's cognitive schemas, distortions, and affects (weakness, vulnerability, and fear) represents a betrayal and therefore a loss of attachment. As Reiker and Carmen (1986) state:

> Therapists fail to realize that the victim's subjective experience of separation or loss of the delusional image of the good parent brings with it the feelings of abandonment and annihilation. (p. 368)

In fact, the individual's sense of "security" lies in an attachment which is characterized by anxiety. The individual remains in the self-critical, anxious mode to maintain the sense of attachment to a disturbed alcoholic or codependent parental figure.

Beck distinguishes between generalized anxiety disorder (GAD) and depression. In the former, the individual experiences anxiety about interactions that carry a risk of being dominated, devalued, rejected, or abandoned. The self-image fluctuates according to the degree of risk, ranging from a sense of competence and high esteem to childlike helplessness and vulnerability.

Beck sees depression as a stable part of character with anxiety related to behavior and fluctuating self-image.

The significance of the interpersonal frame is underscored. This is an important factor in explaining why so many of our patients enter treatment because of difficulties in their intimate relationships, difficulties forming or maintaining close ties, and fears of having children. Many report having achieved a measure of limited security and adjustment by living alone or carefully controlling the degree of intimacy. Others have maintained relationships, but with alcoholics, drug abusing or otherwise dysfunctional partners with whom intimate bonds are not possible. As one patient stated:

> I've never chosen a healthy partner. I always blamed my loneliness and problems on my boyfriends who were always drunk. As soon as I picked a healthy partner, I lost all my confidence and began to have anxiety attacks. Now I see myself as the problem.

The desire for more, the longing for closeness, frequently prompts individuals to seek help. It is often the attempt to step out of the security of one's isolation that triggers the anxiety, cognitive and affective regression, and psychopathological symptoms.

In the next section, we will examine the key issues emerging in the course of the long-term ACA group that illustrate the predominance of the cognitive, defensive adaptations that become the core of adult psychopathology—the framework that provides an isolated defensive illusion of security by limiting and restricting cognitive and affective awareness and expression. These defensive adaptations include denial, control, all-or-none thinking, and the assumption of responsibility.

DEFENSIVE DIMENSIONS OF ADULT PERSONALITY

In Part One I emphasized the overwhelming significance and dominance of defensive maneuvers in the alcoholic family. In looking at the impact of parental alcoholism on individual development, it quickly became clear that the defensive strategies characterizing the family are not simply "defenses," mechanisms utilized to ward off affect or perceptual clarity. These defensive adaptations emerge in adulthood as central issues or even structures—dimensions of adult personality—coloring all aspects of individual development. Many of the major issues or problems brought to treatment, for example, depression, anxiety, problems in forming close, intimate relationships, are related directly to these defensive adaptations. Acquired in the service of survival in the family, they are now a severe impediment to mature development. As Reiker and Carmen (1986) suggest in regard to abused children:

> Defenses utilized by both child and adult victims later form the core of the survivor's psychopathology.

As noted in Part One, the defensive adaptations or "overlay" often become the sense of self—the "false self" that develops in the interest of survival.

Reiker and Carmen (1986) echo Miller's (1984) concern about the loss of self, noting that abused children are deprived of the experience of separateness, a sacrifice of the self in order to maintain ties to others in the family. They cannot experience their own feelings as separate from parental needs and therefore grow up devoid of self-protective mechanisms and more vulnerable to abuse and exploitation (p. 364).

Ted, the 23-year-old now adult child of an alcoholic father spells out these issues early in his treatment.

Ted feels the burden of alcoholism falls disproportionately on children. His mother didn't learn her behavior from his father or model from him. But the kids—he and his sibs—know nothing else. They learned only how to behave unsuccessfully.

Ted says the children in his family learned an abnormal form of reality. They had no prior experience to inform them that something was wrong. Ted developed a feel for what was appropriate in his family, for what was right or wrong in that world and it didn't carry over. He finds himself lost, insecure and frightened in the world outside his family. He is sure he's emotionally immature but he doesn't know what to do about it.

Ted is extremely worried about what he calls his own lack of control and inability to regulate *his* behavior. He is hyper-excitable and overly happy—emotions used to cheer up his depressed family. He has no idea what behaviors go along with loving someone and, if he can't predict the reactions of others, he is always unsure how to behave. Ted feels tremendously insecure socially and especially in developing close relationships outside his family. He is certain he is just as moody and lacking in emotional controls as everyone in his family. So he maintains a vigil on himself just like he did with his family.

Ted feels terribly young—young at least in the world outside his family. Ted says matter of factly that his father's drinking interrupted his development in the fifth grade. He had to think and behave like an adult for his survival so he missed what he calls the jumble of emotions of adolescence. Now out of the family and an adult by age, he often feels like a beginner, a small child, terribly needy, very emotional and lost at sea in an adult world.

Ted reflects that up until now he has had no choices. His relationship with his father and his father's alcoholism was all consuming. He and others did whatever their father wanted. There was no thought of opposing him. Ted said with great sadness that only his father's death allowed him to live. Ted said what countless others echo—his father created the struggles for Ted to surmount. He had to respond to his father or desert him. Now his struggles are his own.

The defenses required for survival and attachment in the family become the essence of the false self, also developed in the interests of meeting parental needs and of maintaining attachments. As such, the individual has no sense of anything beneath the defensive core and cannot step out of it to reflect on it. Very often the process of treatment involves a central focus not only on "breaking down" defenses but on breaking down the false self. These defensive adaptations—denial, an emphasis on control, all-or-none thinking, and a sense of responsibility—are enduring and highly resistant to challenge. Thus the major work of treatment, individual and group, involves exploration of these core issues as defensive adaptations in the past and present, and as structures or traits that influence the individual intrapsychically and interpersonally as an adult.

ORIGIN AND MEANING OF DEFENSIVE ADAPTATIONS

In our long-term group work, these adaptations appear early-on as defenses, utilized in the service of warding off anxiety and other affects related to the group or emerging quickly from the past. For example, the emphasis on control and the dominance of the all-or-none cognitive frame reflect the individual's strategies for reducing vulnerability, uncertainty and ambiguity, feelings all too reminiscent of the early family environment and feelings about the present as well.

In the advanced group, the same issues persist but now reflect deep problems themselves or dimensions of personality that are more central to the individual's behavior and characteristic attitudes. They now appear as "inherited" aspects of the family's defenses, cognitive style, and attachments.

All developmental processes are affected by the predominance of the primary defensive mechanisms in the alcoholic family. Denial, rationalization, perceptual distortion, projection, a maladaptive emphasis on control, and all-or-none thinking characterize the family's relationships and equilibrium. They also influence the individual's acquisition of knowledge about the self and the world. Children acquire these mechanisms as their own by sacrificing their own view of reality and identifying with the parents' preferred view instead.

In describing the family's "style," Reiker and Carmen (1986) note that the "child's task is to accommodate to a family in which exploitation, invasiveness and the betrayal of trust are normal and in which loyalty, secrecy and self sacrifice form the core of the parents' value system." Reiker and Carmen suggest that the "victim's survival is dependent on adjusting to a psychotic world where abusive behavior is acceptable but telling the truth about it is sinful" (p. 364).

They add that the adaptation occurs by altering the perception of reality and thoughts, feelings and behavior so all are congruent with family norms and expectations. These mechanisms of alteration —denial, changing the affective response, and changing the meaning of the abuse—along with the emphasis on control and all-or-none thinking, maintain the family's attachments and organize the individual's acquisition of a personal identity—the sense of self in relation to self and others.

Reiker and Carmen note characteristic patterns in abusive families including rigid and often contradictory rules for the behavior of members. There is disregard for personal privacy within, but a facade of secrecy and silence is maintained for the outside world. There are often sharp dichotomies between good and bad and between what one says and does.

All of these characteristics reflect a strict judgmental, evaluative, cognitive style, required to maintain the family's sense of security as a whole and to maintain attachments to one another.

So critical is the need for attachment to parental figures that children will deny or alter their perceptions and their personal identities, indeed sacrifice them, to identify with the defenses, beliefs, and values modeled by their parents. As such, they identify with disturbed thinking and behavior in order to maintain attachments. Reiker and Carmen (1986) note that children will alter their perceptions, registering an abusive parent as good, because the child must rely on that same parent for comfort. The need for attachment overrides all else.

The pattern of sacrificing the development of one's independent identity in order to maintain attachments has been described by role theorists although not labeled as such. The various role adaptations—hero, mascot, lost child, and clown in Wegscheider's schema (1981) or the responsible one, the adjuster, or placater in Black's configuration (1981)—all describe the *reactive* defensive style of interpersonal relationships adapted to sustain attachment or the illusion of attachment with parental figures or surrogates.

These defensive adaptations shape interactions with others and structure the development and interpretation of self-knowledge as well. However, the same defensive adaptations that permitted childhood survival become the structures that now limit the adult. A patient makes this point well:

> I have a deep sense of myself as needy and vulnerable. But I have an entirely different "face" I present to the world. That "face" of competence, strength and even defiance isn't real, but I rely on it anyway. The facade is the basic structure of my support of myself.

We have examined the course of almost ten years of long-term group and individual therapy noting the themes that emerge repeatedly as deep issues from childhood and problems in adulthood (Cermak & Brown, 1982; Beletsis & Brown, 1981; and Brown & Beletsis, 1986). The long-term view also reveals that these same themes operate as structures for individuals and the group, providing a limited sense of safety. It is critical to recognize that the defensive adaptations which dominated and structured childhood development have now become central problems, in essence, the core of adult psychopathology. Exploration of these defenses becomes the foundation and the structure for examining developmental issues of attachment and identity formation in the next two chapters.

DENIAL

Denial is a primitive, cognitive defense mechanism utilized extensively in the alcoholic family. Denial operates as a major structuring mechanism, dictating what can be known, acknowledged, and incorporated into the individual's view of self and family. In Part One, I emphasized the significance of denial as an organizing mechanism of the family's knowledge about itself. I illustrated the range of denial that exists about parental alcoholism from total to partial and the impact on the individual and the family.

Denial of parental alcoholism includes denial of perception and the affect congruent with it. It also necessitates an illogical or faulty explanation of what has been denied. As such, denial is more than a blocking of perception and affect and a corresponding narrowing of cognitive and affective range of what is absorbed or taken in from the environment. It also involves faulty construction—the act of reasoning. Individuals must not only deny what they see, hear, and feel, but they must also construct faulty explanations for what is really happening. Attachments in an alcoholic family are built on sharing the family's point of view—denying, to some degree, parental alcoholism and adapting the reasoning that explains it.

As noted earlier, that reasoning frequently involves the creation of another problem. There must be a way to explain increasing drinking, erratic or violent behavior, mood swings, and memory lapses that both explains the reality and denies it at the same time. That "explanation" may involve the creation of "another problem," someone or something outside the family, such as a stressful job, or someone within.

Almost always, denial of parental alcoholism requires not only a narrowing of cognitive and affective range, but also a distorted view of the self. As many others note (Reiker & Carmen, 1986; Guidano & Liotti, 1983) children need to maintain an image of their parents as good for the parents' sake and for their own. In altering their view of reality, children accept responsibility for what has been denied and begin to see themselves as bad. Interpretation of self and other and the developing sense of their own personal identities is, thus, constructed on this base. Many children give up early on, acting out the sense of internal badness and despair. Others cling to the hope that they can become good and, thereby, fix the parent who will then be available and loving to the child. The sense of being deeply bad prevails as a foundation of the self and structures the child's adaptation to others and perceptions about the world. These individuals grow up seeing themselves and others in a way that repeatedly reconfirms the view of self as bad. What must be denied cannot be incorporated into one's view of reality or one's sense of self (Mahoney, 1977). Jim illustrates the mechanism of denial or "defensive exclusion" (Bowlby, 1980) within the group.

Angry and exasperated, group members finally confronted Jim about his behavior. Either he is in the center of everything or he's "asleep," sitting through the group with his eyes closed. Surely he must be very anxious.

Jim always denied feeling anxious. This time, however, he wondered if it might not be so. In reading the summary every week, he realizes he has missed important things in the group. Sometimes he wonders if he's received the wrong summary.

Ultimately he could see that reading the summary filled in the empty spaces he experiences each week in group. Indeed, he is so anxious he must exclude a great deal from his awareness.

The impact of denial is also reflected in the lack of trust of one's perceptions which then interferes with deepening intimate relationships.

Brad notes that he often misses opportunities to open up and reveal himself which would deepen a relationship. He worries instead that he cannot trust his perceptions of the relationship. His feelings may be too intense or he has attributed more closeness than is actually warranted.

Members then agreed that to reveal themselves or to be open to deepening experiences is equal to feeling wrong, out of control and overly exposed.

DICHOTOMOUS ALL-OR-NONE THINKING

One of the most all-encompassing and persistent defenses also functions as an organizer, structuring incoming and outgoing perception and affect in a way that minimizes ambiguity, inconsistency, and uncertainty. Unfortunately it narrows and distorts as well.

As noted earlier, dichotomous thinking is consistent with the primitive defense mechanism of denial. It is also a symptom of anxiety disorder (Beck, 1985). However, it is more than a symptom. It is also a cognitive style that diminishes anxiety as much as it stems from it. Dichotomous thinking insists that there are rules. There is a right and a wrong, a good and a bad, and the problem lies in finding the right or the good in any particular setting or situation. Dichotomous thinking eliminates the need to deal with vague, uncertain, or unpredictable perceptions or feelings. It eliminates the need to integrate apparent opposites or complexities with many contradictory dimensions. All-or-none thinking also covers deficits—perceptual and affective.

All-or-none thinking is consistent with the central emphasis on control with each reinforcing the other. All-or-none thinking maintains the adaptive belief that the parent is good and the child bad because in this frame, someone has to be at fault.

The structure of dichotomous thinking reinforces extreme

polar positions and dictates reversal as the solution to problems. Thus the only way for the child or adult to relinquish the feeling of being bad is to reverse it: if the child is really good, the parent must be bad. This conception carries with it acknowledgment of deep loss, pain, anger and feelings of abandonment. It also uncovers severe deficits, such as problems with attachment. Within the dichotomous frame, individuals must cling relentlessly to their belief in themselves as bad in order to hold onto the illusion of attachment. No matter how pathological, that illusion covers the more painful recognition of isolation, abandonment, and aching loneliness.

After many years of struggling with her sense of being bad, a patient says matter of factly:

> How can a child feel anything else but bad? The source of the problem? It's the only way to make sense of brutal parental behavior. It's much more frightening for a child to realize that the parent is out of control and incompetent to care for her child.

Another patient struggling with the same awareness reported a series of dreams:

> I am always in a crowd but have no interactions with any of the people who occasionally notice me but most often do not. In another dream I reached out to touch these people and found they were encased in plastic, transparent cocoons that shielded them from contact with each other and me.

Months later, she began to explore her feelings of deep loneliness.

> My parents were encased by their need for alcohol and their denial. They were bounded by the beliefs they constructed to preserve these illusions. As long as I thought I was bad, I could deny the plastic covers and hope to be good enough so they would respond.

All-or-none thinking divides perception and affect into two mutually exclusive categories. It is consistent with the dichotomous categories characterizing family relationships: one is dependent or codependent, dominant or reactive, and most importantly, in control or not in control. Perceptions and affect about self and others are all interpreted within the all-or-none frame.

The dichotomous perceptual frame is also related to attachment. In the group setting, it appears as an "inherited" trait, which on closer inspection, reveals an enduring world view or attitudinal set adopted by children to conform not only to the family's "story" but its preferred method of seeing itself and reality. A group member illustrates the enduring and organizing character of her all-or-none personal and world view, related to attachment.

> Penny described her family as a "true clan" with strict rules for inclusion. There were friends and enemies, insiders and outsiders, good and bad, all rights and all wrongs and never anything in between. Penny identified with this framework as the family's "beliefs" and expressed it herself as a cognitive frame from which she interpreted all events in the group.

> Early in the group she was silent as she assessed similarities and differences between herself and others. She was also afraid to find herself caught in a dichotomized position against another member, realizing that the only solution would be departure. But in the advanced group, she began to take stands, to express the all or none quality of her perception. Indeed, she and others felt stuck when someone had to be right and someone wrong.

The alternative to leaving was to begin to include areas of "grey" which was frightening and painful. Not only did "grey" interfere with her certainty, it also represented a betrayal of family. She needed to maintain the family's defensive cognitive style in order to maintain her attachment to it.

The all-or-none cognitive frame appears as an issue in its own right and as a frame which underlies many of the most important themes emerging in the clinical work of the group, beginning with the break in denial, the acquisition of the label ACA and the decision to join a group. We have described these factors as a first major step in the process of treatment (Brown & Beletsis, 1986). We related this primarily to attachment, emphasizing that ACAs equate breaking denial of parental alcoholism with abandonment. Acknowledging the truth to themselves and making it public by joining a group is a betrayal of the family's secret which most believe will result in rejection by their parents. Breaking denial is also felt as an aggressive act, one of rejection themselves.

Denial and the break in denial are experienced within an all-or-none frame.

> I either go along with the family's beliefs or I am alone.
> There is no alcoholism or there is and I am out of the family.

In the early work of the group, this same theme and its relation to attachment is experienced around the question of "belonging." Most of our ACA patients feel orphaned and alone in the world, standing outside with a yearning to belong and a deep fear of joining. As a group patient stated:

> I need a family to come from and belong to. Drinking is my ticket in.

or

> I am always lonely, isolated and dying to belong. But I just can't.

As she traced her deep desire, she realized that "belonging" in a relationship or in a group implied the loss of herself. "Belonging" also meant that she would become alcoholic like her father or depressed and victimized like her mother.

> Lori often emphasizes her wish to belong to the group in some kind of middle way. She is provocative or angry or she simply reacts to what is directed by others.

The Codependent Dichotomous Response

In the group setting, issues brought in from the outside and those emerging within are often framed by the all-or-none view. It is often this view that is identified as the problem after group members repeatedly find themselves stuck trying to fix another with advice that cannot be accepted. In essence, the problem presented is almost always one that cannot be solved. Either it is not the "real" problem, or a solution requires taking a stand, getting off the balance point that attempts to hold opposing sides while losing no matter what. Paula illustrates:

> Paula said she wanted to bring up an issue that was outside the group, to let the group know she did not expect any answers or anything to be fixed but she thought it was important for people to know about it. She then spoke about the serious, painful difficulties

she is having with her boyfriend. Paula feels constantly controlled by his moods and erratic, unpredictable explosions of rage. Even though the anger is not directed at her, she is frightened for him and for her. Paula is upset with her own reactions—she is constantly on guard and walking on eggs lest she say something that will upset him. But not saying something is equally problematic because they are living a superficial existence in order not to talk about anything that really counts.

Paula quickly saw the all-or-none framework: she loses no matter what. If she brings up issues to talk about, he is upset and he can't stand conflict. If she doesn't bring anything up, he's still upset and so is she because things are superficial and tense.

Paula uses this reasoning to underscore her belief that she doesn't have to do or say anything—just being there causes problems for him. She then noted how much being with him reminds her of living with her father as a child. She didn't have to do or say anything wrong but she got punished anyway and she never knew when it was coming. The therapist noted that that was also the way Paula felt about her in the group. Paula has maintained that the therapist plays favorites and is not fair.

Group members laughed and now talked about how difficult it is to detach or change one's attitudes or behaviors simply by deciding to do it.

The all-or-none position arises repeatedly around the issues of intimacy and dependence.

Toni is really struggling in her new relationship. She can only imagine herself fiercely independent and defiant of his efforts to be intimate or she is totally dependent on him, openly weak and needy and ultimately harmed. There is no in between.

The all-or-none framework is so enduring as a cognitive structure that it affects all levels of uncovering. Brad illustrates how his cognitive set interferes with his capacity for insight, a critical factor emphasized by cognitive theorists (Mahoney, 1977). Individuals cannot achieve a new insight or an expanded level of integration outside of their core beliefs or the structure that shapes them.

Brad feels frustrated. He recognizes that he cannot integrate the exchanges that have occurred because it is not within his framework to understand how two people can have a difference of opinion and not resolve it. Somebody has to be at fault and you cannot put the issue aside until blame is determined. The group's growing ability to tolerate areas of "grey" and increasing complexity is foreign to Brad and a source of anxiety.

Group members emphathized with Brad. Sally said she was always caught in the same all-or-none dilemma around the issue of her "needs."

> Either she had to give up herself entirely to take care of others or she would take care of herself and heads would roll. She is now beginning to find that middle ground where she can have needs, express them and heads *don't* roll, but she's still amazed.

Months later Brad returned again to the idea of his cognitive set as a problem.

> I always have relied on my own observations and assessments to guide me. Mostly it's turned out well. But then I never know what could have been because I never know what it is I don't know. All of my thinking is bounded by the parameter of my world view. I can always feel confident and in control because I assess everything in a way that fits my beliefs. I can't trust myself to expand my vision and I can't expand it anyway since I rely only on my own counsel. I feel safe and sure while I'm missing a lot that would open up my world.

Brad had this insight after being confronted about his denial of the severity of his drinking.

Themes of control and all-or-none thinking are also explored around the issue of autonomy, especially in close intimate relationships.

> Being involved with someone means I lose. I automatically become wrong or selfish if I don't want to give what the other person needs or demands. It's all or none. There's no such thing as negotiation—only right or wrong. I'm getting my needs met and I'm selfish or the other person is using me. There is no such thing as equality or compromise. If I empathize or am sympathetic with another point of view, I lose my own or have to be wrong. There can't be different points of view without my losing in the end.

This issue is repeated countless times in varying interactions within the group. After several years of defensive resistance to allowing for grey, Sandra explored her deep beliefs:

> I need to see myself as a good person, generous, looking out
> to take care of others. To challenge another is to be ungener-
> ous and to step outside of belonging. To hold a different
> opinion, to express it, and to have disagreement is equal to
> being bad, rejected, or abandoned. The other person has to
> completely agree or there is only loss. I simply can't trust
> that there is such a thing as "working it through" to a new
> ground on which we can agree.

Issues of closeness and distance, control and autonomy were explored around the theme of parental visits, again within the framing structure of the all-or-none view.

> Alice reported splitting her parents up during a recent visit as a
> way to restore the peace. She put one in the guest room and the
> other on the sofa. Group members responded with shock, not to
> Alice's control, but rather to the fact that she could tolerate having
> her parents stay in her home. Others then compared notes:

> Wendy's parents stay in a motel which everyone now prefers. They
> drink there if they have to and Wendy doesn't have to deal with it
> in her home.

> Randy can't even tolerate a visit—never mind where his father
> stays.

> I keep wondering if there isn't a middle ground, a structure that
> would permit a greater range of contact for us that wouldn't also
> contribute to overwhelming anxiety? So far I haven't found it.

Because of the rigid dichotomous interpretations required, the all-or-none frame is often a primary source of feelings of loneliness and isolation. Patty illustrates:

> It's an "all-or-none world." Someone is right and someone is
> wrong. In a relationship someone has to give in. I will end up
> lonely and alone. I'm not going to be the one to give up my
> point of view or be wrong.

Patty expands, describing a friend who has "faith" in life:

> My friend just hangs in there. Not too much upsets her. She
> really *believes* things will work out. But I grew up in an all-or-
> none environment and don't possess the faith that things will
> work out if you negotiate or if they're unpredictable. To take a

risk is to step outside of my own predictable responses. If I can't count on me, what have I got left?

The all-or-none need for control surfaced again when a new member joined the group.

It's all or none for Connie. Either she can be completely silent with the newcomer or she can take over, asking questions and dominating. There is no middle ground. And there's really no choice. She can't take over because she always reveals too much of herself when she is engaged. So she must be silent. The new person, sensing the tension, begins to talk, attempting to make everyone else feel comfortable with the hope they will "invite" her in. She presumes the group is silent because she is supposed to talk. But the more she does, the more the others have their worst fears confirmed: the newcomer is threatening, dominant and out of control.

The dilemma of the group's silence continued for several weeks with escalating tension and anxiety. All members refused to talk to the newcomer, seeing themselves as victims to her verbal dominance and control. The therapist's interpretations could not break the impasse until she expressed her own anger:

Members were refusing to see their silence toward the newcomer as actively hostile, instead focusing on their feelings of helplessness. The group is like TV—members expect to find something interesting to watch and are disappointed when they don't like what is on. But they will not change the channel, feeling instead that they must endure what is offered to them.

This interpretation brought up memories of having to respond to the dominance of out of control parents and of being squelched in their efforts to change the channel as children.

CONTROL

In all of our work, we have been amazed at the repeated emphasis on control, identified as a problem in its own right, and as a structure for interpreting self and other. In examining difficulties related to establishing and maintaining intimate relationships, the need for "control" and the impact of control as a structure are central.

With long and deep exploration, individuals recognize that the emphasis on control reflects the need to ward off anxiety and fear and the need to deal with the chronic danger of calamity in interpersonal relationships. The emphasis on control is also exercised in the service of warding off recognition of one's *own* uncontrollable impulses. Underneath the rigid defenses, the individual believes "I am just like my parents—out of control and dangerous."

In the process of uncovering this deep belief, the emphasis on control often increases. The less denial about one's own out-of-control impulses, the greater the need for control. One group member insisted he had no impulse problem and no fear of being out of control. Other members ultimately shared their fear of him.

The emphasis on control is linked to and intensified by the all-or-none view and is often equated with autonomy. Together this frame provides a powerful defense against feelings of vulnerability and dependence. Many ACAs shun reliance on others.

> I take care of all my own needs. To rely on anybody else is to lose control and ultimately be harmed.

Yet she acknowledges the irony that being in control and taking care of her own needs also resulted in harm and self destruction.

> I have always satisfied my need for longing by eating. It's lucky I never liked alcohol. I've got all the traits to be an alcoholic.

The need for control is a constant, routinely structuring underlying perceptions and affect. Frequently the emphasis on control also emerges as a focal issue, the problem itself as Jake illustrates. Members agreed that, in this case, Jake's need for control was a metaphor for them all, representing a deep longing for the safety of a family in which parents could turn their attention away from themselves to focus on the child:

> I still want to invite my mother to my graduation but I've just heard from my brother that she is drinking again. I feel devastated. Jake then described an intricate pattern of recent behavior. He had been consumed with trying to arrange for all members of his family to be present at this important day while also being able to control them. As a child, Jake recalls that his family could never accommodate to his

wishes or let him be the center of attention. He is trying desperately to orchestrate just that, for one occasion, and he is overwhelmed with anxiety.

The group then spoke about the impossibility of controlling others, urging Jake to examine his behavior and unrealistic expectations. As Patty notes:

> If it were my graduation, I'd go alone. It's the only way to insure it's really for me. I always lose because I need to control everything. Any interaction with others means getting through and surviving it—enduring.

In stressing her need for control, Patty also illustrates the structural nature of the all-or-none frame, tied to her sense of control. "Alone" is the only alternative to losing.

The issue of control coupled with the all-or-none cognitive frame, is symbolized most importantly around the issue of alcohol and of "being alcoholic." The question of "being alcoholic" is central to *all* ACAs. Many are already recovering alcoholics who also have identified parental alcoholism as an important factor in their own developing alcoholism and recovery. Others are not sure. They have identified concern about their drinking as a problem which they wish to examine in the context of the identity as the child of an alcoholic parent. They may have struggled already with their own drinking or drug use and they may continue to struggle over whether they are "alcoholic." Identifying oneself as the child of an alcoholic offers the door to explore both.

Many ACAs identify themselves as "not alcoholic" in the initial interview. On closer inspection, it becomes clear that indeed, they are "not alcoholic," based on their drinking, but in fact they are "alcoholic" in their core view of themselves.

These individuals either do not drink at all or they exercise a vigilant control, permitting themselves to drink only under certain circumstances and in very controlled situations. As one individual stated:

> I know I would be alcoholic immediately if I ever stopped watching myself.

In the course of the group's work these individuals, "alcoholic" and "not alcoholic," reveal a deep belief that they are out of control.

> Life consists of constant vigilance, measurement and evaluation with the hope of not "losing it."

Much of the early work in the group and in life outside consists of assessing control. Who's in charge here? Am I in control? Am I being controlled? Am I out of control?

This creates an immediate serious dilemma for most ACAs who enter group. The focus on control and the importance attributed to "having it" have become major defenses. The emphasis on control is also one of the most serious obstacles to achieving close relationships. With such a focus, there is no such thing as valid concepts of interdependence, negotiation, or the idea of "giving a little." Someone is in control and someone is not. There is a winner and a loser.

Being "out of control" is associated with being weak, needy, dependent, and abused. Individuals enter the group believing that the only way they can protect themselves is to maintain control which means they cannot permit themselves to experience any need or vulnerability. Yet many enter the group precisely because they do feel needy, deeply so; or they experience need simply as the longing for a close relationship. The byproduct of the need for control—loneliness—is as painful as the feeling of not having it.

Thus most members enter the ACA group feeling caught in an immediate bind.

> I have based my entire sense of self—of precarious esteem— on the importance of control and now I am coming here every week to let go of it. No wonder this is unpleasant and I so often question if any of this is helpful.

The unconscious link between being out of control and being drunk or alcoholic is enduring. Following a meeting in which he revealed himself more than usual and was seen as "spontaneous" by others Ted reported:

> I felt great after the meeting but then more and more uneasy. It wasn't long before I actually felt hung over. I then experienced all the shame and remorse I used to feel after drinking.

Group members recognized that the deepening of interactions carries the risk of the group's feeling out of control just like their families did. Not only will they "find themselves drinking" as

Ted experienced, but acting on sexual or violent impulses if they discussed them as well.

Feelings

Of critical importance to the question of control and related to anxiety disorder is the notion of feelings, including feeling good and feeling bad. Several members maintained a rigid, negative view of the world, expecting the worst. Life always turned out worse than even the negative expectations so why hope for anything positive?

> The negative view provides a sense of control. I can't be taken by surprise or risk having my hopes dashed. You don't get hopeful in the first place.

> Group members laughed ironically as Sally said matter of factly that she expects things to be miserable and even participates in their being so and she can't will it to be otherwise.

> Rose nodded. Whenever she is feeling good, she opens herself up for disaster and immediately feels vulnerable, terrified and anxious. When she feels inadequate and self critical, the terror is not present. Rose maintains a precarious balance. She wards off anxiety by continuing to feel inadequate and she achieves a sense of control by coming to group and attempting to do something about it. Feeling good is just another experience of being out of control and ultimately harmed.

The next week Rose spoke more about control, criticism and her negative view of herself.

> A large group is out of control for me. On a one to one, I can manage the reaction of the other and thereby avert criticism. In a large group, I can't manage all the variables and therefore run a greater risk of being criticized.

> Others pointed out that Rose also maintains control of potential criticism by reporting things in a neat package and not getting involved in spontaneous interactions. Ultimately she feels isolated. She tells herself that she is boring others, providing the criticism herself that she anticipates from others and so carefully wards off.

Feelings are a mystery and a source of great concern. They are also an important gauge of control. Members recognize that they want to open up, to discover their feelings, even to find out what a feeling is and they are terrified of the first glimmer, rumble, or sweaty palm.

> Something is coming up and I don't know what it is. I can't label it, explain it or control it. But I know it's there because of the rumble in my stomach.

For Jake, the rumble is more like a blast. He is overwhelmed a good deal of the time by intense emotion which he believes is a bad thing. If he opens up a tiny bit, he and others will be overwhelmed. Like others, Jake believes that if he once starts to cry, he will never stop.

> Jake is still silent. There is too much feeling beneath the surface. Wendy wonders whether he has some feelings that are managable.
>
> No, there are no little rivers leading up to the big one that are safe to express.

Ben, who has always felt categorically like Jake about feelings, has the following experience.

> Ben became anxious and insisted again that his feelings would be "overwhelming" if he began to open up. But as he said this, he continued, opening up to the very experience of feeling that had been taboo. Suddenly he had the profound recognition that what he had called "universal truths" about feelings was not true. He realized through this experience that he could feel very deeply and no one would get hurt. He always thought feelings, if unrestricted, would automatically be "bad." But these were not. He was safe and so was everyone else. From now on he knew his version of the world didn't hold.
>
> The rest of the group was as thrilled as Ben. All recognized that his ability to be completely surprised by his feelings in group and allow himself to have them was an exceedingly important step.

It is also an important example of the power of core beliefs to structure one's perceptions, affect, and interactions. Ben believed not only that feelings were bad, having lived with explosive, violent parents, but if he had them *himself,* he would be bad, out of control, unprotected from the violence of another *and* violent himself. By feeling, he opened himself to become the victim and the aggressor at the same time. Only by not feeling and carefully controlling all interactions, could he manage his anxiety, protect himself and protect others from him.

Anger

Anger is often the focal point around which issues of control, feelings, and the all-or-none frame are crystallized. For many ACAs, anger is dangerous—at the core—feeling it and expressing it will result in destroying the very individuals one would like to rely on; the very individuals whose approval must be sought and won; the very individuals whom one needs and must control at the same time. Recognition of anger also threatens to destroy one's self image as kind, generous and caring. And most of all, anger threatens to repudiate denial of one's own overwhelming deep neediness.

For others, anger is prominent, the only emotion safe to experience—the one that predictably creates distance when necessary, establishes limits and boundaries and importantly covers deeper feelings of need, sadness and loss. Openly angry individuals may become the "alcoholic" in the group, potentially harmful, unpredictable and out of control. Seen to dominate and control others through their anger, they are often viewed as the source of continuing tension as the group becomes in reality "just like my family." Members reexperience the fear and sense of impending disaster as the angry person(s) defends against forming bonds with others that would involve mutual dependence or examining internal deep feelings of need.

The defensively angry individual must ultimately do both. If not, the group becomes stalled, unsafe, and unable to function as a supportive unit. Or, the angry person leaves, furious with the group for its failures or ultimately extruded by members who draw the line.

One member struggled desperately for many months caught between a deep wish to belong to the group and identify with other ACAs and a constant feeling of "danger." He rejected other members' feedback repeatedly, attributing hostility and competitive motives to others whom he believed were jealous of his insights. Ultimately he left:

> This group is just like my family, a war zone. And I'm the target. Every week I come here and get shot at just because I can see things so clearly.

The defensively angry individual often reconfirms for other members the validity of their belief in the all-or-none nature of their own rigorously denied anger. The group becomes in reality a "war zone" as members defend against the unpredictable anger of one by tightening their own controls. A cold war prevails. Cooperation and the sense of safety required for individual uncovering work and interpersonal exploration vanish as the group becomes defensive, reactive and closed down in the interest of self protection. Members can recognize a similarity to their past but often cannot maintain the distance required to examine the transference implications of the group's dilemma. The here-and-now has become in reality too dangerous and the defensive climate prevails. For many, this is the story of their lives outside the group. The defensive climate prevails.

Those who deny feelings of anger must also look deeper and question their denial. Chipping away at the all-or-none perception of anger often reduces the need for denial. Members begin to explore anger as an abstract topic and then as a real issue between them. Initially, the notion of anger may be explored in the context of "taking action on one's behalf."

> If I come on time, I will have to start and who knows what will happen next. If I have to initiate, I'll be out of control and that will ultimately equal anger.

For another member "taking action on my own behalf" will always result in being abandoned.

> To stand up for myself is felt by others as hostile and they will leave me behind.

As the group focused on anger, members explored their beliefs about the therapist. Ben expected that the therapist masked feelings of anger toward all of them which she probably felt most of the time. He certainly does. Others are amazed and Dorothy laughs:

> No, Stephanie doesn't mask anger. She knows it's not worth it to feel it. I assume Stephanie knows that being angry isn't good for her because she'd probably hold onto it forever, just like I do.

As the group focused on anger, Tony became frightened. If she became angry, she would have to leave the room in order to stop herself because others would not put the limits on her. She would be left out of control. Stephanie would be just as frightened as everyone else.

After several years in the group, Tony began to feel and express anger toward the therapist who sometimes responded only with interpretations and, on other occasions, expressed her own feelings of anger in response. Initially, Tony was afraid to return. But over a period of months, she began to see that she was actually exploring a "fighting" relationship with the therapist. To her, it remained a mystery how one could have angry "exchanges" and still maintain a relationship. But that is exactly what she was testing now in the group.

In the advanced group, the notion of a "grey" area becomes a major theme, first explored abstractly, then inside and outside of the group as it becomes a working reality incorporated into members' view of themselves and others.

> From the first day Larry joined the group, he focused on figuring out the rules—the rights and wrongs—expected. He quickly demonstrated in his interactions with others a tremendously limited and rigid perceptual range based on a view of himself entirely as a reactor. He assessed others and the world only in terms of "expected" response.

> He was quickly challenged about his emphasis on rules and his all-or-none view. He couldn't imagine any other way of viewing people and situations although this extreme categorical frame was full of danger, especially when it came to anger.

> The first time anger was expressed in the group Larry became frightened. The following week he said it was all he could do to sit still and not leave. It was even harder to come back. His first impulse had been to duck—he actually had sat crouched in his chair.

> This experience brought forth a flood of painful memories about anger—in his home it meant violence, flying plates, broken glass and screaming—a regular part of the family's dinner hour. The most Larry could do then was take his plate and go upstairs. Last week, it was all he could do to "stay at the table" and not leave the group.

> Larry was terrified of anger, everyone else's and his own. Not long after he joined he observed an "angry" interaction between the therapist and another member that served as a grounding point for his work in the group over the next several years. As he said many times:

I knew Stephanie was angry because she said so. But she didn't *sound* angry or behave in an out of control manner. I didn't even have the impulse to duck until it was all over and I realized what had happened. From that point on, I knew there was "something in between" and I wanted to find it for myself.

Two years later he reported the following:

Larry reported confronting his boss about adverse conditions at work. His boss listened to him and though he didn't agree with Larry, he accepted his point of view. He also responded to some of Larry's complaints positively. Larry was exhilarated. He never would have been able to recognize that the problems at work were outside of himself before now. He would have become obsessed and taken on more and more work, focusing all of his feelings internally and blaming himself for his failures. This feels quite different to him, something he never could have imagined when he joined the group. The idea of negotiation, of "middle ground" or "grey" was something that Larry never had any idea about. Either he was not angry or he was angry and it equalled violence. The heart of his work in group has been to explore possibilities that there are shades of grey. Larry joked that the idea of a middle ground has not gener-alized easily to other areas of his life. It seems he has to "turn a switch on" anew each time and it is very hard work to hold off his automatic extreme response and try something new.

In exploring his fear of anger, Rob notes he cannot make fine distinctions in his feelings. His anger is volcanic. He will be "flooded" by it. Thus any feeling or emotional experience that cannot be explained is enormously threatening. There must be slots for all feelings and explanations for everything.

In exploring the issue of anger, Hal realized he experiences no subtle distinction in internal cues. For Hal, any expression of annoyance will escalate to being out of control. When he feels upset, annoyed, or irritated, he has the same internal flow of adrenalin that has always signaled intense anger. He has no sense of internal distinctions between small and large anger—they all equal the same thing. This feeling signals "fight" or "flight."

Rob is frightened of his anger, too, which he controls symboli-cally by "keeping one hand tied behind his back." If others were to get angry, Rob would be at a disadvantage with only one hand.

This insight prompted Rob to begin to look for his own anger, as he decided that his fear of it was a serious handicap for him. As he did that looking, he experienced new awareness. Rob's anger is not just his own, stemming from experiences of deprivation and abuse. It is also the anger of his father. Rob is deeply identified with his father and must therefore exercise constant control—living with one hand tied behind his back—so he does not *become* his father, violent and out of control toward others.

Control Symbolized in Group Themes

The issue of control is frequently raised in the context of interpersonal dynamics in the here-and-now. In one group, members complained about the slow pace and their wish to "loosen" up. The theme of "loosening up" and the issues of internal control and external control were symbolized through discussions of dress.

Today the men spoke about their own feelings of inadequacy and uncertainty, accenting the lack of teachers or role models and what they had missed. They shifted to the subject of control, noting their dissatisfaction with the extreme need for control in the group. Nick said he wants a "looser" atmosphere and Hank removed his tie. Immediately the deeper fear surfaced which Rob expressed:

> Nick will come dressed only in jogging shorts and will sit in the middle of the floor—what his mother would have done. He will be out of control and the group will have to pay attention to him. Nick said his father was the spontaneous, creative person and also the out of control alcoholic.

> The men then spoke about their continuing dilemma: how can they "loosen their ties," becoming more involved and spontaneous without losing total control? Taking your tie off, or "loosening up" means a free for all.

The issue of "pace" was both a theme and a structure, regulating exploration, interaction, and the expansion of insight in the group for many months. If members felt stuck, they often focused on the slow "pace" emphasizing their wish to "loosen up." Frequently the loosening up went too far and anxiety rose.

> Nick arrived late with rumpled hair and a bright turtle neck replacing his usual three-piece suit and tidy hair. Others stopped and stared.

> Now you've gone too far, said Rob. You've upped the ante
> and I can't compete. You're out of control.

As members proceeded in relaxing their control by symboli-
cally loosening their ties, they also expanded their insights. Dan
was very late for three weeks in a row following a fast, "looser"
meeting in which competition was intense. Finally group members urged him to look at the meaning of his behavior. In doing
so, he and others agreed that their unconscious behavior does
have meaning and is observable to others. This recognition feels
like a loss of control.

> If my perceptions, feelings, verbal and nonverbal behavior
> do indicate a lot about me, I have no control at all.

A few weeks later the same focus on control rose again in
relation to competence and competition. Jack and Rob do well
in individual sports but not in team play. In the latter, there is too
much demand for perfection so you don't drag the team down, or
you have to control the others so they don't drag you down. But it
is hard to be perfect as Jack illustrates:

> I have to start out perfectly in any sport or new endeavor.
> I could never put myself in the "learner" mode because I
> couldn't show myself as incompetent. By showing myself as
> incompetent, I risk disapproval from those I can't allow
> myself to learn from but must impress.

Being in the "learners" mode is felt as a loss of control—the
endangered, one-down, the "none" of the all-or-none dichotomy.

> I must know everything—start out perfect. How can I open
> up to learn from models and teachers who will show me how
> to self destruct?

The discussion of "showing oneself" brought the women in.
Wendy said she was angry at Connie for dressing last week in a
seductive way which Wendy felt as competitive and rejecting of
her. Other group members were surprised, pointing out that
Wendy had worn an equally provocative dress several weeks ago.
Wendy was astounded and then embarrassed at what she had
revealed about herself without consciously realizing it. At first
she felt intense feelings of shame and exposure at her lack of

control. With further inspection, she recognized that she wants to be praised, to compete sexually and aggressively and she is afraid.

The group now focused on dress again for several weeks as a metaphor for a variety of issues almost all touching on control.

> Sara said she changes out of her work clothes purposely to deem-phasize her managerial role and her sexuality in group. Hank laughingly agrees that Sara's dress doesn't say too much about her and he wishes she'd "say more." He adds that Wendy is the most unpredictable dresser and the most unpredictable in her mood. She dresses in a way that is most visible and exposed and most threatening to Hank.

Threat is often related to competition. After a series of impor-tant insights and authoritative interactions in group, Connie wore what she perceived to be a nondescript, plain outfit. Sitting in group, she realized that she expected the women to be angry with her progress and initiative so she unconsciously dressed in a way that would communicate her wish not to threaten others.

As the group continued its discussion of loosening up, another member spoke about the danger of being spontaneous.

> I can't afford to take my focus off of others. In a relationship, you have to "cover all the bases" all the time. Otherwise, you will be caught "off guard" and humiliated.

The need for control is also demonstrated around the issue of tardiness. After being in group for sometime, members recognized that tardiness is not coincidental or without meaning. Eventually they discussed their responses to Jake who is almost always late.

> For a long time, they felt they couldn't "start" till everyone was present. Jake's tardiness left the group constantly waiting. Yet they always denied feeling controlled by him, just like they deny that others in their lives are important or have an impact on them.

> Eventually members looked closer, realizing that Jake's tardiness was a source of chronic irritation. But they couldn't comment on it because that might make him mad and he would leave. It was better to have him late than not at all. This discussion prompted Jake to look closer too. He realized he is driven by guilt for failing to respond to the demands of others. Tardiness provides an illu-sion of control. He can choose to respond or not to a situation

(whatever is already occurring in the group when he arrives late) started or created by others.

Much later he looked at another side of this issue. Coming on time and starting opened him up to challenge, criticism or hostility from others for his aggressive demand for the group's attention.

On another occasion the group examined tardiness again.

> It's difficult and uncomfortable to be first which is what happens if I arrive on time. It means I have to stand up for myself and have needs. To "take risks" means to step out of familiar patterns and "dances."

The group recognized how difficult it is to alter basic patterns even though they are unsatisfying or self destructive.

> How can I do things differently and still reconfirm my basic assumptions about the world?

Dan explained his persistence in revealing himself and engaging in deeper feelings. He was always reactive to others and never felt he could keep up with the right words or comments. The ability to do that now is very important even though "initiative" sometimes feels "out of control." Dan does feel he has more control now and can risk deeper feelings without the threat of being overwhelmed as he felt before.

Brad is encouraged by Dan's efforts and hopes to model from him. He thinks about bringing a subject up in the group but does not know where it will go or what he will have to say about it after he brings it up. The need to control whatever happens with him or others is so predominant it keeps him from acting at all.

The group agreed. Brad's control is air tight and members protect it, seeing him as fragile. Besides, what good would it do to challenge him? There is no negotiation, no middle ground: "you accept people the way they are or you write them off."

To help puncture Brad's wall of control, the therapist suggested that he carefully read the summary before group, writing his comments, feelings and reactions on the paper. He might then have more "active" feelings to bring to group. Brad's response was more anxiety.

Silences, tardiness and missed meetings are important mechanisms of control, ultimately recognized as such by group members, as much as they are problems in their own right to be explored in the context of the here and now.

> The group is angry at Connie's need for silence which feels controlling and manipulative. Confronted, Connie feels she has to talk which then makes her responsible for how others interpret her. Chances are, they won't understand and she'll feel more alone, unsupported and unsafe than ever, all because she talked.

> Finally she said her silence reflected her feeling that the group wasn't safe since Dan's tardiness three weeks in a row. The group then looked at their current emphasis on defensiveness and control. Silence, tardiness and missed meetings are all suggestions of a wavering commitment which means others can't go deeper.

The all-or-none frame and the emphasis on control are identified as problems in establishing and maintaining equal, interdependent relationships. They are also the structure that frames the exploration and holds members caught in repetitive patterns of perception and behavior. Members in the here and now cannot see that they are bound by the limits of their perceptions and their defenses while they are labeling these perceptions and defenses as problems at the same time.

Following the discussion of tardiness and commitment, the group explored the issues of closeness and distance and their often mutually contradictory need for both at the same time.

> Sandra realized she was caught in a bind. She wanted to continue the intense feelings of closeness but she also wanted to fall back into her self today. By now she had stopped looking at people and Jake appeared to be dozing. The therapist commented that Jake's dozing was an extreme response to Sandra's wish not to have anyone get too close yet also not lose the closeness all had been feeling recently. The whole group was "on hold," caught up in Sandra's dilemma.

Group members assured Sandra that she doesn't have to "manufacture" closeness in the group in order to keep it alive. Closeness is ongoing or Brad could never have allowed himself to feel the way he did several weeks ago. Brad then spoke about his toddler daughter whose own efforts to deal with closeness and distance have opened up a new range of possibilities for Brad.

> She talks about her aunt and then runs right past her. She hugs and kisses us and then pushes away to go play with her

blocks. She figured out that she can come and go as she pleases because she's assured that we are there. That's how I feel in the group.

Sandra adds that she didn't have that certainty growing up so she is always checking to make sure people are there. Stability or certainty is not an underlying reality for her even in group.

Patty illustrates further the difficulties that arise in interpersonal relationships because of the emphasis on control. She is the center of attention frequently which she likes. In order for her to be at the center, she has to have a problem for which she needs help, but she also has to have it solved so that she does not have any interactions with others. In group, she and others talk about her need for control as a problem, but she cannot yet recognize it in here and now interactions.

As Patty examined the issue of control and its relation to intimacy, she reported the following:

> I have to control my mother's drinking so she has just enough to enable me to be with her. If she doesn't drink at all, or drinks too much, I receive the brunt of her anger. I've learned that having any relationship at all means being responsible for controlling the other so as not to hurt myself.

Any need for distance is felt as a resistance and a rejection of others. Following a discussion of this issue, the therapist introduced the notion that distance might not be such a bad thing. Perhaps members need to explore the ways they can gain distance in order to be able to be alone or deepen their exploration with one another.

This was truly a revolutionary idea that opened members' bad feelings about their need for controlling the level of intimacy with others and how it always feels like an all-or-none proposition. With many months of exploration and testing, Rob came to the following insight:

> I've realized that people will ultimately let me down and it may have nothing to do with commitment. I've got to learn to depend on others and to trust them knowing they will *also* let me down.

The next week Rob was absent. On returning, he told the group it had been important for him to choose as he did. He was committed to the group *and* he chose to do something else. Rob had come to the realization that others will disappoint him and he will disappoint others.

> I've always placed great demands on others to be totally committed to me and I expected the same from myself. Then I'm terrified that I'll be engulfed and will have to leave entirely in order to be free. Choosing to be absent allowed me to try out the idea of a middle ground.

A few weeks later, Nick arrived late wearing a T-shirt inscribed: "marching to a different drum." Everybody laughed.

Self-Blame and the Assumption of Responsibility

The child's development takes place in the context of "reaction to" and by necessity becomes predominantly defensive. A major cognitive mechanism utilized by all children (and frequently adults) to deal with the insecurity of this base is the assumption of responsibility. All children need to believe that their parents are good and they will be taken care of (Kagan, 1984). When reality disproves this basic assumption or places it at risk, the child quickly alters beliefs about the self and world to preserve a belief in parental integrity and to deal with the incongruence of perception dictated by denial (Rosen, 1985).

If there is nothing wrong in this family—for example, there is nothing wrong with my parents—but there *is* something wrong in fact, then it must be me.

> Cindy often experiences deep feelings of need and longing for a close relationship with her mother. She longs to be heard and responded to on the basis of what she needs and asks for. In the group setting, she is repeatedly frustrated and let down by what she perceives to be the therapists' failure to *really* hear her and respond.

> The therapists and other group members point out that Cindy becomes increasingly muddled and vague when she most wants something from others. This observation leads Cindy to tears as she realizes that the lack of "connection" to her mother was evidence that she repeatedly failed as a daughter to be able to get her mother's love. If she could figure out how to be a better daughter, her mother would become available.

This sense of responsibility—it is my fault, I am bad—allows the child to feel needed and provides the illusion of security about the parents' well being and availability. The child experiences the absence or loss of parental attention as a *response to* something bad about the child. The child thus shifts the center of control and often attention from the parent to the self. This mechanism provides an illusion of security because it leaves the parents intact as available and caring figures and places the responsibility for problems on the child. The child then focuses on "fixing" him or herself—becoming perfect—believing that parental love and care will then be forthcoming.

The feeling of responsibility also may be an expression of survival guilt and a defense that provides an illusion of control. Feeling responsible reflects a sense of omnipotence, often adopted early by children to ward off recognition of helplessness and fear.

> If I caused all this trouble, then surely I could fix it too. That way there was hope.

The theme of responsibility reappears frequently within the group as a defense and as a problem itself.

Sara is struggling again with the pain she experiences whenever she longs to have a good life; whenever she determines to go after what she wants for herself. Stephanie wondered what it would be like for her if she did have a good life and she started to cry. She would feel guilty and she would need to be punished for wanting a good life. To be successful is also to become responsible for the family she left behind. She doesn't want that responsibility. She repeats her belief that she is a bad person anyway who doesn't deserve good things and good relationships.

Other members spoke about similar feelings—guilt, responsibility, and a deep sense of being bad. Group members talked about their inability to step out of the feelings and beliefs they learned about themselves as children from parents who felt very badly about themselves. Paul suggested that taking the responsibility for what was wrong was the only way to cope as a child in a situation that was intolerable and unfixable. Bob added that his mother told him he was to blame. He wondered how he could have grown up feeling anything other than he was doing it wrong and he was bad.

Group members continued, recognizing they were dealing with very painful feelings of being tightly bonded to the very bad feelings their parents had about themselves and communicated to their children.

Sara sighed. Is there no end? She realizes she lives her adult life driven by the ties that bound her to her parents.

> As a child I was deeply wounded and bleeding as a result of my parents' inadequacies and behavior with me. I don't expect the reality to go away but I would like to be an adult who, though scarred as a result of these experiences, is no longer bleeding.

A few weeks later Paul continued, demonstrating his sense of being deeply bad and, therefore, responsible, this time for the negative treatment he receives from others.

> Paul spoke about always worrying about the reactions of others and always being certain he is not OK to begin with. He recognizes he approaches every situation or every individual with an idea of trying to please that person while expecting to be criticized and ultimately fail.

Pam describes in detail just how Paul makes these beliefs a self fulfilling prophecy.

> You are like an abused child in the group. You believe you are bad and you proceed to figure out how to please others. But since you believe you are bad and expect to be criticized, you end up making it happen. First you are not direct and second, you have no idea what you want from others because you have no sense of yourself that would permit you to have needs or wants. Everything's related to and interpreted through others.

> No wonder you are always anxious in settings with a lack of structure or a lack of response to you. Immediately you assume you're doing something wrong, while others are waiting for you to be direct about what it is you want or need so they *can* respond to you. Instead you grow more confused and uncomfortable sensing you are failing to guess right about what others want. You end up actually being criticized or left out.

The sense of being bad is also related to attachment, identification with the parent's sense of badness and the shame experienced for parent and the self. Grace illustrates:

> I am so lonely. Being alone is a reminder that I have failed but it is also the only time I feel good about myself. I long to have a close, loving relationship. But it's just a fantasy. As soon as I'm with someone, I feel wretched about myself. It's a sense of not being good enough. No matter what I do, my bad breeding shows. It's a constant source of humiliation because I don't know what it is I don't know.

The sense of being bad extends further to the issue of responsibility as Grace illustrates when a recovering alcoholic joined the group.

> I don't want anything to do with you. I don't want to take care of you, to have a relationship with you. Once I care, I have to take care of you and you will need a lot. You might drink and then you'd be unavailable to help me. I'd be stuck. I'd feel responsible, I couldn't fix you and I'd lose you too. I would rather be alone by choice than risk caring and be abandoned.

Jim feels "out of control" today. His wife broke her arm and he believes he must automatically become responsible for her.

> I don't know how to get control. Simply by being "involved" with other people I open myself to become responsible for them, endangering myself at the same time from their crazy behavior.

The issue of responsibility is also raised repeatedly in relation to competition.

> Being good at something, or being "better" makes me responsible for the bad feelings others will then have about their inadequacies. For me to be better in here, to have more insights than the therapist, is equal to being alone and separate. And what's more, my insights will result in the breakup of the group.

He then recalled being the one who repeatedly set limits on other family members and ultimately broke the family's strong denial of his mother's alcoholism and physical abuse. Following his confrontation, his parents separated and the children were sent to relatives.

The issue of responsibility arose again around the themes of attention and competition. After being the focus of admiring attention for other group members the previous week, Patty felt guilty and frightened.

> I loved the attention but immediately felt sorry for Grace and Jane. I should not be making progress if they're not. And if I'm getting the attention, it means automatically that they're being criticized. Positive strokes for me equal implicit negatives for them.

> I'm responsible for their bad feelings. But if they'd been the ones getting the goodies, I'd also have been responsible for being left out and criticized implicitly myself. It all boils down to this: any relationship means someone will feel good and someone bad and I'm responsible.

Several years after this incident, a similar one occurred. By now, Patty was able to take a firm stand on her own behalf and register her perceptions of a person or event as accurate for her even if others saw it differently. Remnants of her all-or-none frame and her sense of responsibility crept in as group members explored areas of "grey."

> Patty insisted her view was right for her although it didn't have to be right for others. Then the group focused on Bob, who held the other "opposing" view. Members offered support and sympathy to him.

> Patty tried to remind herself that she could have a different view. But, as she later noted, she had "lost it." She began to feel awful about herself and enraged at the group. Their support of Bob was an implicit criticism of her. By being sympathetic with him, they were indicating that he was "right" and she was wrong.

> She raged. By having a different perception she had alienated others whom she now perceived as critical and hostile. She was alone and responsible for having caused it.

The issue of responsibility remained a central theme for Patty and others as it merged into the other main issue of all-or-none thinking.

> Patty started the meeting with a "confession." She had not read the summary because she knew there would be something she didn't want to see. She wants to hold onto her hurt feelings and

especially to her belief that someone has to be right and someone wrong. There has to be somebody at fault. Patty realized after last week's meeting that she can't empathize with another point of view because it automatically makes her wrong.

The group then struggled with the idea of "differences." Abstractly, they can acknowledge that differences can exist and everybody doesn't have to see, feel and think the same. But it doesn't hold up in reality. Seeing things differently carries the threat of losing the person or relationship if the differences can't be resolved.

The group then gingerly returned to the issue of differences among themselves. Immediately, they smoothed the rough edges, determining that their differences were really insignificant and due to circumstance.

The therapist was amazed. She pointed out that members were whitewashing their differences in an attempt to achieve quick agreement. By explaining away their disagreements, they would not have to deal with the reality of their differences and explore how to continue a relationship when no one accepts fault, no one apologizes and differences remain. Group members felt extremely anxious which Patty interpreted:

> Differences will result in abandonment. Plus, I can't tolerate the loss I feel while waiting to resolve the difference. It's better to patch it over and take the blame. Then at least I've got the relationship.

The question of differences is also related to control.

> Chris is struck that two people can have different reactions to the same event. He always has believed that he can predict how people will feel and therefore gauge his behavior according to his predictions. If two people can react differently, his theory is destroyed and he does not have the power he thinks he does. Suddenly the world becomes unpredictable and frightening again.

In looking at the issue of differences, group members also realized that the sense of responsibility is tied closely to attachment.

> Carl is unable to detach himself from his sense of responsibility for his family and his guilt. It's guilt for being OK to begin with and for failing to take care of everyone else.

I've been punishing myself since leaving the family, for having been OK and for failing to help them. I think it's also a way to hold onto them. You know, I was just trying to save my own neck. I couldn't take care of them and I was also the one holding them all together.

Carl recognized months later that he maintained a defensive attachment to his brother by the belief that he might be able to do something different now or that he could have done something different in the past. By holding onto his guilt and sense of responsibility, he keeps from abandoning them once again. Much later, Carl spoke about how alone he feels and how desperately he needs a family.

In this chapter I have outlined the defensive adaptations that structure the individual's sense of self and relationships with others. These maneuvers also provide the link between the systems perspective and exploration of individual development. In Chapter 5, we turn to the latter, examining the impact of parental alcoholism on attachment.

Chapter 5

The Impact of Parental
Alcoholism on Attachment

ATTACHMENT: THEORY BUILDING

Major dynamic and developmental theorists (Bowlby, 1980;
Mahler, 1975; Erikson, 1963; Miller, 1981, 1985; and Blos, 1962)
agree on the significance of attachment as the base for healthy
human development. The road to mature, independent separation and individuation—the development of a healthy self—is
built on successful early dependency relationships outlined by
Mahler et al. (1975) as the symbiotic stage and by Erikson (1963)
as the establishment of basic trust, in simple form, the expec-
tancy that one's cries will be understood and needs attended to
through a predictable process of mutual communication and responsiveness between infant and primary caregiver, typically the
mother. All theorists agree on the importance of certainty, predictability, and stability of the care-giving figures. Disruptions in
the accuracy, empathy, timing, and certainty of the response can
have serious consequences on all aspects of later development.

Bowlby (1980) underscores the significance of attachment as
he notes that the goal of life is a primary affectional bond. He
adds that individual actions can be best understood as they relate
to attachment behavior.

Miller (1981) notes that "true autonomy is preceded by the
experience of being dependent." She outlines the severe consequences for children whose narcissistic parents occupy the center
of attention and require sustenance from their children to resolve
their own internal conflicts. From her object relations point of
view, Miller describes how the child exists to reconfirm the narcissistic parents' value or point of view and as such becomes a
tool or extension of the parent. She is unequivocal in her estima-
tion of the damage: Parental narcissism, that is, the dominance of

138

the parents' needs at the expense of those of the child, leads to a loss of self rather than autonomous development. True separation cannot occur at any point in development without the foundation of attachment and dependence, based on the centrality of the child's needs and the parents' accurate responsiveness to them.

The importance of the environmental point of view emphasized in the first section surfaces again. The alcoholic family is organized around the dominance and centrality of the parents' needs—the alcoholic's growing need for alcohol and the nonalcoholic's (if there is one) need to control the alcoholic. Both parents are frequently overwhelmed with their own anxiety and need and, therefore, inattentive or marginally available to focus on the needs of their children. There is a chronic underlying fear held by all that things are, or soon will be, out of control.

We have stated elsewhere (Cermak & Brown, 1982) that childhood is short-circuited or nonexistent for these children whose primary needs are secondary to those of the parents. Children learn to experience and express their dependency needs in reaction to the uncertainty or random capacity of their parents to respond.

Children may develop a precocious pseudomaturity often demonstrating emotional and practical role reversal with one or both parents. Children assume responsibility for the parent (including feeding and clothing) and for parenting younger siblings. Indeed, the alcoholic is frequently the number one child in the family with all others responding to the dictates and needs of that individual(s).

In the alcoholic family, attachments are built around and governed by the centrality of the alcoholic and the denial of parental alcoholism. In Miller's terms, the child exists to confirm for the parents not only that they are good, but that there is no alcoholism as well. The latter requires the child to adopt the same distorted logic and reasoning maintained by the parents to sustain their denial.

Lidz (1973) outlined a similar theory in relation to the development of schizophrenia in children. He suggested that the parents' struggle to maintain their own precarious emotional balance leads them to shape the family environment rigidly to match their requirements. They must structure the family environment in a way that allows them to maintain their own view of themselves and their often precarious emotional equilibrium. Lidz notes that the parents' insistence on altering family members' perceptions and meanings, as noted earlier in relation to language, creates a family environment filled with "inconsistency, contradictory meanings and denial of what should be obvious" (p. 68).

Like Miller, Lidz emphasizes that the children must subjugate their needs to the parents' defenses. The child's conceptualizations of experience are in the service of solving parental problems rather than of mastering events and recognizing their own feelings. Further, the acceptance of mutually contradictory experiences and meanings requires paralogical thinking. The parents' lack of awareness of "the child's needs and the masking of the true nature of intrafamilial situations distort the child's meanings and reasonings" (p. 69).

The child must perceive the family as the parents dictate, which forces the child to either repress or deny his or her own feelings and needs or feel unwanted. Perceptions must be distorted to fit the family's mold. Facts are constantly altered to fit the emotionally determined needs of the parents rather than the child, a key point also emphasized by Miller.

Rosen (1985) emphasizes the centrality of cognitive structure as a framework influencing other aspects of development. For example, he suggests that affect never appears in a vacuum, but rather is always channeled by the cognitive structure present at any particular stage of development. Rosen outlines a theory of cognitive psychopathology, accenting problems in the child's acquisition of knowledge about the self and the world. He and others (Guidano & Liotti, 1983) focus on the cognitive and affective problems that result when a child accommodates to a parent's needs, feelings, and defenses.

To a large extent, the degree of psychopathology and the level of cognitive and affective development achieved and demonstrated by parents greatly affects all aspects of the child's cognitive, affective, and social development.

Rosen focuses on the difficulties and arrests in cognitive function that occur in response to parental problems. He, Miller (1981), and Lidz (1973) all speak about the loss of self that occurs when a child must become parent-centered. These authors note that parental egocentrism blocks a child both from progressing through the development stages and from acquiring the meaning system of the broader culture as well.

Egocentrism does not accommodate to reality but rather requires a distortion to meet the individual's own needs. The denial required in the alcoholic family and the centrality of the parents' needs also require distortion which produces a conceptual deficit. Thinking becomes paralogical.

In addition, Rosen points out that inconsistent or ambiguous parental views cause children difficulties in learning to decenter from their view and, therefore, difficulties in coordinating their view with others. This leads to deficits in thinking conjunctively—the ability to join two attributes of an object or relationship.

Rosen suggests a clear link between a child's level of cognitive development and emotional experience. Since cognition gives structure to emotional experience and expression, the level of cognitive structural organization will influence the nature and range of emotional life and vice versa.

Rosen continues, suggesting that there is a clear relationship between childrens' level of cognitive developmental maturation and their ability to fathom mechanisms of psychological defense. The better the cognitive abilities, the better the social and emotional competence.

Primitive defenses cannot be deciphered in an alcoholic family precisely because attachments are based on maintaining the defenses and the beliefs supporting them. Most important, Rosen suggests that defenses correspond to the level of cognitive development. Denial is consistent with preoperational or concrete operational thinking which includes reversible thinking, primitive projection, and ego splitting.

Families bound by a predominance of denial will also exhibit more primitive levels of cognitive development consistent with the denial. These same families may demonstrate higher order cognitive development in areas where denial is not required. Thus one may find skewed families and individuals within—members can operate at a level of formal operations with hypothetical reasoning, combinatorial thinking, and higher order reversible cognition while regressing to a more primitive level of paralogical, concrete thinking when denial or distortion are required.

Thurman (1985) notes that children integrate the cognitive and affective realities of parental illness in different ways depending on their age, level of cognitive development achieved, and defensive needs.

In the therapy group, one sees a wide range of cognitive and affective levels and abilities as well depending upon the particular issue or subject and the degree of threat to one's denial.

Rosen (1985) further suggests that the regressive pull of a strong preexisting notion is too great for children to be able to integrate contradictory self-observations. They will retain the preexisting belief. Children need to fit new experiences in with prior expectations to form patterns and make sense of them. What doesn't make sense is selectively unattended to or repressed.

The need for denial, the centrality of other primitive cognitive defense mechanisms, the arrest or regression to levels of cognitive operation consistent with the defenses and the need to fit all experiences—cognitive, affective, and social—in with prior expectations results in a very narrow cognitive frame or equilibrium or a constant sense of disequilibrium based on the mismatch between perceptions and explanations of reality.

Given this theory, we would expect that children of alcoholics would be arrested in cognitive development. As cognitive theorists note (Guidano & Liotti, 1983), the cognitive developmental counterpart to denial is a preoperational or concrete operational level of cognitive organization, characterized by literality, concreteness, and all-or-none thinking. We would expect, therefore, that much of the incongruity and complexity to be mastered in the higher development stages cannot be integrated except through the more primitive cognitive frame consistent with denial and concrete operations.

In clinical work, the primitive mechanisms appear in areas of conflict which often dominate much of the individual's life. The defensive maneuvers described in Chapter 4 correspond to earlier cognitive levels of organization. Many ACAs utilize their intellectual strengths in careers that demand the highest level of cognitive competence. Yet these same individuals feel impoverished in emotional and personal development. In the group, they can discuss abstractly the properties of a good relationship but they cannot experience one. Quickly, the group reveals a cognitive and affective compartmentalization. Individuals regress to earlier levels of cognitive development and defenses in areas of core conflict. Thus it follows that the centrality of parental alcoholism and the degree of denial required become key determinants of the degree to which primitive cognitive patterns predominate. To what degree can an individual bypass conflicting areas of personal or interpersonal development and proceed with the tasks—affective, cognitive, social—intrapsychic and interpersonal—of normal development?

Also relevant to the alcoholic family is the concept of "masking" (Spiegel, 1953). To defend the parental equilibrium, one or both parents conceals a disturbing situation within the family, acts as if it doesn't exist, and expects the child to ignore the situation and collude in denying it. After breaking their denial of parental alcoholism, ACA patients begin the painful process of reconstructing events and relationships in their family of origin—as they actually were—relinquishing the "mask" of collusion required to maintain the parents' precarious emotional balance and sustain attachment. This relates again to the significance we attribute to the break in denial, signaled by the patient's acquisition of the identity and label "ACA." Patients equate acquisition of the label and the decision to seek treatment to abandoning their parents. At the same time, they fear their parents will reject them for their aggressive act of breaking the family denial (Brown & Beletsis, 1986).

The break in denial is often followed by intense feelings of isolation, loneliness, and depression as the realities of childhood become clear. The break in denial precipitates a recognition of profound loss, not necessarily for what one had, but for the illusion of attachment, an illusion that was maintained by the family's denial and core beliefs.

> In a newly formed therapy group, a member experiences profound sadness as she recognizes the longing for her first family. As she thinks about the reality of parental alcoholism, she tells the others that it didn't matter. The whole family stuck together, believing that they were a close ideal family. The belief shared by all that everybody loved each other provided the illusion of a tie that, in fact, was precarious at best.

> A female patient repeatedly rejects deepening feelings of trust and attachment to male patients and particularly to the male co-therapist. She maintains her view that men will ultimately fail her, demonstrating the primacy of their own needs and their use of her to meet them.

> Her rejection is categorical. With a failure in empathy by a man, she is once again let down, vulnerable and needy. So why allow herself to ever long for closeness and attachment with a man? After many repetitions and deep hurt, she notes that even if her father had been sober he could not have put her needs first—he did not have the capacity to care for others—his own needs were always overwhelming.

The emphasis on denial early in development and the distorted reasoning necessary to maintain it form the base for disturbances in the cognitive component of attachment as well as the affective bond. Children learn that the maintenance of their attachment to parental figures is based on sharing the family's point of view—in essence—there is no alcoholism.

Parental Egocentrism

Lidz (1973) elaborates on parental egocentricity noting the parents' inability to recognize that the other person, the child, has different feelings, needs, and ways of experiencing. Thus "the egocentric parent cannot properly accommodate to the child and his or her needs but rather must assimilate the child to the parents' needs, requiring the immature child to fit himself to the parents' orientation—to see the world as the parent needs to have him see it" (p. 74).

Lidz notes that the child, in contrast to the parent, is open and sensitive to the needs and feelings of others precisely because he or she needed to adapt to the parents' needs. The egocentricity of both parent and child are reciprocal but while serving to protect the parents' emotional balance, actually leave the child vulnerable. Directed by the parents' needs, the child has not invested his or her energy and attention to self-development. The child then needs the egocentric parent in order to maintain a sense of self, false though it may be.

Further, the child believes he or she can affect his parents by his thoughts and feelings—separation, for example, will kill them. Lidz emphasizes that the child is more parent-centered than egocentric "but his feelings of being central to his parents' lives lead to feelings of being central and important to everyone . . ." (p. 75).

Lidz' explanation is extremely useful in understanding the apparent contradiction many ACAs experience: They are extremely important—central to their parents' lives and nonexistent—not recognized nor heard on their own behalf. They are needed and valued to meet parental needs and expectations, but long to have needs of their own. In essence, they long for role reversal—to be the child with a caring, attentive parent responsive to their needs.

Meg cries as she thinks about the overwhelming needs of everyone in her family. She's been thinking about the therapist lately, wondering if she's OK. If not, Meg has to be on the watch to take care of her and protect her. Meg then speaks about being a parent to both of her parents:

I have to constantly set limits on both of them. I told my father to leave me alone when he was drunk. I never had a chance to be a child. I wish I'd had an opportunity to be a 12 year old.

Dan shares a similar memory:

I can remember planning how to get something I wanted from my father. He was so unpredictable. I'd have to behave very carefully for days in advance so as not to upset him. I always thought I could "manage" my father's reactions to me by being on good behavior myself. When I'm with my father the negative pull is so great I lose my good feelings and get drawn in to meet his needs. I can't remember an occasion when my father felt sympathetic with what I needed or was talking about.

The theme of the group now centered on the loss of self to a powerful parent whose needs are greater than those of the child. Meg feels the power of her mother's attitudes and beliefs in her new relationship:

Every inch I give makes me feel like I'm capitulating to the enemy.

As Dan spoke of "managing" his relationship with his father, Gloria added:

It's like the "marketplace" of human relationships. Everything is bartered to get anything in return.

In the affective sphere, children may reflect a close but insecure attachment, and later identification by taking on the feelings that belong to the parents but which they—the parents—are not themselves feeling. Intense feelings of anxiety, shame, humiliation, or embarrassment may provide a lifeline to a parent otherwise emotionally unavailable or unresponsive. The child may indeed experience him or herself as a real lifeline, providing life to the parent who is out of control or emotionally "dead." Members of an advanced group provide examples of their identification with behavior, beliefs, or parental affect in order to sustain attachment.

Sally entered the group expressing a deep, intense, and unyielding anger toward her alcoholic father, now generalized toward all men. She progressed in the group, examining many issues but insisted repeatedly that she would never relinquish her anger and no one should ask her to examine it.

Sally's rigid position was badly shaken when a recovering alcoholic male entered the group and expressed a desire to resolve his own anger towards his alcoholic father. For months, Sally diverted his efforts, focusing on her distrust of him because he was alcoholic and a man.

Eventually the group bypassed the deadlock and as others began to look at their anger, she explored her own:

> I realized that my tie to my mother is based on my being angry with men. But it's not my anger, it's hers. I identified with the anger and contempt my mother must have felt for my father but never expressed. If I stop feeling angry with men, I'll betray her and lose my relationship to her.

During the same period of the group's work, when the emphasis was on attachment, another member explored her unshakable belief in her badness expressed and reinforced through constant self-criticism and self-punishment. After a particularly painful episode of self-flagellation, Sandra reported the following:

> I suddenly had this feeling that if I altered my belief about myself—my badness—I would abandon my alcoholic mother and lose my tie to her in the process. It's impossible. I know how my mother feels in my bones—"I am my mother." I walk in her shoes. I have always felt the criticism that belongs to her but which she constantly gave to me.

Recognizing the strength of the bond and Sandra's inability to relinquish it, or go around it or stop her self-criticism, the therapist suggested that Sandra begin to think about herself as a "recovering self-hater." With this frame, she acknowledged her inability to control her self-attacks and the reality of her mother's self-criticism and hostility. She can hold onto her own bad view of herself but stop the attacks.

This framework is based on the alcoholic's acknowledgment of loss of control of drinking, relinquishment of efforts to control alcohol consumption and change in identity from nonalcoholic to alcoholic. The individual accepts the identity as an alcoholic and relinquishes the behavior becoming a "recovering alcoholic" a day at a time (Brown, 1985).

While group members laughed at the idea, they also recognized the serious implications. Sandra could maintain her tie to her mother by maintaining her identity as a self-hater (just like her alcoholic mother, though denied by her and projected onto Sandra), but she could relinquish the behavior.

Sandra consciously practiced, reminding herself as soon as she began a self-critical barrage, that she is a "recovering self-hater." She reported with amazement that it was extremely difficult and painful to interfere with her critical attacks. While terribly painful, they were also familiar and even comfortable as they paradoxically strengthened her sense of primitive attachment to her mother.

Harvey provided another illustration.

Harvey entered the group "knowing" the therapist had an agenda for him. According to her belief (projected by Harvey) she would get Harvey to see himself as an alcoholic like his father. In so doing, she would win the battle for control of his autonomy. For Harvey, it was all or none. If he wanted his mother's affection, he had to see the world exactly as she did. There could be no difference in point of view.

The core issue emerged in the group: Harvey could sustain a relationship with his mother by staying in the battle but he could not make a decision about his own drinking. He longed for the tie to his father but could not see himself as alcoholic to get it.

Not all patients consciously experience a deep affective or cognitive attachment to a parent. Many have achieved a stable but limited adjustment by fiercely disidentifying and dissociating from any recognizable aspect of parental belief, affect, or behavior. These patients are often emotionally flat and actively resist any transference experience or interpretation. They may have survived predominantly through the role reversal (Bergmann, 1985), assuming parental responsibility for parents and siblings. Any feelings of need threaten the dissociation, bringing them too close to the neediness the parents experienced and they, of course, might experience themselves.

The process of hearing other group members begin to feel and remember is threatening and enticing as the deep longing is intense. A patient illustrated:

> Mark resisted experiencing or acknowledging any feelings about the therapist for several years. Instead, he focused his positive feelings and longings for closeness on a female group member who regularly expressed her deep feelings openly and honestly. Whenever the focus was on Mark, he shifted it to Carol who repeatedly found herself feeling for others what they could not feel for themselves. Mark realized he needed Carol—a sister—to feel so he could identify with her and awaken feelings in himself. Eventually Carol resisted and Mark became depressed. He had failed again to get her to be what he needed.

Mark could not establish a parental transference for the same purpose. As he stated angrily: He had survived by dissociating himself from an emotional attachment to his parents. Being in group was a constant bind. Mark needed to maintain *his* parental identity while, at the same time, opening up his feelings as a child. To Mark, the feelings of a child were those of his alcoholic parents. To identify with them would be to sink into hopelessness, need, and despair.

Role Reversal

In having to alter their perceptions, members speak about the loss of self, a core factor in Miller's theory of parental narcissism. The loss of self is further reflected in group themes emphasizing role reversal. Members echo Searles' (1975) convincing argument that the essence of therapy involves the patient's efforts to teach the therapist how to hear and respond to the patient in the way that was lacking in childhood. In recalling their childhood and their current relationships, group members speak as parents who have failed at this very task.

> My mother was supposed to teach me what to say and how to respond to people but, in fact, I had to teach her. The problem is, when I do respond or suggest something to her, it feels so aggressive. If I know something she doesn't, it's a betrayal of her.

It took months and months of examining role reversal for Carol to realize that she could not have any needs because her mother failed to meet them and she could not meet her own because that was a betrayal. Then if she tried to meet her mother's needs, she felt guilty.

Several months later, Carol focused again on the theme of role reversal coupled with identification. The parents' need is so great, the child is frightened hers will be just as overwhelming.

> I alternate between feeling angry and terribly needy myself. I know what my mother must have felt. How can I be angry with her for being so cold and unavailable when she couldn't help it? She was always so needy.

> I remember waking up to hear her sobbing uncontrollably, drunk and begging forgiveness. I felt so helpless in being able to take care of her. You know, I was the child, I was the one who needed care and protection, but I had to comfort her repeatedly and tell her it was OK.

As Miller (1981) suggests, the narcissistic and needy parent pays attention to the child to obtain reassurance about the parent's worth, not from an interest or empathic response to the needs of the child. Group members' response to the movie "Shattered Spirits" (Robert Greenwald, 1986) provided another example.

> Sara did not feel sympathetic for the male at any point until the very end of the film. She had a glimpse that this father cared about his family when he was able to cry and recognize that he was not ready to come back to live with them. Sara said later that she never had any sign at all that her father cared about her or anybody else. Once again, she felt the intense anger at his tremendous preoccupation with himself and alcohol to the injury of all those around him.

> Brad agreed. He noted how much time and energy all the other family members had to pay to the alcoholic and to his treatment. Brad and others wondered when, if ever, the family members get to pay attention to developing their own lives or looking at their own needs. Margaret echoed this question, wondering whether children of alcoholics, as adults, can ever learn to give themselves the care and attention they never received as children.

Ben illustrated the emphasis of parental need as well, discussing his fears of dealing with his father as a sober parent.

> I feel worse about my father being dry than I did when he was drinking. I'm worried about seeing him. He won't be "insulated" by alcohol and therefore he'll be more vulnerable to what I might say. I feel very protective of him and am afraid I'll be destructive or hurtful.

Next the group looked at the issue of need and the sober parent.

> How can you have anything wrong with you or have needs as the child of a sober alcoholic? What do you do when you've been deprived of a parent all your life and your mother gets sober? Ben commented:

> It's harder to be rejected by a sober parent than a drunken one. But their needs are just as great.

Ben continued, anticipating a visit to his father:

> I just want to see what he's like. I'm not interested in "getting" anything from him. I hope I can create an atmosphere that will be safe enough for him to talk and maybe reflect back to my childhood. I'm actually afraid of what I have to learn about myself from a sober father. I was a difficult child who needed a patient father.

The group explored role reversal further around the issue of drunk versus sober parents. Kim noted:

> My father stopped drinking late in his life and it was very difficult for me. I couldn't accept the change in his behavior and I didn't trust his newfound sobriety and new beliefs. And I didn't know how to take care of him anymore. He seemed more lost to me than when he was drinking and needed my attention.

Paula nodded:

> It was much easier to deal with a drunken mother because I could be angry at the drinking. Her drinking also gave me a sense of being grown up. I treated her like a naughty child and could attribute her criticism of me to the alcohol.

> She got sober a number of times and didn't change at all. She demanded more. She expected praise and approval for her good behavior and she had no sense that she had anything to make up for with me or the family. I can't imagine what it would have been like had she gotten sober for any length of time, joined AA and found God. It would have been awful to feel so resentful and angry for what I hadn't gotten with her redeemed and sober!

Often it is difficult for group members to recall or feel the pain associated with never successfully helping the real parent so they could become the functional responsible parent the child needed. Members often start with a discussion of what they needed as children from their parents, but they inevitably shift to what their parents needed from them and how they failed to provide it.

Boundaries and Limit Setting

ACAs recall the centrality of their parents' needs and the feeling of being constantly overwhelmed by them. The sense of themselves as parents, responsible for out of control, unpredictable children, is reflected in the group setting as a constant need to set limits and maintain boundaries. The theme of limit setting is reflected in transference interactions with other group members and the therapist, and in sharing their common experiences of the past. The following detailed examples illustrate the notion of limit setting within the context of parental narcissism and role reversal as the base of child-parent attachment.

role reversal as the base of child-parent attachment.

> Neither Martha nor her mother can step out of an unhappy but mutually binding relationship. Martha has been linked and identified with her mother since childhood. She admired her mother's energy and activity while her father was more passive and withdrawn. Her mother directed her childhood, molding and producing the very kind of child she wished: a model of good behavior and deference to her mother. Martha carries on this tradition to this day—she is still obedient and deferent, trying to be a good daughter.
>
> Martha always ends up failing to meet her mother's needs. There is never a situation in which Martha doesn't do her best to please her mother but she still ends up having to set limits which her mother feels as a grave disappointment.
>
> Martha is so locked into feeling inadequate and unsatisfying of her mother's needs that she cannot shift her point of view to see her mother's behavior as the problem. To challenge her mother's authority would be equal to "divorcing" her. She is locked into a view of herself as a daughter who is failing to adequately parent her mother. The need to set limits with her mother is a constant, painful reminder of her failure.

This example further illustrates the centrality of alcohol as the binding agent in attachment between child and parent. Another patient illustrated the centrality of alcohol as well in attachment and boundary definition. As she anxiously anticipated her parents' visit, Pamela thought about drinking and the fact that her father would be sober for the first time.

> I always get through visits with my parents by drinking with them. Alcohol is clearly the tie that binds us, but it also establishes the limits. Boundaries between us could be defined and tolerated as long as everyone was drinking. I am afraid my father will be just as fuzzy, overwhelming, and enveloping with me sober as he was drinking. I get swept up by him and lose my clarity. Drinking always helped. There was something between us that somehow established the limits.

Following the December holidays, members expressed their discontent at being controlled by the uncertainty of parental visits. Patrick spoke:

> I am resigned to the fact that there is nothing one can do about the rights of parents. The therapist wondered where it is written that children can't set limits with their parents.

The notion of attachment and boundaries is illustrated by another patient.

> My mother was an alcoholic all my life but I was very close to her. I never could have cut the apron strings had she not become a "drunk." Ironically, my mother did the "cutting" by becoming emotionally unavailable to me as she turned more and more toward alcohol. My mother was such a mess, I left, going away to school as she had wished.

Ironically, her mother's alcoholism provided the only out for Martha while it was also the restraint to her leaving. As Martha said in group:

> How could I leave such chaos and really create my own life? I was constantly on call to pick up the pieces in the family I couldn't leave behind.

Within the group, members experienced the same powerful sense of role reversal and the need for limits in their interactions with another member who disturbed the group's cohesion and deepening process as he repeatedly demanded and diverted— directly and indirectly—the group's attention onto him.

Members discussed Jake as a metaphor for their most important relationships with each examing their reaction to him in the group setting. Mandy sets limits by ignoring him or tuning him out which is what she does with her mother. Sherri would really like him to leave but she can't acknowledge this wish to herself or others because she would then have to give up her fantasy of the group as a happy nurturant family. So she tolerates his intrusions.

The group then shifts to discuss the importance of being a child. They recall the high expectations they had for themselves and the need to be little adults. They worry that they seek the approval they needed from their parents from their own children inappropriately. Members recognize that they were never able to say that something was intolerable in their first families. Mandy summarizes:

I approach all relationships with the expectation that I will fail to get my needs met and I will end up having to set the limits and therefore reject the other person. Then I feel alone and abandoned which I have done to myself by failing to meet the other person's needs and ultimately drawing the line.

Another member reacted to Jake in the following manner:

You remind me of my mother who was so childlike and vulnerable. Whenever we point out your intrusiveness and your need for attention, you quickly accept our feedback and become apologetic. Then I feel guilty for setting the limits and have to make it better for you, still denying the fact that I feel hurt and needy too and want you to listen to *me*.

The issue of limits arose within the group in relation to sexual attraction between members.

Hal spoke again about his attraction to Bonnie, who attempted to silence him and then repeated her belief that she is sexually amorphous. Being asexual solves the problem of who's going to set the limits. If Hal is attracted to her, she must set the limit. But she can't do so without rejecting him and losing him as the strong, caring male she desires. She then thinks about her real family:

> If things are out of control in my family, it must be my fault.
> I failed to set a limit somewhere just like I failed repeatedly
> to control my parents' behavior.

The introduction of a new member raised the issue of control and limit-setting again. In an advanced, vulnerable group, a new person is often seen as powerful, well-defended, and potentially harmful.

> After expressing their distrust of the new person, group members
> discussed the unpredictability, and inconsistency of parents and
> their inability to trust authority or parental figures. As stable and
> consistent as the therapist is, group members still maintain a vigi-
> lant stance, waiting for her to become unpredictable or disappoint
> them. Sara has been in the group five years and is still waiting
> for disaster. She missed her personal development because she
> needed to have her "eyes open." She needed to be watchful and
> vigilant because those around her were so out of control. It was her
> responsibility to stop them if she could, stay out of their way or fix
> whatever was wrong.

The group continued with an intricate discussion of trust, ne-gotiation, and limit-setting as parent and child. Hal and Sid noted that they were always the responsible ones, having to be careful of the greater authority of the other person whether parent or child. They then talked about the need for children to "push" authority figures to find out the limits.

> Do they push Stephanie? No, what good would it do? You will just
> be seen as a negative, uncooperative, bad person if you express
> dissatisfaction.

Sara then related back to her parents.

> I couldn't push my mother because she was so overwhelmed,
> anxious, and so involved with her own needs she couldn't be
> available to me. In fact, she was constantly pushing against
> me and I set the limits.

The introduction of a new member raised the same issues for another member in another group.

Connie is concerned about the new member. She knows she will feel inhibited and begin to withdraw, a painful response that feels completely out of her control. But she cannot reveal herself to newcomers because of possible surprises. She then recalls her family:

> There was no room for me. Mother was the important one whose emotions were most prominent and central. Mother came first. I was expected to help my mother deal with her feelings. When my brother had a bad accident, my mother's emotions were more important. I felt repeatedly rejected when I tried to get emotional support. If anyone else has a need, I have to be quiet.

Again, the introduction of a new member raised the issues of limits and control.

The group discussed their anxiety about a new member and suddenly Patrick felt panicked:

> "Is there a rule in this group about smoking?" Patrick imagined that the new person would arrive and be a "puffing maniac," blowing a smoke screen in his face and engulfing him. Patrick insisted that the therapist set a no smoking rule before the newcomer arrived. If Patrick could successfully control the new person's imagined smoking, he could reduce his anxiety and feelings of powerlessness about her arrival. His anxiety about being overwhelmed overrides any interest he might have in this new person—what will she be like, what will she bring to the group, which parent was alcoholic and how might she be helpful to him? He must be on the defensive instead.

The issues of role reversal and limits also arise around the "management theme" noted in Chapter 2. The "too controlling" mother in the group became the focus for this discussion.

> Paul can't focus on anybody or anything today because he is so concerned about Mary. He needs to ask her how she is because he is worried about her and because he needs to ward off the consequence of not asking her. If left alone, she will later explode. But Paul also runs the risk of asking her a direct question and having her be angry for the question. There is no way he can assess what she needs from him at the moment that will satisfy her and insure his protection.

Paul had no sense of "setting a limit"—actually restricting his mother in some way. His notion of limit setting was reactive and manipulative: How to anticipate the needs or reactions of another so as to avoid intrusion or attack.

On another occasion, Paul experienced the same reaction with another female group member who had "demanded" a hug from his after the preceding meeting in order to "patch up" the differences between them that were not resolved in the meeting. Paul was enraged the following week.

> You not only demanded a hug, you then said it wasn't enough and demanded a longer one which I gave you. I didn't want to but I couldn't say no and I couldn't negotiate. Paul then recalled his inability to set any limits with his mother or to get her to hear. So he kept raising the severity of response in order to get her attention. He is now very frightened of the depth of his anger.

Paul continued to struggle with the issue of limits within the group, terrified of the level of escalation he would have to reach in order to successfully limit someone else. He marveled at Becky's easy ability to define her "boundaries."

> Becky informed the group that she was emotionally worn out from last week's deep involvement and today wanted to limit questions from Stephanie. Paul was astounded. If he needed to stop Stephanie, he would have to get angry and shout. He has no control over interactions so must angrily push the other person away.

> Other members were also astounded. They realized they all shared a belief that it was not OK to come to group and express a wish not to talk about something today.

Boundaries, limits, and control evolved as central issues for another member who wished deeply to "belong" but was terrified of "belonging" at the same time.

> Bob reported that he was still thinking about leaving. He is intolerant of others asking him questions and of having to listen to others express themselves with words he doesn't like, such as "mushy" or "warm inside." Bob wants a way to shut people off. Someone else's empathy or wish to deepen a relationship with him is threatening because he has no sense of boundaries or limits and does not feel he can stop the exchange. He can't tolerate listening to people's problems in the group and being unable to fix them or stop them. This is just like his life outside and growing up.

The central difficulty for Bob emerges: he cannot join the group and stay detached. But he needs to be detached as a way of controlling his and others' emotions and the degree of involvement. Setting limits is not acceptable for him so he has no choice but to feel trapped, impatient, or leave.

In response to Bob, Paula joked that if "Mr. Right comes along she would give him a place in her garage and even supply him with a heater. But she would retain her right to bring him in only when she wants."

The group members reaffirmed the importance of being able to set limits and the impossibility of totally controlling others. What is the middle ground?

Many of these examples illustrate the paradox described by Lidz (1973). The parents need the child to confirm the parent's view and provide an emotional bond as well. The child develops a sense of self as a parent responsive to the centrality of someone else's needs. At the same time, this leads to a narcissistic, omniscient view of the self as necessary to the survival of another.

Occasionally, a group member will exhibit a strong need to be the center of attention, or at least involved in all interactions, in order to sustain the illusion of attachment. Underneath is the more dominant feeling of "not existing," of being "wiped out" by parental figures, directly through critical attack and chronic hostility or simply by the centrality of the parents' needs. The feeling of "not existing" is also an expression of the individual's recognition of the parents' lack of emotional awareness and availability to the child. The need to constantly maintain the illusion of an emotional bond serves to ward off recognition of the lack of one with a primary parental figure. Ron illustrated:

Today the group focused on Ron's need for constant attention. He must include himself in every interaction or he feels bored or angry. In including himself, he personalizes or over interprets what someone else is saying, thereby giving meaning to himself and shifting the focus of the group to him. Ron recognizes he is uncomfortable if he feels left out. It's like he is "not there." Ron can't be quiet though others urge him to try. The feeling of being left out is so intense—it reawakens feelings of being left behind and the loss of all his family to alcohol which he experienced so frequently.

On another occasion, Ron wondered sadly whether anyone would ever miss him if he didn't keep showing up at the places he belongs.

Much later in the work of the group Ron became able to examine his drive for attention and engagement in the context of exploring the "quality" of his relationships and interactions to others in the group. He acknowledged and felt the accuracy of the therapist's suggestion that he gives the appearance of relating with others but, in fact, he does not. Rather, he uses others as a "mirror" to learn more about himself. Interactions are not reciprocal or of the kind that build. He frequently feels empty and others feel used.

The other side of the intense need for "contact" and constant engagement is the inability to experience any at all. Many ACAs have few memories of childhood and little affect, feelings of their own, or appropriate affective response to the feelings of another. These individuals often seek treatment because of severe interpersonal problems, especially difficulties establishing and sustaining intimate relationships. As one emotionally flat ACA put it:

> How do you communicate a feeling of emotional involvement with others when you don't have it or can't give it yourself?

This same individual spent a good deal of time in group figuring out the right way to respond, since he had no internal feelings to guide him. He felt and was seen by others to be "tuned out." With careful exploration, he came to realize that his emotional withdrawal and isolation were necessary for his survival as a child. His parents were most often drunk and out of control emotionally, demonstrating wide, fluctuating extremes in mood and behavior. Emotional insulation was his only protection against feeling constantly out of control himself. Yet as an adult, his emotional withdrawal was felt by others as a problem.

Further exploration within the group revealed the double bind he felt with his mother. She was often upset that he refused to be engaged with her and was so uninvolved and inactive. Yet he was also supposed to be an "ornament," seen but not heard. His mother wanted no part of him.

Matt was frequently amazed at the intense feelings other group members experienced in relation to the female therapist. He saw Stephanie only as her "real self" and a spectator in the group. It's almost impossible for Matt to imagine seeing her any other way. In fact, he was a spectator himself.

In the group, Ron got bored or upset if he didn't feel a

"connection," the very emotional component that Matt lacked. No matter what Ron said or did, he didn't feel he had gotten what he wanted from Matt. And Matt kept feeling baffled—he didn't know what it was that Ron was asking for.

The difficulty in sustaining an emotional attachment—in group language a "connection"—was experienced by Hannah. She believed she was "empathizing" with others who, instead, felt she was "grabbing the focus." She and others were eventually able to see that establishing similarities between herself and others was equal to having a "connection." But as soon as she saw the similarity, she shifted the focus onto herself and everyone else felt "ripped off." She was repeatedly seen as needy and demanding, "attaching" herself to anyone in the group, while she maintained that she just wanted to establish a relationship.

Deep Need and Dependency

The focus on the child as parent and the assumption of responsibility for failing—both to fix the ailing parent and to be good enough to get from the parent what the child needed—often serves defensively to mask clear recognition of one's own deep needs. The dominant emphasis on control (Cermak & Brown, 1982) and the emphasis on establishing boundaries and setting limits on the needs of *others* also masks one's own deep feelings of neediness and the strong belief that I also will be out of control, intrusive, demanding, and aggressively voracious if I allow myself to feel a need and dare hope to have it met by another.

A central theme and core work of the advanced group involves chipping away at the defenses that mask recognition of need but which also severely restrict the individual. Relinquishing the view of oneself as a parent, in "control" and responsible for others is fraught with anxiety. "I will be left hanging, attacked for my neediness and damaging to others."

The deep need to feel safe, cared for, and listened to nevertheless exists and forms the foundation of much of the group's deepening work, especially in relation to attachment.

Primitive Attachment and Symbiosis

The notion of primitive attachment, so close that one is "boundariless" in relation to another is often discussed as a wish, but more often as a fear. The notion of "merger," a term used by members, is fraught with a sense of danger. Relinquishment of control, of vigilance, to the care and protection of another is not safe, though the imagined freedom and gratification is sometimes openly desired. In identifying themselves as children—children of alcoholics—members accept permission to feel their dependency needs, although they actively ward off in themselves and others the regression that is also permitted and required (Brown & Beletsis, 1986). A group member demonstrated the conscious longing to be cared for and the nature of her close "merged" bond with her mother which dictates her assumption of the parental role. Gloria described her lifetime fantasy that she could make everything right for herself and everyone else too.

> My mother did outrageous things but always thought the problems belonged to somebody else and not to her. I was the opposite. I grew up believing there was something wrong with me—I was never quite good enough. It is central to my view of myself and I got it from my mother. But it's not just that I'm part of the "everybody else" who's got the problem. It's deeper than that. I feel like my mother must have felt underneath her anger and outrage. As long as I define myself as the one with the problem, I can feel close to her. It's painful, but feeling good about myself also carries with it a great sense of loss.

> Still, I long for someone to care for me, to praise me and cheer for my successes. As a child, I used to fantasize that I was an orphan, adopted by a new family so I could "start over again" or begin a new "slate."

She repeated the same cycle in the group: she achieved new insights, felt better about herself—got a new "slate"—but always returned to the fact she was not good enough and really had done nothing at all. As Lidz noted, Gloria accepted her mother's defenses in order to have a relationship with her. As she uncovered more in her reconstruction of the past, Gloria experienced a deeper and clearer sense of her close tie to her mother.

> The more I open up, the more I experience myself as the "falling apart mother" which is the role my mother always played. She commanded our attention through her drinking and her dramatics. I don't know how I felt as a child. I felt

only my mother's feelings, or the one's she should have been
feeling, which were so deep and out of control.

The group then discussed the notion of "leaving" their parents
behind—giving up the feelings of parents or the view of self necessary to sustain the attachment.

> The idea of "leaving" my mother is terrifying. It's like leav-
> ing a very important part of myself. My mother is the only
> source of my self definition. I built my identity from her
> knowledge and view of me. My whole sense of myself is
> linked to her acknowledgment of me, which was always crit-
> ical and punishing. So that's who I am. When I'm down on
> myself, I know I exist.

On another occasion the group focused on "mother" and Gloria
extended her insights:

> If I feel angry or punishing toward my mother, it's like pun-
> ishing or doing away with my very own self. I feel so much a
> part of my mother and understand her so well that to attack
> her is to attack myself.

Gloria's empathic identification with others served her and
others well in the group.

> Jake is struggling with illness and feels beaten down by the world.
> He works hard, is on the brink of achieving and then something
> awful happens. He knows he feels terribly needy but he can't
> express it, much less really feel it. If Gloria were there, things
> would be OK. She would lend Jake her own deep feelings about
> herself. And she would be upset on his behalf which he can't do for
> himself.

Like most group members at all stages of the groups' work,
Jake believed he could only experience his emotions alone.

> That's how it was growing up and that's how it is now. You
> didn't dare feel any need. There wasn't anybody there.

Group members often return to the painful question: did they
ever have anyone to talk to? Many fantasized an ideal special
family to which they could belong which would lend legitimacy
to themselves and a sense of normality. Several had the fantasy of

becoming adopted and several actively wished to belong to another family. Along with these wishes came the recognition that they desperately needed someone to talk to.

The contrast or conflict between a deep sense of need and a sense of responsibility reappear hand in hand. Gloria continued her uncovering, feeling upset and out of control.

> My feelings are pouring out as if they had no end. But I'm perplexed because my memories of my childhood don't seem that bad.

Group members then helped Gloria think about what it is like for a child in a family with an alcoholic. Gloria sobbed as she experienced a deep and painful longing and a strong recognition that her parents could not provide for her. Later on she added:

> If I gave up the notion that I was to blame, I would have to recognize my parents' inadequacies and I couldn't do it. I needed them to teach me about myself and the world.

Other members and the group also examined issues of need and longing with their parents.

> I am beginning to feel a sense of detachment from my mother. I have carried my mother's sadness and depression and I don't have to feel for her anymore.

Rose then spoke about her own deep neediness and her feelings of responsibility at the same time.

> I can't blame my boyfriend for anything because then I couldn't continue to idealize him as the one who will take care of me. If I blame him, the taking care of myself is up to me and I'm left alone once more.

Issues of deep need also arose around themes of loss and deprivation.

> Sue describes her mother as childlike and vulnerable, frightened much of the time and therefore unable to model or pass on a sense of safety about the world or maternal protection for Sue. She experiences a constant nagging, deep loss. When she thinks of herself as a small child, she feels frightened and tremendously

deprived. She experiences the therapist as weak, frightened, and withholding.

She does feel cared for by another member. He is a model, someone who has something to teach her. It is this lack of modeling that seems central to what she missed as a child.

Sandra also experienced a continuing sense of loss.

> My mother was depressed because I had too many needs. If I could have been better, less needy, then my mother might have been able to be more giving.

The group now spoke of loss, of important possessions and relationships, and their own tremendous need for a caring parent who was never there. They discussed their efforts to separate—practically and emotionally from parents—because the relationship was so destructive and damaging rather than supportive and giving.

The group focused on the loss of what they never had, the deep need that continued in the present and the fear of trying to get it from parental figures. A member described a newspaper article chronicling the experiences of an abused child. Group members became very sad as they recognized their parents weren't competent in caring for them.

The longing for a parent who cared was expressed by another member after he saw his therapist at a concert in which the member was playing.

> I knew you had come especially to hear me play. My mother used to forget my recitals or she'd come in order to catch someone else who'd be there.

Rejection of one's dependency needs is necessary to protect not only against the sense of loss, but also against disappointment related to the parents' unpredictability and inconsistency. Many recall not the loss of what might have been, but the repeated disappointment experienced with the emotional withdrawal and detachment of a parent during a drunken episode.

Group members can allow measured need in themselves but it must be controlled and the caregiver constantly monitored for signs of withdrawal or disapproval.

> If I am too needy, I overwhelm others who must withdraw to protect themselves. I end up having caused my own abandonment.

Another member entered the group openly contemptuous of needy people, believing "you have to be able to take care of yourself and you ought to be able to control yourself too!" As time passed, Henry expressed his envy of the warmth that Bob and Jim received from others. At first, he believed that the group was against him, threatened by him, and actively withholding their support. Members challenged Henry repeatedly noting that he was always angry and guarded. He felt just so much of himself and then was angry for the lack of response. After this pattern occurred several times, Henry thought about need.

> Being needy equals being out of control which equals being drunk. I used to feel disgusted by my father's need. He was so helpless and out of control when he drank.

Henry realized that he maintained an angry tone to protect himself from feeling needy or communicating need and especially to insure a sense of control. Several weeks later he spoke about the consequences of having needs and experiencing them.

> My family and I lost at least two decades in our emotional and personal growth as individuals and as a family due to my father's alcoholism. It was a tremendous loss to me—an enormous consequence of my father's preoccupation with taking care of his own needs first. I can't imagine putting my own needs first though I often wish someone else would do so on my behalf.

Another member experienced the same desperate need for control of himself and others and his contempt of need and longing in others. Ray reported a dream.

> I'm driving a car carefully with two small children. Mysteriously, the car gets itself out of control and I'm in an accident. No one is hurt, but I'm incredulous that this event can occur when I'm being so careful.

Ray then linked the dream to his difficulties revealing himself in the group.

To open up is to have needs. If I reveal myself, I'll be out of control and someone will be hurt.

Dependency in the Group

Core issues of deep needs and dependency are experienced as major themes in the group's work and reflected in the transference as well. The need for a reliable, primary, stable figure of attachment with whom close bonding, mcrgcr, and symbiosis can be experienced were strong. As the group advanced in its work, members looked to the leader to serve this role and to the group itself which became a "holding environment" (Winnicott, 1953, 1960), a structure which provided stability and predictability and a "home"—the place or "object" that represented a new "substitute" attachment, a parent who was missing the first time around. It is a parent whose ego can be borrowed for the most basic early needs of bonding, one who can stand still while group members move back and forth testing the bounds of closeness and distance and their own control. Members need a "parent" who is comfortable and competent with self and world and who will gladly teach them. Finally they need a parent and a structure that will "let go," but remain intact as they move away.

The intensity and progression of these issues was demonstrated when a new, openly needy, and overtly dependent member was added to an advanced group whose members were at that time struggling with issues of boundaries, limits, and the nature of intimate attachments and extreme fear of their own needs.

Within her first meeting, Marsha was identified by others as the "typical female victim" needy, helpless, and waiting for the ultimate rescue. This angry, negative assessment followed Marsha's description of her life with an alcoholic parent and an abusive alcoholic husband from whom she was now separated. With one exception, members immediately labeled her seductive and manipulative. The exception, a male, was sexually attracted to her and experienced a profound desire to comfort and protect her. His acknowledgment of these feelings was jeered by others.

The group's anger and rejection of Marsha escalated over a period of several weeks. Members attacked her for her inability to take action on her own behalf and refused to listen at the next meeting to reports of actions she had taken. As one member put it:

You want to attach yourself to me like glue. I'll never get
away from you or your neediness.

Other group members felt stopped with the power of the victim's stance.

My needs are always second because she is so needy and
helpless. I have to be concerned about her or feel guilty for
being angry and critical. There's no room for me. Her needs
are overwhelming and take up all the space.

During this period, another member was having great difficulty at work. In the group she described her efforts to deal with
her helplessness by being angry and exerting control. The group
recognized that they needed to reject Marsha because they could
not tolerate their own passivity or neediness.

I have two choices: to be a helpless, passive victim loony or
totally in control which leaves me feeling isolated and unhappy.

The group realized that Marsha was overwhelmed. She was
difficult to ignore because she looked so needy and frightened.
Her presence called for the attention and protection of others
who in turn became enraged.

Occasionally several members empathized with Marsha,
sensing how frightened she was and the no-win situation she was
in. The group would not accept an openly dependent person
who hoped to have her "needs met." The more they rejected
her, the harder she tried to find a way to please. Finally, a member interpreted:

The group is "staying away" from Marsha. No one wants to
be pulled into the parental role of taking care of her and
that's the only relationship possible.

Following this very disturbing, turbulent period of the group,
members began to explore their own feelings of need expressed as
a wish, not for a caring parent, but for a stable group structure.

Stephanie took a different seat today which Dan found upsetting. He stressed the importance of keeping things the
same while he is in the process of changing.

The group then spoke about the recent disruption with a new "uncontrollable member."

> I need you to control the group, make it stable, keep new needy people from entering, and keep old members from leaving. I can't imagine going away for a vacation and finding the group here when I return.

Ultimately, through many angry meetings, group members articulated the painful dilemma:

> I feel caught holding together a fragile group and needing to maintain control over the degree of intimacy as well. I feel in danger of becoming fragmented and losing everyone and equal danger of becoming too close and being swallowed up.

As the members focused on their need for stability, they also spoke of the group summary which serves many as an object substitute or representation of their attachment to the group, individual members within it and/or the therapist.

> I realized it's really important to me. I look forward to its arrival each week and, in fact, if it's late, I find myself very aware that I'm missing it and watching for it. I keep all the summaries. They're a reminder of who I am and useful, especially as a gauge for my progress. It's also helpful to go back and read if I'm stuck and don't know how I got where I'm at.

Several other members also talked about keeping their summaries and referring back to them. Bob throws his away.

> I don't want a reminder of this group! To me, the group is a "necessary evil"—it is important but looking at that summary makes me feel needy and dependent.

The group regained a sense of safety and comfort as members spoke about the structure and stability of the group and the summary. Then they raised painful memories of abandonment.

> I want so desperately to feel safety and trust in the group but I'm terrified. The group has been a "rock" for me but now I'm in a frame of mind where my "rock" can turn to mush. The foundation no longer seems secure.

> I have counted on the group to keep me "on track." My
> security rests on my belief that the therapist has a support
> system of her own to keep her "on track." If I don't rely on
> this "rock", I'm afraid I'll lose sight of reality and become
> involved in somebody else's "cultish" view of the world. My
> family became "cultish" and deviant as we reacted to my
> father's alcoholism.

> As a child in that family, I fell deeper and deeper into the
> skewed beliefs they now held and I was unable to tell that
> anything was amiss.

The focus of the group then evolved to a discussion of members' great need for something to rely on and their fear of relying on anything because it can be so harmful. As a child, Dan relied on his parents and look what happened. As he thought about relying on another person—the therapist—he realized the uncertainity of that as well. He then thought he might start believing in God or attending Al-Anon.

The group then spoke about the importance of a belief in God, or a higher power because of the reality of their lack of control in the world.

> I can't believe in God because I can't "let go" or "trust" that
> I'll be taken care of. As a kid, God was vengeful and punish-
> ing. As soon as I am happy, God will take it away or the
> ground will turn to mush.

In this chapter, we examined the impact of parental alcoholism on individual development beginning with attachment theory, using the frameworks of Bowlby (1980), Mahler (1975) and Lidz (1973). We outlined the serious consequences for a child whose attachment to a parent is grounded in parental egocentrism and the role reversal required to continually satisfy the needs of the parent(s). The child has difficulty developing an independent sense of self and struggles as an adult with severe concerns about personal boundaries in relationships with others and feelings of deep need and dependency which must be continually denied. Gratification of need always resulted in harm or disillusionment. Parents needs are central and the child's sense of attachment rests on accommodation. In the next chapter, we will continue our theory building, examining the impact of parental alcoholism on identity formation.

Chapter 6

The Impact of Parental Alcoholism on Identity Formation

In Chapter 5, we examined the notion that parental alcoholism operates as a governing agent in the process of attachment between parent and child. I focused on the role reversal that frequently results when parents are dominated and absorbed by the primacy of their own needs, in this case, to deal with their own alcoholism or that of a partner or spouse. This is an absorption that makes them unavailable, or at best randomly available, to their children.

In this chapter, I extend the theory development by examining the impact of parental alcoholism on identity formation. I continue to build the integrated theory that attachment and the development of self-knowledge—one's personal identity—necessary for all human development, are founded on the maintenance of the family's core beliefs. These beliefs (i.e., the family's "story") are based on denial of alcoholism, or the explanations adopted and incorporated to explain it if it is not denied.

According to major cognitive theorists (Guidano & Liotti, 1983; Rosen, 1985), denial of perception results in denial of affects which together result in developmental arrests or difficulties. In the process of ongoing development, the child constructs a personal identity (Guidano & Liotti, 1983) that confirms beliefs about the self and others necessary to maintain attachment, facilitate identification, and maintain the family story, often all contrary to reality. Maintenance of denial and the resultant distorted perceptions about the world then structure subsequent cognitive, affective, and social development. In a circular fashion, the distorted view of self is maintained because of the strength of attachment to the parental figures. Thus cognitive, affective, and social development are inextricably bound to relationships with key attachment figures. It is this interrelationship and interaction that is critical to understanding the difficulties in treatment and the inability of children of alcoholics—young and adult—to step out of the family's "story."

The need for attachment operates unconsciously and overrides all other concerns. Recognition of this need provides a base for understanding the serious intrapsychic and interpersonal difficulties that are impossible to alter or correct by conscious intent. The link between cognitive and affective development and attachment also provides a base for understanding the transmission of alcoholism through the behavioral and cognitive processes of imitation and identification. In this chapter, I focus on the acquisition of knowledge about the self (i.e., the formation of a personal identity) (Guidano & Liotti, 1983). How do children acquire beliefs and what are the beliefs that shape and ultimately address the question "who am I?"

PERSONAL IDENTITY AND THE DEVELOPMENT OF SELF-KNOWLEDGE

Cognitive theorists emphasize how the acquisition of knowledge shapes adult emotional experiences and behavioral patterns (Guidano & Liotti, 1983). Reflecting the influence of Piaget (Greenspan, 1979), they agree that the progressive construction of self-knowledge is developed through action by the organism on the environment and interactions in response to the environment (Guidano & Liotti, 1983). Individuals obtain self-knowledge by developing theories about themselves (p. 35). These evolve into concrete and well-defined beliefs about the self that regulate the individual's behaviors and perceptions in the world (p. 61). Beginning in infancy, the child develops a core of basic assumptions which must not be disproved. These assumptions become the base for further knowledge development and are known as the personal identity, the most fundamental and basic beliefs about the self.

Guidano and Liotti stress that the maintenance of one's perceived personal identity is critically important to the developing individual. In essence, individuals cannot function without a stable self-representation. To maintain a stable personal identity, individuals begin to be selective in what they register so that only information which is considered to be in keeping with the structured self-image is retained and incorporated. Thus the individual's way of seeing reality is increasingly anchored in a manner consistent with the view of self.

The development of self-knowledge is rooted in the interactions of the child with its environment and particularly with key figures in that environment. Those figures of attachment, typically the parents, exert a profound impact on the child's core beliefs and subsequent cognitive structural organization. As Guidano and Liotti emphasize, parents are *the* world and the only one possible. The attachment to parents is an emotional bond without alternatives.

They further emphasize the importance of attachment to identity development, suggesting that "every pathological feature of attachment will be reflected in developing self-knowledge" (p. 104) and that the "nucleus" of self-knowledge is formed before the child is able to remember and reflect on it. They stress that a distorted self-concept, developed in the service of maintaining an attachment, will influence all elements of subsequent developmental processes. These distorted self-conceptions remain anchored to forms of prelogical thinking typical of childhood and consistent with denial which are difficult to alter or make explicit after adolescence in the form of conceptual and critical knowledge (p. 105). Guidano and Liotti further note that the distorted elements of the self-concept then function as tacit rules, coordinating thinking, and deductive reasoning on the basis of the mythical and dogmatic "logic" to which they are bound. Most importantly, the child and later adult remains anchored to patterns of organizing reality that were typical of primitive thinking. Guidano and Liotti note that these primitive cognitive patterns are characterized by unidimensionality, globality, invariance, and irreversibility. These characteristics are often reflected and demonstrated in the long-term group therapy process as all-or-none thinking, an enduring primitive cognitive style that affects all perception and affective integration and social development.

In an alcoholic family, attachment to key parental figures is based on shared perceptions and identifications with the parents' beliefs which frequently center on the denial of alcoholism. Thus denial of alcoholism is a major organizing principle structuring the family's attachments, level of cognitive structural development, perceptions about reality, and related affect and the development of one's personal identity.

THE SIGNIFICANCE OF DENIAL

In Part One I examined the relationship of denial to the family environment, accenting the primary role of denial in maintaining homeostasis. In Chapter 4, we looked more closely at denial as a major defensive adaptation. Now we look at denial again, this time in relation to its impact on the child's perceptions and developing identity.

Guidano and Liotti (p. 38) emphasize that the exclusion of environmental data by parents exerts a profound influence on cognitive and affective development. In an alcoholic family, the denial of drinking or its consequences forces children to refuse the testimony of their own developing senses in order to accept the parents' point of view. To the degree that denial is necessary and to the degree that it is central to the family's attachments and perceptions, to that degree will the children begin to be in conflict with their own perceptions.

This results in a state of cognitive and affective disequilibrium. The world (or the family) does not make sense or have meaning and is therefore not predictable or manageable. With disequilibrium, individuals must revise their schemas—change their core beliefs or basic assumptions—or exclude contrary information and perceptions from their awareness in order to cope with the disequilibrium. As these theorists note, children cannot alter their core beliefs, primarily because they are defined by and bound to parental attachment figures. They must, therefore, refuse incoming data that challenges these core beliefs or begin, like their parents, to develop illogical or distorted explanations to explain contradictory information.

The exclusion of data leads also to the exclusion of well-defined feelings from the emotional repertoire. Rosen (1985) suggests that cognitive development determines affective development. Guidano and Liotti (1983) concur, although they emphasize that cognitive and emotional development proceed together, reciprocally influencing and determining each other. For the child of an alcoholic there is a denial of both perceptions and affect which must be maintained and which becomes part of the core personal identity. This results in feelings of unreliability toward one's own sensorial, intuitive, and intellectual abilities and the development of basic mistrust of others' intentions (p. 39). As noted (Cermak & Brown, 1982), we identified the mistrust of one's perceptions and the mistrust of others as key issues in the early phase of group therapy treatment.

In order to incorporate and support the parents' denial, the child must exclude a range of emotional experiences from the self-image so the personal identity will be consistent with the image the parents prefer or consistent with the family's story—the beliefs that maintain the attachment and structure identity formation. The need for exclusion creates a feeling of unreliability to recognize and define one's own internal states (p. 40). One cannot have feelings about a reality that does not exist.

We have seen that the child adopts the parents' point of view that there is no drinking problem in the family. This is in conflict with the child's perceptions. The child must also adopt the explanations and beliefs necessary to maintain the denial. In building our theory, we now add the recognition that distortion is two-pronged: first, there is denial of perception and affect and second, there is distortion of belief and construction to explain what has been denied. As Lewis (1977) notes, anxiety then develops because of the mismatch between the cognitive organization and the actual information to be mastered. Reality as explained does not match the child's perception.

The management of this conflict and the continuing maintenance of denial require individuals to narrow and distort the environment until behavior appears adequate to it rather than changing their understanding and enlarging their knowledge till they can cope with the larger, real environment (Craik, 1943). Ultimately, some individuals develop a rigid attitude toward themselves with their interactions stereotyped and repetitious. The assimilation of new experiences will be progressively hampered as they become more maladapted and out of sync with their environment.

PERCEPTION, BELIEF, AND ATTACHMENT

Rosen states (1985) that when the child's interpretation of reality differs from the parents' explanation, the child will alter his or her view to conform to that of the parents. A group member with an intense need for a nourishing parental attachment demonstrated:

> Shirley and Peg became very angry accusing each other of excessive demands and misperceptions of the other's intent. They maintained their anger for one meeting.

During the second meeting, Shirley agreed that Peg's view was the correct one and apologized for her misperception and resultant failure to be responsive to Peg. Other group members were aghast, pointing out to Shirley that she had altered her perception—equally correct in their view—in order to cover the anger and patch the relationship. Shirley couldn't tolerate the challenge:

> I felt so alone and isolated after confronting Peg. I began to feel so responsible for her anger and so sorry I had seen things differently. I decided that she was right.

Group members insisted that Shirley look closely at what she was doing: changing her view of reality to stop the anger. Shirley cried:

> I would do *anything* to keep others from being angry with me. It's a much better choice to give up my position and to feel responsible for others than to risk having them be angry.

Members further demonstrated the impact of attachment on perception as they registered their responses to the television movie "Shattered Spirits" (Greenwald, 1986).

> Dan was very much affected by the movie as it brought back tremendously painful feelings of living with an alcoholic father. He was amazed at how angry he felt at his own father for the arbitrary, erratic outbursts of anger and manipulation. Dan also feels upset with himself for "buying into" all the distorted reasoning and manipulation.

> Dan feels tremendously affected by living with someone who was so out of control and who so dominated the way the family behaved and explained reality. He has had to struggle hard as an adult to understand what is real for him. He has had to struggle especially with his own fears of being "out of control."

Following this same movie, members of another group spoke about coming to terms with whether or not they had a problem with alcohol.

> Sara asked Brad if he would mind telling her how much he drank. When he responded, Sara heaved a sigh of relief and said "that's not so bad." She had become very worried that she would have to change her positive feelings about Brad because he has decided he has a problem with alcohol. Sara was afraid that she would have to lump him into the category of "alcoholic" which includes her

father and several other men she knows. These are people who are angry, manipulative, self centered and selfish who have never given her anything. She does not want to characterize Brad this way and, therefore, lose him as an important person for her.

Sara could see that her need to know how much Brad drank was actually an expression of her fear of the loss of him. If Brad had told her that he drank a huge amount, she would probably not have believed him in order to hold on to her positive view of him. He has been open and caring for her in stark contradiction to her beliefs about alcoholic men. If he decides he is an alcoholic, she will either have to change her view about alcoholics or lose her close relationship to him.

On another occasion, group members discussed perceptions and a deep wish to be able to get a "true" family history from their parents.

Today members spoke of "coming home," examining what it would be like to return to their parents as adults, removed from the interactions that prevailed during childhood, question parents about personal and family history and get an objective response. The importance of standing outside the family was emphasized. Karen still has no sense of distance or "separateness" and cannot conceive of getting historical data from her mother that might be objective and accurate.

Members then spoke about keeping journals as children to record their perception of events and, in essence, write their own family chronicle. Rereading their journals as adults, they find big holes. Perceptions or feelings related to parental drinking or abuse could not be recorded. Instead, there are gaps, codes, or "news, sports, and weather." Karen continued:

I have diligently kept a detailed journal of important events
in my children's lives so they will have a record of it later on.
I long for a clear picture of my childhood but I know I can't
get it from my parents as reporters.

Members concluded as a group that parents constructed a view about the family that was different from the children's. Now group members discussed the impact of critical, sadistic, or supportive teachers and supervisors, a thinly veiled reference to their parents and to the therapist in the group.

It is so hard for me to hold onto my own view or feelings as legitimate. Whatever my supervisor says is automatically the truth. I have to change my view to fit hers and then I feel so stupid. That's why it makes no sense to become angry or disagree. I always have to adjust my point of view to solve the disagreement.

THE ASSUMPTION OF RESPONSIBILITY

Like denial, the assumption of responsibility reappears as a central aspect of environmental accommodation, defensive adjustment, attachment, and now again as an important part of identity formation.

The child develops a personal identity that permits the reality of drinking behavior along with the denial of that reality to be maintained. As noted earlier, this process often involves the assumption of responsibility for the problem that is denied. Rosen explains that children lack an appropriate sense of the source of causality and therefore see themselves as the cause agent. If the parent does not have a problem with drinking, then there must be something wrong with the child. This belief in the child's responsibility is adopted by the child to cope with the disequilibrium or is actually advocated by the parent and accepted by the child.

The importance of the parental attachment is critical to understanding the mechanism of responsibility. Children will reconfirm their beliefs even with continuing evidence to the contrary. They may try to do better but to no avail since the real problem does not change. Still, they cannot eliminate attempts at resolution even when they are useless. Many developmental theorists note that children need to protect their relationship to the parent, maintain parental approval, and reduce unconscious guilt. It is difficult for children to feel they are wrong, but it is worse to recognize that those they must depend on are wrong or incompetent to care for them.

When children assume responsibility, they may develop a pattern of self-hatred, self-criticism, and self-abuse in response to the conflict of having caused the problem and then being unable to solve it. Or they may narrow their range of cognitive and affective involvement in the environment. They may become knowledgeable in one well-defined area, high achievers but impoverished in their range of cognitive and emotional development. A patient illustrated her growing recognition of the significance of her assumption of responsibility to her adult self-destructiveness.

> A few years ago I saw a movie about slavery. People were marching in a line with each whipping the one in front. I almost fainted and had to leave the theater. Now I suddenly see why. These individuals assumed responsibility for having caused their plight and were exorcising the demons from within and punishing themselves at the same time. That is how I've spent my life: punishing myself for what I caused at home and could not fix.

Burt identified with the sense of responsibility:

> I remember feeling an intense drive for perfection and an inability to achieve it in my family. On weekends I cleaned the house, moving around my parents as they sat there drinking.

Burt realized he was chronically upset with the loss of control he felt in group which reminded him of his family.

> I'm always looking for structure, for rules, for something in here. I'm so anxious about the therapist because I can't tell what she's feeling or thinking. This is just like my life—a state of chronic anxiety. If there's a cyclone in Bangladesh, I caused it.

The child of an alcoholic defines problems in a way that is consistent with the subjective representation of reality. Events are not seen as consequences of behavior but rather as confirmation of the deepest beliefs—often I am bad. In areas where denial is necessary, it also may interfere with progression to higher levels of cognitive development including cause and effect reasoning and logical sequencing.

The need for denial and the assumption of responsibility for what is denied require enormous adjustments in ongoing cognitive and affective development. Core beliefs necessary to maintain denial and therefore attachment now structure subsequent cognitive and affective development. In this manner, the deepest beliefs about the self—often contrary to reality—are maintained, reaffirmed repeatedly, and strengthened. This conceptual framework explains how Gloria in Chapter 5 could feel a closer bond to her mother when she herself was feeling badly.

SOCIALIZATION

Rosen (1985) suggests that many children do not learn the rules of the culture from their families. In a family with an alcoholic parent, children cannot learn the rules of society because the family is bound by denial which requires increasing isolation from a culture whose rules might challenge it.

Beginning in latency or preteen years (Brown, 1974), children in an alcoholic family begin to recognize that the world at home is different from the world outside. That difference is related to alcohol, beliefs about alcohol, and drinking behavior. One of our patients explained:

> The children in my family learned by observation an abnormal form of reality. I had no prior experience to inform me that something was wrong. So I developed a feel for what was appropriate in my family, for what was right or wrong in that world and then I found it didn't carry over. As an adult, I found myself lost, insecure and frightened in the world outside my family. I'm sure that I'm emotionally immature but I don't know what to do about it.

As children realize the drinking behavior of the parents is not typical, they may suddenly develop intense feelings of shame, humiliation, and a feeling of being a deviant outsider. They may become more defensive and more isolated from the rest of the world, lest somebody discover.

> When I was about twelve, I invited several close friends to spend the night. I was excited but soon humiliated. My friends' faces registered disbelief and dismay as they watched my parents drink. They had never seen anyone drunk except on TV. They were frightened but giggled to hide their fear.

> I felt so humiliated. I was embarrassed by my parents and defensive on their behalf at the same time. I wanted the approval of my girlfriends and to be just like them and I was also angry at them for laughing at my parents. So I became much more protective and secretive about my family. I must hide the truth. There became an inside world of alcoholism to which I belonged by birth and there was an outside world to which I strived to belong as well. I had to overcome and hide my origin and birth to belong to this normal world.

As Guidano and Liotti (1983) note, self-concepts in childhood are still connected to the specific familial contexts. The child develops a self-view that is consistent with the family's representation of reality—its "story." With adolescence and the onset of logical deductive thinking, the individual becomes progressively more competent to structure the personal identity as independent from the familial context.

The child in an alcoholic family is bound by denial to maintain the connection to the familial context. Her move to separate with be fraught with anxiety as she perceives the outside world to operate on a different view of reality.

Often the adolescent and the adult ACA feel caught between two different worlds and two different representations of reality. ACAs in treatment often express the view that they could not operate in the world outside without transgressing the family's beliefs. Bound to a pre-logical, all-or-none cognitive frame, individuals in the ACA therapy group are often struggling with which view is correct. They feel pulled toward familial attachments, maintained by denial and the family's core beliefs and they feel an equal pull towards separation and independence represented by affiliation with the culture outside the family. But to separate and join the world outside is to betray the family's beliefs and therefore lose the core attachments.

For many of our ACA patients, the inability to separate—emotionally or physically—from their alcoholic families of origin, is what brings them to treatment as adults. While developmental difficulties may be rooted very early in problematic attachments with difficulties in bonding or subsequent problems in childhood and latency, adolescence, marking the onset of identity consolidation and separation, heralds a critical point in the child's development.

IDENTITY FORMATION

Adolescence is the time when identity formation takes center stage (Erikson, 1963). It is the time when the various elements of multiple identifications begin to merge into a stable, more mature, autonomous sense of self. The adolescent tries on various identities and constantly questions "who am I?"

Under the best circumstances, this developmental task is turbulent with great fluidity in affective experience and expression.

It is a time when socialization is a more dominant factor, as the child attempts to integrate the values and the culture inside the family with those outside. The adolescent masters or attempts to control many of the emotional ambiguities and wide inconsistencies through the cognitive move into formal operations, the highest level of cognitive development which includes formal logic and abstract reasoning abilities. Most importantly, the advance to this level includes combinatorial thinking, the ability to merge apparently contradictory or polar opposites and therefore to integrate much more complex ideas and information about the self and the environment. In the affective sphere, the young adult can scan the range of feeling, determining what is real and integrate opposites.

The predominance of primitive defense mechanisms and adaptations in the alcoholic family—especially denial—interferes with the progression to these higher levels of cognitive development in areas of conflict. Denial limits the range of what can be recognized, explored, and ultimately integrated.

The cognitive counterpart to denial is a preoperational or concrete operational level of cognitive organization. Therefore much of the incongruity and complexity to be mastered in identity formation cannot be integrated except through the more primitive cognitive frame consistent with denial and preoperational and concrete operations. (Love & Schwartz, 1987)

Using Erikson's developmental stages to trace the impact of alcoholism on development, Beletsis and Brown (1981) indicated that impairments in early childhood developmental tasks such as the establishment of basic trust, difficulties with autonomy and self-control, and mastery so interrupt the path of normal development that the preadolescent is in no way emotionally prepared to negotiate the adolescent tasks of identification and separation. The predominance of defensive adjustment requires major accommodations through the developmental stages that result in serious impairment. The developmental groundwork required to successfully negotiate the tasks of identification and separation is either missing, full of deficits, or dominated by defensive accommodations necessary to sustain early attachment or the limited adjustment that has been achieved.

Thus individuals approaching adolescence are often ill prepared to begin the process of detachment and separation-individuation. While many difficulties occur in the earlier stages, and individuals may well be arrested at an early stage of development, a crisis may not occur until the onset of adolescence.

Our clinical evidence (Brown & Beletsis, 1986) indicates that many adult children of alcoholics are arrested at the adolescent stage of development. Their attachments to their parents are based on distorted beliefs and perceptions about themselves and others. Adolescence demands action in the form of identification. Identification cannot proceed without addressing the incongruity of the core beliefs and behaviors or acting out an underlying identification with the reality of parental belief and behavior, for example, drinking alcoholically like the parent while denying that any problem with alcohol exists.

Children of alcoholics cannot negotiate emotional separation because they lack an adequate base of attachment from which maturation and separation can occur. The difficulties in early attachment and the childhood accommodations required make autonomous separation impossible. Not only does the adolescent not have the emotional base and maturity, but he or she as parent to the parent cannot leave the real inadequate and needy parent behind. Thus individuals seeking treatment feel guilty about betraying their families (by breaking denial of alcoholism) and for wishing to separate. At the same time, they feel a deep longing for a dependent bond, missed or impaired so early in their development. Thus the move toward separation simply cannot occur.

Many patients who experience themselves as the "hero," the model child, or the "survivor" are also bound to maintain the primary attachment to their original family by survivor guilt. Every step forward in their development is met with guilt and self-punishment.

> It is such a struggle for me to be successful. I don't know why I'm the one who got out, but it often feels terrible. I think about my younger sister who was so scapegoated by all the family and I am drawn back in to try to help her. But I never can. Still, I have to try or I feel too guilty getting better myself.

As treatment progresses, it becomes clear that in addition to the accumulated developmental deficits and the guilt associated with leaving a "sick" family behind, the major roadblock to autonomous development and separation is the necessity to develop an independent identity. It is this need which causes the adolescent crisis or arrest.

Alcohol: An Organizing Principle in Identity Formation

In a family in which denial of alcoholism has been the central organizing feature of the family's attachments, including cognitive, affective, and social organization, the development of a stable, integrated, independent identity that by-passes the issue of alcohol is impossible. The denial of parental alcoholism, the defensive mechanisms necessary to maintain the denial and the reality of the organizing function of alcohol, represent a serious stumbling block to the adolescent tasks of identification and ultimately separation.

Throughout our clinical work with adolescents and adults, it has been clear that one of the most central critical questions to be answered in identity formation is the issue of determining, often unconsciously, whether one is alcoholic. The reality of parental alcoholism and its denial are so central to the family's "story" and to its bonds of attachment that no child can separate without "passing through." As such, we have come to regard the question of "being alcoholic" as part of the developmental process. In some families, the issue of alcohol is the central focus around which identity formation occurs. In others, it is one of several.

The notion of alcohol, and being alcoholic, as central to the developmental process of identity formation is a critical factor in understanding familial transmission, that is, the passing of alcoholism intrafamilially from one generation to another. While there is likely to be a genetic factor in transmission (Schuckitt et al., 1972; Goodwin et al., 1977), there is also no doubt that environmental and psychological factors play a significant role as well. The cognitive theories of Guidano and Liotti (1983) offer a theoretical base to explain what our clinical evidence strongly suggests: becoming alcoholic (actively) or "being alcoholic" as a deeply rooted core of one's identity whether acted out or not is part of development for all adults who grow up with an alcoholic parent. Examination of the theory illustrates this dynamic and clinical examples reinforce it.

Imitation and Identification

Guidano and Liotti (1983) stress that identity formation—the core of knowledge that constitutes the self—is the accumulated result of knowledge organization that has been structured beginning with early experiences. Imitation and identification are central to this process of development of one's personal identity.

Guidano and Liotti suggest that imitation is the behavioral side of modeling and identification the cognitive side, possible only with the acquisition of rules and beliefs. According to Piaget (Greenspan, 1979) and others (Lewis, 1977; Santostefano, 1980), behavior, that is, the action on the environment, is the earliest form of knowledge construction. Imitation is one aspect of that early form of action. The infant first mirrors and actively imitates mother's expressions and actions. Imitation is an early, important cornerstone of attachment and cognitive structuring.

Identification is a more advanced aspect of modeling. The individual actively selects aspects of the model's attitudes to imitate and reconstructs these data on the basis of the cognitive structure he or she already possesses. Because of the importance of attachment as Guidano and Liotti stress, the tendency to assume a model's viewpoint and behavior does not depend on outcome. That is, contrary evidence from the environment or maladaptive consequences of the behavior or identification do not alter it. Rather, the individual continues to evaluate self and environment on the basis of the early cognitive schemata. In the alcoholic family, these center on a belief in control and denial of parental alcoholism, along with core beliefs about family members necessary to support and sustain denial.

The beliefs about self, constructed on the assumption of responsibility, and positive, idealized beliefs about the parents both required to maintain denial, are also resistant to change. These beliefs structure subsequent actions on the environment, attachments, and perceptions about the self and others. At the center is alcohol, a primary organizing principle of behavior and identity formation, expressed in adolescence and adulthood.

Adolescence is a time of fluctuating identity (Blos, 1962) and the trying out of adult behaviors in preparation for emotional and physical separation and adult identity. In an alcoholic family, the tasks of identification and separation are profoundly influenced by, and often centered on, drinking. Depending on attachments, cognitive structure and the level of denial (and genetic factors not yet understood), children of alcoholics may imitate the alcoholic parents. As one of our patients stated:

Drinking tells me that I belong.

Many recovering alcoholics who are also the children of alcoholics report that they were alcoholic from the first drink, never having the internal experience of control. For these young people, behavioral loss of control was immediate.

They also identified with the beliefs and attitudes of their parents, structured to maintain denial and secure attachments within the family. Thus their behavior is in immediate and continuing conflict with their personal identities. Having accepted the denial in the family, these individuals believe, like their parents, that they can control their drinking. Evidence to the contrary must be explained in other ways. They, too, develop the "thinking disorder" (Brown, 1985) characteristic of active alcoholism and its denial, now related to their own drinking. Peg illustrated:

> Peg recalls her beginning awareness of an inside world and an outside world in which the rules and perceptions of reality didn't match. For her, the adolescent tasks of identification and separation occurred around the central core of alcohol. In adolescence, Peg began to drink primarily with her family. She got drunk regularly, with them and just like them. But she also denied any problems with alcohol. She maintained that she, like her parents, had control, a faulty belief that allowed her to maintain the illusion that she and her family were not outsiders in the world away from home. By identifying with them and imitating their behavior, she could maintain her attachment to them and function in the world outside, although this attachment precluded her healthy individuation and separation. Ironically, drinking like her parents also was the developmental milestone that allowed her the illusion of autonomy and separation. As a young adult, she was drinking alcoholically while attempting to establish her own life. She married an alcoholic and both organized their lives around alcohol. They were already severely disabled by their advanced alcoholism, mirroring an identification with and imitation of the advanced alcoholism of all four of their parents.

Another patient illustrates the adult resolution of the issues of both imitation and identification reflecting the underlying attachments and identifications that maintained it.

> Both of Ted's parents were alcoholics for as long as he could remember. Ted became an alcoholic too, drinking compulsively from early adolescence until he stopped and entered AA in his late twenties. In the process of group psychotherapy, his conflictual identifications with both parents emerged. For much of his early work in therapy, he felt fragile, emotional and subject to the control of others. He tied these feelings and his sense of himself as "passive" to his identification with his mother. As a child, he frequently intervened

with his father on her behalf, creating a disturbance which redirected his father's anger away from his mother onto him.

After several years, he shifted his stance dramatically, now becoming aggressive and critical of more passive or openly dependent group members. His anger escalated till he became frightened of himself and concerned with his destructive potential. He soon began to examine his identification with his father's angry, violent outbursts, until now concealed from him by his stronger overt identification with his more passive "victim" mother.

These are the children of alcoholics who become alcoholic themselves. But many do not behaviorally model after their alcoholic parents. Our clinical experience indicates that those who do not imitate their parents' drinking behavior may still have identified with the dominant beliefs of these figures. One of our patients illustrates the impact of identification without the behavioral imitation of excessive drinking.

Sara, an only child, idealized her severely alcoholic mother. As she remembered her childhood, she recalled her mother's dramatic flair and her capacity to be the admired and envied center of attention. Sara also recalled her mother's angry, critical attitude toward her. Sara identified with and internalized her mother's hostility toward her. She was compulsively negative and self critical, engaging in a constant barrage of punitive attacks on herself. As long as she maintained the negative attacks on herself, her idealization remained intact.

As she progressed in treatment, she began to speak about her fear of her mother's anger toward her. She soon realized that although she had been frightened of the attacks on her, she had been more frightened for her mother whom she saw as unstable. Having internalized her mother's hostility towards her, she increased the angry attacks on herself, now feeling responsible for her mother's erratic, angry behavior.

As an adult, she perceives others and the world as idealized but fragile. Sara needed to exert constant control over herself and others in order to protect them from her.

With several years of therapy and increasingly self punitive behavior, Sara realized that she maintained her sense of close attachment to her mother by identifying with her mother's projection of hostility onto her. She felt chronically out of control emotionally and completely dominated by her compulsive self abuse and criticism. Ultimately, she could see that her chronic depression and erratic bursts of emotionality equalled her mother's drunken, out of control behavior. Altering her negative stance equalled abandoning her mother and her own dependent attachment to her.

For individuals who do not imitate the alcoholic drinking behavior, denial of loss of control is an important piece of their identification. These individuals either do not drink at all or exercise hypervigilant control over their drinking, lest they become just like the alcoholic. These individuals believe that becoming alcoholic is inevitable—that underneath their conscious control, they are already alcoholic and just waiting to act it out. A patient illustrated:

> As an adult, Michael emphasizes the importance of intellectual and emotional control. Michael grew up in an atmosphere of constant tension, the potential of violence and chronic loss of control by both parents a constant. His father was a violent alcoholic and his mother suffered periodic psychotic episodes.
>
> In the group, he exhibited little tolerance for the expression of emotion and felt immediately responsible to fix anyone demonstrating helplessness or need. As the group advanced, he grew more anxious and exerted more control, obstructing the progression of the group into deeper exploration and emotional expression. As his anxiety grew, he realized that he believed deeply that he was out of control. Just like both of his parents, any expression of his feeling would result in his becoming violent or crazy. Any expression of feeling by others required his assumption of responsibility and unsuccessful efforts to fix the other.

In a family in which both parents are alcoholic but deny their behavioral loss of control, the possibility of alternate models for identification is minimal. Children cannot challenge their view of the world without an independent model and, therefore, an alternate figure of attachment.

In a family in which only one parent is alcoholic, the nonalcoholic parent may also support the denial. Several studies suggest that children identify with the more dominant parent (Burk, 1972) or the parent with whom the child has the most intense relationship. (Guidano & Liotti, 1983) Often the alcoholic is the most dominant central figure regardless of behavior or actual authority.

In families in which denial is minimal, or in which the nonalcoholic parent is a viable figure for imitation and identification, children may not imitate the alcoholic behaviorally (genetic factors precluded). They may, instead, significantly imitate and identify with the attitudes and behaviors of the nonalcoholic parent. This attachment often centers on a maladaptive emphasis on self-control which must be maintained by a rigid and narrow range of cognitive and affective experience. A patient illustrated:

> My key problem growing up was a lack of role models. My father was never able to cope and my mother's behavior was always a reaction to my father. She was always trying to control him or us and exploding just like him when her efforts failed. He's been dead quite a while and my mother still doesn't know how to regulate her behavior. She over-reacts, can't control her anger or put things in their proper perspective. I never saw mature responsible behavior.

It is well established that many children of alcoholics marry alcoholics, replicating an identification with the nonalcoholic and the relationship patterns modeled by both parents. Often, the adult child will choose a mate who needs to be fixed or "controlled." Many hope to be successful with their own alcoholic partner after having failed to help their parent.

Many children of alcoholics report clinically that they have chosen dysfunctional mates, alcoholic or not. In treatment, they realize that they had no examples of mature relationships characterized by a respect for autonomy and interactional interdependent partnerships. They have no sense of give or take and continue to perceive relationships in an all-or-none fashion—dominance or submission, weak or strong, right or wrong.

The nonalcoholic parent is often viewed by the children as more disturbed than the alcoholic—more angry and out of control with no excuse. The nonalcoholic may be seen as passive and unprotective of self and children. Identifying with the alcoholic and maintaining the belief in self control is often the most appealing resolution to an identity conflict in which there are no viable figures for positive identification and ultimate separation.

The issue of "no viable models" is a serious one creating an unconscious all-or-none block as the push for identity consolidation and separation approaches. Adolescents in treatment and adults retracing their development within the transference outline the crisis occurring in adolescence: to identify with either parent, alcoholic or nonalcoholic, is equal to insuring self-destruction or the repetition of pathological patterns of attachment based on their own early attachment and later identification with the relationship patterns of parental models. Unfortunately, such recognition is unconscious. Instead, pathological identification (imitating alcoholic drinking behavior or addictive disorders), developmental arrest, or limited and circumscribed maturation occurs.

BECOMING ALCOHOLIC: A DEVELOPMENTAL MILESTONE

Over the course of ten years of work with children of alcoholics we have witnessed the centrality of parental alcoholism as a governing agent in identity formation in working with adolescents who are struggling directly with establishing their identities and in work with adult children of alcoholics who have suffered the consequences of a pathological identification or the consequences of being stuck warding it off. We see overwhelmingly in our clinical evidence that there is no way around it. *Alcohol, or being alcoholic, is central to identity formation.*

The Adolescent Struggle

In working with adolescents whose parents have been identified as alcoholic and whose parents are already recovering, we see the significance of the question of "being alcoholic" more clearly than for those whose parents are still denying alcoholism. Regardless of the degree of denial however, all are struggling with how to incorporate parental alcoholism and/or its meanings into their own sense of personal identity.

Children cannot "not identify." The process of identification is occurring continuously from birth, often unconsciously. Thus children must incorporate or accommodate to the reality of parental alcoholism, its denial or explanations in some manner. It is extremely difficult, if not impossible, for children to step out of the denial process of the family to recognize and label parental alcoholism while it is still being denied within the family. It is too threatening to the child's developing ego and sense of belonging to the family to step outside. Thus, despite greater awareness and prevention programs, often the only adolescents in treatment as identified children of alcoholics also have parents who are in treatment. Even then, the central role of alcohol to the family's identity and individual's identity remains intact.

Nineteen-year-old Michelle sought treatment in a group for young adult children of alcoholics. Her mother was a recovering alcoholic, sober for six years. Her father, also a recovering alcoholic, had been sober for one year. Her older brother, 24, was currently in treatment for chemical dependence in an inpatient program that emphasized family involvement in the therapeutic process. Michelle lived too far from the family to participate in the treatment program but she agreed readily to seek treatment on her own in response to her parents' suggestion.

In the evaluation interviews Michelle spoke about the centrality of her parents' alcoholism to her childhood and family life. Her mother had been an identified, sober alcoholic since Michelle was thirteen and her father's continuing active alcoholism had been the focus of much denial which could now be acknowledged since he too had identified himself as an alcoholic.

Michelle stated matter of factly that being alcoholic was a part of belonging to her family. She already had experienced a turbulent adolescence with her "rebellion" centered on the issue of her drug use. Through her early adolescence, she maintained that she was not like her parents because she was not an alcoholic and she was not having difficulties with alcohol.

As she separated from her family and her older brother entered treatment, she became more concerned about the centrality of the issue of alcohol in her own life. While she maintained she was not like the others, as she progressed in treatment she wondered repeatedly: do I have to be an alcoholic and then a recovering alcoholic to belong to my family?

For adolescent siblings, Kevin and Donna, family issues of dominance, authority, and control were played out around the issue of alcohol. Their father had been in on-again, off-again treatment for alcoholism for seven years and was now severely disabled, suffering from malnutrition and liver disease as a result of around-the-clock drinking. He had been diagnosed a "failure" and was believed to be dying.

In describing his unpredictability and erratic behavior, the children denied any emotional impact or difficulties themselves. They agreed to talk to someone only if they could come together.

The children presented a history corroborated for the most part by their mother in which father's alcoholism had been *the* central problem in the family for many years. The parents ultimately separated and divorced because of the father's drinking. Custody was awarded to the mother for the same reason. However, following the divorce, the father became sober and after a year successfully won visitation rights and later alternating custody.

Recently he had begun to drink again and the children's living arrangements now fluctuated according to whether father was currently sober.

They insisted that the unpredictability of this arrangement and their father's erratic emotional and practical availability did not bother them. They had, in fact, rejected all previous attempts to acknowledge the existence of a "problem" and seek help for it. They now could label and speak about their father as an alcoholic but they refused suggestions to attend Alateen. To seek help for themselves was equal to abandoning their father.

In the course of treatment, Kevin and Donna both demonstrated a strong identification with their father's role as the failure in the family. Both bright, they were failing in school. Donna was also using drugs and sleeping during the day in similar fashion to her father's behavior while on a binge. Both denied vehemently that they had any problems with drugs or alcohol or any fears about their addictive potential. Yet, their roles in relation to others in the family and school environment were just like their father's role in the family—the failure. Kevin and Donna both rejected a conscious identification with their father, while imitating his drinking behavior with a symbolic substitute.

Both were staunchly defensive on their father's behalf. Any acknowledgment of pain, loss, or damage had to be dismissed or explained away. Their failures represented their attachment to their father. Their agreement to enter treatment reflected their efforts to represent her to their mother and the world.

Beth, 15, was referred by her parents, both recovering alcoholics, for behavior problems. In the initial interview, Beth indicated that the realities of her parents' behavior while drinking (they had been sober for five years) could not be discussed in the family although their identities as recovering alcoholics and their involvement with AA could be talked about and, in fact, was a source of pride for all.

Once in treatment as the child of alcoholic parents, she began to talk about the realities of what happened to her when her parents were drinking and her own fear that she was going to be just like them. Her acting out subsided, but she remained terrified that ultimately she would be out of control herself.

As the years passed, she struggled with bulimia and then her own drinking. Beth always had been seen as the "strong one" of the four children and temperamentally much like her aggressive father whom she greatly admired. She wanted desperately to be in control of herself in a way that her father had failed.

Another example provides a final illustration.

As an adolescent, Warren felt caught between his divorcing parents. Although both were alcoholic, only his mother was identified and labeled as the "problem." He was told by his father to take care of his mother and younger siblings but then felt rejected by him for doing so. His mother accepted Warren as a substitute husband displacing her bitterness and anger onto him. Warren felt hopeless and terrified. He began chronic drug and alcohol use in late adolescence finally entering treatment in his late twenties.

> I always knew I was going to be alcoholic. There was never any question.

With several years of recovery, the central theme of Warren's work in therapy evolved around issues of early attachment and identity. By recovering and calling himself an alcoholic, he had cut the tie to his father and mother. He often felt lonely and orphaned with an intense childhood sense of longing for a stable, nurturing family to belong to as an adult.

The Adult Struggle

In the deepening work of the ACA therapy group, issues of identity formation also take center stage. ACAs who have themselves become actively alcoholic and those who have not, share the symbol of alcohol as a central feature governing their own identity formation.

Belonging and Being Alcoholic

One of the most important ways the issue of identity formation is expressed is around the theme of belonging—in the group, to one's family and in the world. When a new person joins the group, members frequently compare family data, such as which parent was alcoholic—which then may evolve to a discussion of whether they belong in the group.

> Ray's primary image of his father is not as an alcoholic because his father did not start drinking heavily until Ray was a teenager. Patsy shared this view. Her parents' poor marriage, poor communication and alcoholic drinking were always there but not publically acknowledged until she was 18 and out of the home. Therefore, do they belong in the group? Others nodded a vehement yes. Sonia said

the image of herself as coming from a bad family or a sick alcoholic family is deep and that children in these families carry that identification in a very deep way.

Sonia longs to identify herself with a higher social class, adding with humor that bad taste is an inherited trait. No matter what she does, her bad breeding shows and is a source of humiliation.

Sonia's wish to identify with a higher social class expresses her longing to feel better about herself and her need for a model to show her how.

> I determined early on that I wasn't going to get involved with anyone who had family problems. It's better to be alone than be in such a painful environment.

Members continued their discussion of belonging for several weeks as Ray resisted actively joining the group. Ray had always "explained" his father's alcoholism as a "minor" matter which allowed him to preserve his idealized view of him. "Belonging" to an ACA group threatened to disturb this positive image. Couldn't he deal with the realities without having to feel angry or sad?

Bonnie, another member, challenged Ray, suggesting that he might be denying some major difficulties or feelings. After all, he had joined a group explicitly for children of alcoholics. She knew something about the issues of belonging and denial herself. She had been in the group for a year before she figured out a way to belong and still be uncertain if her mother was alcoholic. With more time and further exploration, she realized that confusion about her mother's drinking was directly related to confusion about her own. These issues became quite clear when her mother stopped drinking.

Bonnie remembered feeling surprised and confused about how to interpret this new action of her mothers. Bonnie had been so firm in denying that her mother had a "serious" problem with alcohol that she couldn't explain to herself why her mother would need to stop. Since her mother never fit Bonnie's idea of what an alcoholic was, Bonnie could never allow it to be true. Her mother's decision was an immediate threat to Bonnie's denial of her own drinking and her own inability to decide if she is alcoholic.

Over the next few months Bonnie looked differently at her own drinking, recognizing that she had begun to need alcohol. She could now see that drinking provided insulation against overly intense interactions and her own emotional responses. Much of her emotional life gets buried every day in her carefully rationed two glasses of wine. But how does she decide if she's alcoholic?

Over the next year, Bonnie fluctuated, deciding that she was an alcoholic for a period of time, then drinking, after deciding she wasn't a "real one." When she was drinking she was also much more confused, not only about her own identity but about her feelings and perceptions as well. Finally she decided drinking was not good for her—just as it had not been good for her mother—and she stopped for that reason. She no longer needed to determine once and for all if she or her mother are alcoholics. After this decision, she no longer questioned whether she belonged to the group.

She remained abstinent but the question of "being alcoholic" continued. Prior to a visit from her mother, she became confused again.

> I don't want to be like my mother and I am afraid to see the ways in which I am. It is painful to have needed her so badly and never have gotten her.

Bonnie is frightened by her sudden recognition of her deep longing for attachment and covers it:

> My goal in life is not to be an alcoholic like her.

Being alcoholic is also linked with issues of dominance, control, aggression or simply an active stance in relation to others. This theme is almost always experienced within an all or none frame as Sandra illustrates:

> I have tried desperately not to be like my mother who was so passive and depressed. But then I must be like my father. When I think of myself as aggressive, I also wonder about the possibility that I might be alcoholic like him.

Andy illustrates the polar opposites in terms of identity. He, too, has been struggling with the issue of belonging and commitment to the group.

Andy described his severe difficulties integrating two opposite internal views of himself. One is the quiet, passive, self protective individual and the other is the free, expressive, active successful man who is also out of control, violent and a drinker.

His difficulties belonging to the group reflect his fear of choosing one side over the other. Not taking a stand and feeling like "nothing" is the only way to avoid choosing a negative, harmful identity, either way he goes.

Andy's indecision and internal split were also reflected in his choice of career and commitment to it. He had always dreamed of being a professional athlete, but a back injury stopped him on that path in his late teens. Next he envisioned himself as an entrepreneur, successful, and hard driving. Now in his thirties, he still has fantasies of himself as an aggressive executive. But in reality, he has chosen other "jobs" that have no "career track" and no competitive components. He feels as if he's marking time until he "goes after" his real goal.

Whenever Andy describes his internal ambivalence and career dissatisfaction, he also wonders whether he is really alcoholic and just waiting to act it out when he someday lets go of his control.

Andy missed several meetings after straining his back again in a recreational game of soccer. When he returned, he related the following:

> For many months in this group I have left in tears, longing to feel closer to my father but terrified. I started going to AA meetings and listening carefully to older men, hoping I could identify with what my father would have been like if he'd ever stopped drinking. I even had the crazy thought that I might become a recovering alcoholic before I go through being alcoholic myself. I didn't feel too differently from the alcoholics at AA. One night I left a meeting and started drinking. I drank for three days and couldn't stop. I didn't even want to. Being alcoholic is there, waiting for me.

As these conflicts became clearer to him, he realized that he expressed both "parts" of his identifications in the group. He most often felt frightened and self-protective expecting others to be critical and abusive toward him. He also was frightened of his own emotions, particularly anger and aggression.

> I need to protect myself from the potential danger of the group's response to me and I also have to protect the group from the bad person I really am—the violent, abusive, free alcoholic. That person is also the successful executive who tears down his colleagues.

As Andy deepened his exploration of these issues, group members again raised the question of whether they were alcoholic.

Penny said she liked to drink because it breaks down internal barriers and her resistance to feeling. But she's worried about it too because she does not want to be an alcoholic like her parents. She and her husband have established a rule—two drinks per night and no more. Now she's concerned about needing those two drinks every night but she also wonders what's the matter with it?

Brad always wonders why his father accepted such a mediocre job and asks himself whether he will accept being mediocre as well. Was his father's drinking related to his passive acceptance and lack of aggression? Andy and Brad chuckled. Alcohol allows Andy to act and Brad to be passive. Sandra added:

> My father was the alcoholic and the active one. The rest of the family waited for his next act or for the consequences of his behavior. The alcoholic identification is the more active and therefore more appealing. Identifying with action gives me a much greater sense of control than the reactive, passive and protective stance of the nonalcoholic.

The theme of belonging also comes up around visits home, reflecting the centrality of denial, its impact on perception and the continuing longing for attachment and identification.

Brad was frightened to come to group today. Because his visit home this time had been a good one, he expected he could no longer belong to the group. Sonia joked that his membership was still intact because he had not gotten too much. She then spoke of the difficulty of having a good exchange with her parents because it automatically nullifies her feelings and perceptions about the negatives in the past. She automatically questions her own perception if her mother is in a good mood.

Sonia hangs onto the slightest kernel of something positive as evidence of her parents' care. Beth has a good conversation with her mother and immediately questions the realities of her mother's alcoholism she has worked so hard to accept.

On another occasion Brad spoke about "attending to" another person. He's decided that listening and being attentive are part of being a good friend. You listen carefully and try to feel what the other person is feeling.

Sonia shudders. This has always meant the loss of her own perspective and the possibility of getting her needs met. To listen carefully is to lose herself in the process. As she speaks of this all-or-none dilemma, she hangs her head low.

> I don't want to be involved in the group now. I need to get control and must actively shut you out. If I listen, I lose myself and end up harmed. There's no middle ground.

The Symbol of Alcohol—The Alcoholic in the Group

Issues of identification and the meaning of alcohol were accented when a new member, an ACA and a recovering alcoholic, joined the group. Jack described his reasons for joining the group in response to members' questions. His mother was the alcoholic. She beat him up and was unavailable to him because of her drinking. He, in turn, became an alcoholic and as a result, came to have a much better understanding of his mother's difficulties.

Sonia listened impassively and hung her head. She then told him of her dislike and lack of trust for alcoholics and her anger at them as well. She does not want to welcome Jack to the group nor attempt to establish a relationship with him. Even though he has stopped drinking, he might start again and then she would be obligated to take care of him.

Several members took this opportunity to update the group on their own drinking. They were glad to have Jack there because it raises the issue again. But Sonia and Jeff were not so pleased. They needed to reject Jack as an alcoholic in order to maintain their anger and rejection of their parents. When Jack suggested the possibility that alcoholism is a disease, Jeff responded angrily.

> I was unable to control anything in my life as a child. As an adult, I finally have some control and can exercise it on my own behalf. I won't be drawn back in to feel sympathetic.

Sonia concurred:

> For me to recognize my father's alcoholism as a disease, I would have to give up my anger. There is no way.

Jack remained philosophical. He realized members were angry with him because he symbolizes the alcoholic in their lives.

But he maintains that they also cannot understand their parents because they haven't been through it.

The group felt disrupted and split after this discussion. Jack's presence pushed issues of identification to the surface. The question of "being alcoholic" related to identifying with one's parent was now a constant theme.

After a few weeks in the group, Jack missed a session without calling. Sonia was furious.

> As soon as he said he was an alcoholic, I knew he would be unreliable. Here's the evidence.

Patsy felt quite differently:

> I decided to stop drinking this week. I think I did it to support Jack so he would keep coming but I also know I needed a model for myself. It is not OK to be an alcoholic in this group.

Members explored this viewpoint. They decided that it was OK to be concerned about one's drinking, but, indeed, it was not OK to be an alcoholic. Patsy realizes that being alcoholic and going to AA means she will lose the support of group members and her husband as well. She would continue to drink (with him) if it meant the relationship would survive, though she also recognizes sadly that that would mean the loss of herself.

Patsy then asked Sonia what it would mean to her if Patsy decided she was alcoholic.

> If you're going to see yourself as an alcoholic then I must hold the same beliefs about you. I could no longer trust you.

The issue of "being alcoholic" and what it means became a central theme in the group's work for many months ahead. It was a painful period for Sonia who felt that Jack arrived before she was ready to deal with what he represented.

> He is a real threat for me. If he's going to be in the group I must form a relationship with him and therefore allow positive feelings. But he's an alcoholic so I have to reject him.

Sonia struggled for months to "let Jack in," hold onto her anger and her disidentification at the same time. She recognized intuitively that she had to stay and struggle. She longed to be able to form a close relationship with a man but could never relinquish her position of control to allow a "give and take." Any areas of "grey" brought a sense of panic and an angry return to her limited all-or-none categorical rejection of men.

It was several years before she could contemplate relinquishing her anger and acknowledging her deep longing for her father which was underneath.

> I've been thinking about my father a lot. I am beginning to believe that maybe alcoholism really is a disease. There were people who loved him so he must have had some positive qualities. But I never saw anything lovable. I saw only the shell of a man around his disease.

Jack had to leave the group prematurely because of a job transfer. After his departure, members shared their feelings of great loss and their sense of Jack as the "alcoholic" in the group:

> Sonia thought the therapist was very protective of Jack, more so than anybody else—she believes Stephanie would not be as protective of her nor so available. Brenda agreed adding:

> The drinker becomes the most important person and the one who gets the attention. After disasters have been taken care of, there is no mothering left for the other children.

A few weeks later, members continued their reflections, recognizing how much they missed Jack:

> Jack was special because he went through something more devastating and disastrous than anybody else.

Jack was an inspiration because he "hit bottom" and got to the other side. As Harvey noted:

> I don't believe I could survive that "bottom." I have not experienced the pain that Jack did so I don't deserve special attention.

Members agreed that they admired Jack but so feared "hitting bottom" themselves that they invest all their energy in warding off disaster and controlling themselves.

The Longing to Know

In examining the issue of identification with their parents, group members outline their need to fill in holes or gaps in their sense of themselves that represent the self-destructive or abusive parent. Before emotional separation and adult autonomy can occur, individuals must integrate parts of the bad parent, so long warded off, or find acceptable parts to align with.

In the advanced group, focusing on members' deep identification with an out-of-control parent and a longing for a different family or different view of the parents, the pull toward attachment and identification is strong.

Brad spoke of his admiration for his father and his fear that he will be a "souse" just like him. By piecing together bits of early family history Brad has determined that he had two talented parents. But all he saw was withdrawal, depression, and a sour attitude toward the world. Brad cried, feeling a deep sense of loss for what he didn't know about his parents.

The rest of the group shared Brad's sadness. All experienced the loss of what their parents might have been or what they were underneath their problems.

Marshall saw a picture of his father as a child, laughing and splashing with the garden hose. It made him sad thinking of him as a spontaneous and happy child. Marshall knew him only as emotionless and withdrawn. He worries that he is like his father—not someone whom others will find likeable. He is recognizing more qualities about his father in himself, particularly the tendency to blame others and be angry.

Over the next few months Marshall became sadder and more depressed as he thought more about his father. Putting up the family's Christmas tree this year was unbearable. For the first time, he recognized that his childhood Christmases were unhappy. He remembered his father isolating himself in the den or sitting by himself in a corner unavailable to the children.

Marshall cannot see how he is different. He tells himself he doesn't drink and doesn't abuse his children but it doesn't help. The more he looks, the more closely he resembles his father.

The need to disidentify and to reject the parent is ultimately recognized as the very tie that binds—the defense that maintains the individual in an arrested state of development. Jack's entry into the group highlighted the rigid defensive positions of others who were forced to examine the paradox: the all-or-none position that had allowed them to survive now prohibited their full development. They had to begin to explore a broader view of their parents in order to move ahead.

Rather than strict disidentification, the group now focused on filling out their views of parents—actively searching for positive qualities they could identify with that would allow them to feel good about themselves rather than bad.

> I've been looking around in antique stores lately, thinking about what I might collect. My mother had a wonderful collection of porcelain figurines which gave her much pleasure. I remember how closely she guarded her figurines and how much care she took in cleaning them. Through all the battles and all the broken dishes, I never saw a broken piece of porcelain.

In this part, we examined the dominance of defensive accommodation to parental alcoholism and its impact on developmental issues of attachment and identity formation. In Part Three we will highlight these same core issues in the process of repair and recovery.

PART THREE

The Process of Recovery

In Part One, we looked at the environment in an alcoholic family describing "what it is like." Next, we examined the impact of the alcoholic and nonalcoholic parent and the home environment on individual development, accenting the dominance of defensive adaptation and the relationship of parental alcoholism to attachment, identity formation, and separation. In both parts, I utilized several theories or analogous models to build a dynamic, theoretical framework for viewing adult children of alcoholics. This integrated theory draws on traditional models of alcoholism, systems, cognitive, and dynamic developmental theories. We have looked at defensive adaptation and the development of psychopathology as well. Now we will link the first two parts to develop an integrated theory of recovery for ACAs.

At this point, I refer to my text on alcoholism (*Treating the Alcoholic: A Developmental Model of Recovery,* Brown, 1985) as a companion piece—the theory and the practice which served as a model for examining ACAs. In developing a theory of recovery for alcoholics, I emphasized the importance of alcoholism as a central organizing principle in the alcoholic's life, structuring behavior, cognitive patterns, and identity formation. The centrality of alcohol and its relation to identity formation form the core for the process of recovery, which centers on a predominantly cognitive process of construction of a new personal identity and reconstruction of the old based on accepting the reality of loss of control of one's drinking and the new identity as an alcoholic.

In developing a theory of recovery in alcoholism, it was necessary to expand on previous theories which focused only on drinking. Recovery, if examined at all, was viewed as static. The new "continuum" defined recovery as a process with developmental stages. The process includes an integration of behavioral, cognitive and dynamic theory and practice.

201

Recovery from alcoholism is a process of breaking denial, acknowledgment of loss of control of drinking, and new knowledge construction and reconstruction, incorporating the realities of the past and the present into a new personal identity as an alcoholic.

In this part, I will outline a similar theory of recovery for ACAs utilizing the same model and framework of stages: drinking, transition, early recovery, and ongoing recovery. As I have already stressed, alcohol as a central organizing principle and its impact on defensive adaptation, attachment, and identity formation form the core.

The critical difference in the process of recovery between alcoholics and ACAs lies in the nature of the object of attachment. The alcoholic is "attached" to alcohol; the ACA is "attached" to the alcoholic. The ACA may also be attached to the nonalcoholic parent (if there is one) and to alcohol as the central organizing principle in the family's beliefs about itself, individuals within the family and relationships with the outside world. For the child of an alcoholic, the processes of development are bound to and structured by the emphasis on alcohol and the beliefs maintained by the family. The centrality of alcohol as an organizing principle must be incorporated into the new personal identity as the adult child of an alcoholic. This incorporation and restructuring of one's identity is the core of the process of recovery.

In this part, I will develop a theory of recovery using the stages of recovery in alcoholism as a model. Next I will focus on each stage—drinking, transition, early recovery, and ongoing recovery—outlining the task of treatment for the child and adult. I have combined the first two stages, drinking and transition, into one chapter emphasizing pre-treatment and preparation for recovery. While the tasks of these stages are different and the stages separate, the break in denial and preparation to accept the label ACA are central to both. It is difficult for individuals to be in formal treatment designated for adult children of alcoholics if they do not yet identify with the reality of parental alcoholism. These individuals will benefit greatly by attendance at self-help groups or short-term educational groups to help them determine whether their parent is, indeed, alcoholic. The long-term interactional therapy group requires an ability to acknowledge parental alcoholism, even though that reality may remain painful and even uncertain at times.

In early and ongoing recovery, individuals are still dealing with the break in denial and the label, but within the context of formal treatment. In Chapters 9 and 10 I will integrate the work of the long-term interactional therapy group to illustrate the process of treatment and the developmental nature of recovery.

In Chapter 11 I reflect on the whole, defining progress as a developmental process of "growing up, growing out and coming home."

Chapter 7

The Process of Recovery: Theory

The idea of a distinct group "children of alcoholics," especially "adult children of alcoholics" is so new that there are almost no previous models or theories to review, expand upon, or use as a frame of reference, especially related to treatment or recovery. As I noted in the first chapter, the "idea" has been accepted rapidly; the practice—offering treatment to ACAs—has also developed quickly. ACAs can now find outpatient education, support, and long-term uncovering psychotherapy groups in many areas as well as ACA 12-step programs and ACA Al-Anon. Treatment is offered to individuals who identify and label themselves as ACAs in inpatient programs as well. Previously geared only to the alcoholic or chemically dependent person, treatment centers are expanding their programs to include codependents and ACAs as primary patients, separate from the alcoholic. But theory still lags far behind.

Black (1981) was a pioneer in legitimizing the concept and the practice through her theories of role and her workbooks for children. Other individuals and organizations (Morehouse, 1984; Wegscheider, 1981; *Children Are People and Kids Are Special*) have developed workshops and curricula for increasing awareness and knowledge about parental alcoholism and its effects on children. Much of this work has fallen under the rubric of "prevention." There is still no theoretical base.

Recently Gravitz and Bowden (1985) developed a theory of recovery based on stages which serves as a general guide to therapists and patients outlining what to expect in the process of recovery. Cermak (1985, 1986) also offers guidelines for understanding adult children of alcoholics theoretically and in practice.

Theorists and clinicians at the Stanford Alcohol and Drug Treatment Center combined practice with theory development for ten years. Previous work (Cermak & Brown, 1982; Beletsis & Brown, 1981; Brown & Beletsis, 1986; Brown, 1985; Brown, 1986) provides the basis for this book.

In my earlier book on alcoholism (Brown, 1985), I applied the model to families—codependents, spouses, and ACAs—defining the task of therapy for patient and therapist at each stage of recovery. In another work (Brown and Beletsis, 1986), we defined a process of recovery loosely called "growing up, growing out and coming home." As the name suggests, we emphasized in this model the familial, developmental nature of recovery and the emphasis on reconstruction of the past to facilitate healthy adult development and recovery. In this paper, we highlighted the significance of attachment based on maintaining the family's denial and the arrest in development and problems in adulthood that result. Treatment involves breaking denial and beginning a process of reconstruction which necessitates challenging the core beliefs that bound the family together, structuring identity formation, and other developmental tasks.

This process signifies a break in attachment and the beginning of separation-individuation, this time based on a new identity and new beliefs about the self constructed during the course of therapy. Such intense personal exploration, regression, and new construction can occur *only* within the context of a new attachment that provides a safe individual and a safe "holding environment" (Winnicott, 1953, 1960)—the attachment and the structure—from which reconstruction can proceed. In this section, I will build on this initial formulation, illustrating how the long-term therapy group, individual therapy, an ACA 12-step, or Al-Anon group serve these functions.

With all the excitement and acceptance, there is pressure for "quick" results. How long is recovery? Unfortunately, the emphasis on time reinforces the notion that there is a "start" and a "finish," a time when ACAs can expect to be "fixed" or now "normal." This concept significantly distorts the emphasis on process and misses entirely an appreciation of the issues I have raised so far in this book: the centrality of parental alcoholism as a governing agent in the child's development, particularly affecting attachment and identity formation.

The centrality of parental alcoholism and its impact on the child and now adult become incorporated into the adult view of self in the process of recovery. In long-term therapy, individuals examine cognitively and affectively through the reconstruction of the past and work within the transference how the environment and the distorted beliefs about the family and the self, formed to sustain attachment, affected their development, and now continue to affect them as adults. The process of treatment involves examining the ways in which childhood experiences and attachments affect their beliefs, values, attitudes, defensive behavior, and patterns of attachment as adults.

A COGNITIVE THEORETICAL BASE

The first two parts outline the critical issues emerging over long-term treatment for ACAs. What stands out repeatedly is the emphasis on denial, distortion of thinking and perception, construction of beliefs about the family and the self, and the dominant emphasis on defensive adaptation by the family and the ACA. Particularly pertinent to the latter are the *cognitive* defense mechanisms of denial, all-or-none thinking and perception, an emphasis on control and a sense of responsibility. Like the alcoholic, the emphasis on denial and the beliefs necessary to maintain it form the structure—the central organizer—against which identity formation takes place. In my book on alcoholism (Brown, 1985), I utilized the cognitive theories of Piaget as a base for building a theory of recovery based on the relationship of cognitive schemas—beliefs about the self and world—to the development of self-knowledge or identity formation. The more recent work of cognitive theorists (Guidano and Liotti, 1983) illustrates the translation of Piagetian theory into clinical theory and practice. Cognitive theory forms the base for understanding the process of recovery for ACAs as well.

Cognitive Equilibrium

Individuals in an alcoholic family and the family as a whole are bound together by the centrality of parental alcoholism and the shared denial of that reality. Denial requires the systematic exclusion or distortion of environmental data, resulting in a narrow range of what can be assimilated. Everyone in the family must reject incoming perceptions that challenge the denial or the core beliefs that maintain it.

Individuals and the family become more and more limited in what they can absorb from the environment and what they can express cognitively and affectively according to the need for denial. Like the alcoholic, the codependent (coalcoholic parent and child) develops the alcoholic "thinking" disorder, that is, the beliefs and explanations or rationalizations necessary to deny alcoholism and explain it at the same time. The emphasis on denial and the systematic exclusion or distortion of data result in a narrow range of cognitive and affective equilibrium. Reality constantly threatens to disturb the tenuous balance. Greater distortion is required to maintain it. All information from the environment and internal perception and affect must be filtered through the interpretive barrier of denial. Consciousness, cognition and affective awareness, and experience are all constrained or distorted.

Cognitive theorists, particularly Piaget, view development as a process of interaction between assimilation and accommodation. The former is the "taking in" and integrating of environmental data or stimuli into an existing framework or schema, while the latter involves a change in the schema or structure in order to incorporate the new data. Equilibration is the process of achieving a balance between the two. Cognitive growth is viewed as the ever-widening expansion and flexibility in the range and depth of what is assimilated and accommodated.

Disequilibrium occurs as a normal part of development, particularly in relation to accommodation as the structure shifts to achieve a new balance. The fluidity, flexibility, and range of these cognitive processes are severely impaired by the emphasis on perceptual and affective denial and distortion.

The consequence for children and adults is a narrow range of cognitive and affective experience, with rigid defensive adaptation required. As one patient said to another who was examining his all-or-none view of the world and his inability to comprehend any other possibility:

> You are your defenses. Your whole sense of self is tied up in the battle for control of your autonomy. Only when you're defending do you feel alive. Underneath your defenses there is nothing but the threat of collapse.

As Kegan (1982) says, resistance and defense are utilized in the service of warding off the threat of the constructed self's collapse. Any data that threatens: (1) denial of parental alcoholism, (2) the beliefs constructed to maintain it *and* preserve attachment, and (3) the defensive adaptations that now provide the structure of the self, must be excluded.

Defining oneself as an ACA is the very step that threatens all three levels and directly threatens the collapse of the constructed self.

THE PROCESS OF RECOVERY IN ALCOHOLISM

Overview of Alcohol as the Central Organizing Principle

Throughout the process of theory building in this text, I have referred to my first book (*Treating the Alcoholic: A Developmental Model of Recovery,* Wiley, 1985) as a reference point. In the next few pages, I review the basics of that new dynamic model of alcoholism which again serves as a framework for examining stages in the process of recovery for the ACA.

In building a theory of recovery in alcoholism, I focused on alcohol as the central organizing principle, ordering the construction of a view of reality that maintains denial of drinking and explains it at the same time. With the break in denial and acceptance of loss of control, the alcoholic enters the transitional phase into abstinence. Central to the theory of recovery is the continuing focus on alcohol as the organizer of a new construction of reality based on the new identity as an alcoholic.

The individual begins a process of new knowledge construction and reconstruction of his or her core identity in the past and the present. The process of reconstruction involves acknowledging and incorporating the reality of the past in a manner that is congruent with one's new identity as an alcoholic. This reconstruction process is what is known in AA as developing one's "story" or "drunkalogue."

The process of new construction occurs through the course of early and ongoing recovery. It involves incorporating the reality of one's past into one's story in the present as well. "Who I am" today is continually defined and redefined according to uncovering self-exploration ordered by the new identity as an alcoholic.

The process of recovery involves the integration of behavioral, cognitive, and affective components with the particular mix and intensity of focus varying according to length of abstinence, stage of sobriety, and emerging issues.

The individual in recovery alters basic behavior, changing from drinking to not drinking and going to AA meetings instead of bars. The changes in behavior are *congruent* with the cognitive change in identity: the shift from seeing oneself as nonalcoholic to acknowledgment of alcoholism. The new identity and behavior then order the new construction providing a structure for the integration of affect from the past and the present.

According to cognitive theorists (Rosen, 1985; Thune, 1977) the process of recovery centers on a reorganization of logic and knowledge structures. Loewald (1960) and Noney (1968) suggest that the provision of a new conceptual framework which facilitates new cognitive and affective connections is the most important factor enabling patients to see themselves differently.

In line with cognitive theorists, the greater the need for denial—of alcoholism—the greater the restriction of cognitive and affective range. The individual cannot see nor integrate information from the environment that challenges the "story" constructed to preserve denial. The break in denial of alcoholism and change in identity open the process of cognitive and affective expansion because the need for restriction is eliminated. The new story incorporates the realities of the past and the present, ordered around the central organizing principle of the new identity as an alcoholic.

The process of ongoing recovery is one of gradual expansion in self-knowledge built on the new foundation of behavioral change (abstinence) and new identity (alcoholic). Continuing self-exploration, including the uncovering and integration of beliefs and affects, characterizes the unfolding process within the bounds of what the *current* defensive strategies and cognitive frame can incorporate (Mahoney, 1977). Cognitive expansion permits the incorporation and integration of old and new affect as well.

The Process of Recovery: ACAs

The process of recovery for ACAs follows a similar progression to that described for the alcoholic (Brown, 1985). Denial of parental alcoholism organizes the range of cognitive and affective experience that can be incorporated. The child develops a sense of self and family congruent with the beliefs required to maintain denial and preserve attachments. If alcoholism is not denied, the child cooperates in the distortion of belief, perception, and affect required to maintain the family's balance, however pathological that may be. Where alcoholism or other problems are long standing, that balance is the "normality" that children grow up with and incorporate as their own view. When parental alcoholism or other problems are of recent origin, the new balance may be seen as "abnormal."

The active codependent position is one of response to the dominance or directives of another. The child "fits" in behaviorally, cognitively, and affectively in a way that maintains attachment to the dominant parental figure(s).

The child adapts on many levels as Part Two outlined. Early issues of attachment, including the building of basic trust, symbiotic bonding, and emerging autonomy are affected by the realities of a chaotic, uncertain, and out-of-control environment *and* the nature of the parent-child relationship. Core issues in identity formation and later separation individuation are also related to the same issues: the environment and the particular nature of the parent-child bonds.

The third level is *defense.* The child and family develop a constellation of primitive defenses, characterized by a predominance of denial which maintains beliefs and attachments but also structures the individual's developing perceptions about self and others. As indicated, the defenses often become the sense of self, a facade covering deficits in development of the real self or a cover that protects the individual from discovering or displaying the real self that would be identified with parental pathology.

The analogous process of recovery through the stages unfolds in levels and stages. The ACA in the "drinking phase" is bound by continuing denial of parental alcoholism and "codependent" behaviors and beliefs that maintain attachment. The move from the drinking phase into recovery is characterized by the break in denial. The individual, as a child or adult, "sees" that the parent is or was alcoholic, a recognition that profoundly affects the individual's entire view of self and world. Many individuals may move no further than recognition. They receive no treatment nor exposure to the shared experiences of others. Recognition in itself may be extremely beneficial but they may also maintain core beliefs about the self and patterns of behavior that are defensive and maladaptive in their adult lives outside their families.

The transition phase involves a beginning incorporation of the recognition of parental alcoholism, clearly and definitively, into one's sense of self. Like the process for the alcoholic, the incorporation is one of "fits and starts" with the ACA shifting back and forth from acknowledgment of parental alcoholism to denial. The individual may spend months or years in the process of breaking denial and confirming the reality through incorporating evidence from the past and present. As cognitive theorists (Guidano and Liotti, 1983) note, this process of reconstruction and new construction involves making tacit knowledge explicit. The reorganization of one's beliefs and attitudes towards reality follows the reconstruction of personal identity for the ACA.

The process of early recovery parallels the task for the alcoholic as well. The individual begins a process of construction of a new personal identity based on acknowledgment of parental alcoholism and the new identity as the child of an alcoholic. The individual focuses on reconstruction of the past, altering the family story to accommodate the reality of parental alcoholism. The individual also focuses on behavior change, learning to alter behaviors that supported denial or maintained "codependent" attachment.

At the heart of recovery are the tasks of detachment and disengagement, not only from the behaviors that supported and maintained the codependent position, but from the very attachment itself. While the alcoholic "detaches" from the reliance on alcohol, the ACA detaches from the destructive reliance on attachment to the alcoholic and nonalcoholic parents. The ACA detaches from the beliefs and behaviors that maintained the attachment. The process of recovery is continually threatening for the ACA because it represents a loss of the parental bond.

It is difficult, if not impossible, to sustain the uncovering process and new identity construction without a new attachment and a holding environment that provide the safety and the structure for reconstruction. Through the process of long-term ongoing recovery, individuals will strengthen the identity and examine the difficulties in their own adult lives related to the childhood experience of living with alcoholism. Issues of attachment and identity formation are critical. So, too, is the challenge of defense.

The core of ongoing recovery and uncovering psychotherapy for the ACA is the challenge of the defensive structure, a process of unfolding characterized by ACAs as one of "incremental risk." Individuals ultimately challenge the very structure that has both protected and limited them.

Significance of Dynamic and Cognitive Theory

The process of recovery for ACAs involves challenging the deepest core beliefs about others and the self that were constructed to preserve core attachments. It involves establishing a new attachment—to therapist, group, or ACA-12 step program—that will provide the safety and the framework of new beliefs that will structure the process of ongoing recovery. The core of the new attachment and cognitive frame is acknowledgment of parental alcoholism and the identity as an ACA.

The process of recovery involves an expansion in cognitive and affective equilibrium with greater range and flexibility grounded in the new schemata of the identity as an ACA which organizes perceptions and affect, reconstruction, and new construction. As denial of parental alcoholism and the beliefs that maintain attachment are challenged, the individual can relinquish more primitive cognitive distortions and defenses characterized by preoperational thought, global absolutistic, and irreversible thinking. Cognitive maturity is characterized by the capacity to incorporate multiple dimensions, relativistic and reversible thinking. In essence, multiple levels and meanings and areas of "grey" are now included. The individual can also incorporate and tolerate greater complexity and range of emotion.

Thune (1977) indicates that AA therapy for the alcoholic involves more than a shift in understanding about the essence of the self. It must also lead to the resolution of paradox. Individuals discover that what is paradoxical and problematic is only so when viewed within one body of presuppositions about the self and world. For the ACA, that body of presuppositions involves the beliefs and defenses constructed to maintain denial and attachment.

In outlining the importance of the "story," Thune (1977) emphasizes that what is altered are not isolated meanings, patterns, or implications, but a total body of structural integration, definitions, and understanding of experienced reality. Through the process of relabeling and reanalysis, the past and the present acquire formerly lacking pattern and coherence. This process of total reorganization occurs under the direction of the new identity as an alcoholic or the ACA. As Kegan (1982) notes, the process of redevelopment involves moving from the security of the old self through unchartered waters toward the construction of a new self.

Cognitive theory is an important cornerstone because it provides a guide to the processes and sequences by which a child or adult comes to know about the self and the world. Cognitive therapy involves not only challenging and altering core beliefs, but eliminating feelings based on inaccurate or arbitrary interpretations that are maladaptive (Rosen, 1985). But the challenge of core beliefs and elimination of feelings grounded on maladaptive cognitions is not enough. A focus on the development of attachment as outlined by dynamic and developmental theorists, specifically how those beliefs structure and maintain a core attachment, must be integrated as well. In the process of recovery for the ACA, the challenge of faulty, distorted, or maladaptive cognitions involves a continuing threat to attachment. As such, cognitive and dynamic therapy proceed hand in hand. The individual acquires a new object of attachment—the therapy group, ACA 12-step or ACA Al-Anon, the principles of Al-Anon, and/or a belief in a higher power, that provide the structure for challenging old beliefs and ordering new ones.

The alcoholic relinquishes the object of attachment—alcohol— entirely and relies heavily on the substitute attachment and dependence on AA. The ACA or codependent may not relinquish the attachment to, reliance on, or active relationship with the object— the alcoholic—or alcoholic and coalcoholic parents. Thus the process requires relinquishment of an emotional attachment and the behaviors and cognitions based on the distortions while not necessarily abandoning the relationship. Finding a working balance between a strong new identity and real involvement with actively alcoholic and codependent parents is often the central struggle of recovery. How can I maintain an attachment while altering all the beliefs that maintained it? We will now examine the process of recovery according to the developmental model of alcoholism.

Chapter 8

Preparation for Recovery: Drinking and Transition

DRINKING

The stage of alcoholism, or family alcoholism, in which denial is intact and operative as the central organizing principle for the child and ACA is called drinking, just like it is for the alcoholic. Active parental drinking is the "what it was like" part of the story, the experience of growing up with an alcoholic parent(s). For the recovering ACA, it is the "real" story, the "true" story, reconstructed after denial has been lifted. But during the actual "drinking phase," there is no story of alcoholism. There is only denial and the behavior and beliefs constructed to maintain it. During the drinking phase, for the ACA, there is active codependency—the central organizing principle of alcohol, its denial and the reactive, responsive position to the centrality of the alcoholic. The task of the drinking phase is the challenge and erosion of denial.

Drinking: The Child

It is extremely difficult, if not impossible, for the young child in an actively alcoholic home to challenge parental denial or the distorted beliefs necessary to maintain it. The child develops his or her concept of "reality" of the world from the parents' point of view. And for the young child, the world is the home and the family. Not until school and really not until latency or adolescence does the child learn about the larger world outside the family. So, the parents' reality becomes the child's reality, no matter how much it doesn't match the child's own perception or experience. When it does not match, the child will alter perception and belief in order to make his or her perceptions fit the parents'. As one patient stated:

> I counted on my parents to define reality for me. Turns out
> most of reality was a collective lie.

As outlined in Chapters 5 and 6, young children attached to disturbed or healthy parents will learn from them, consciously and unconsciously, through imitation, and identification, who they are and who they are to become.

Adults, reconstructing the stories of their childhood to include their parents' alcoholism, tell of their efforts, at first direct and then indirect, to challenge the parents. They recall asking Mommie not to drink so much and being told it was not so; or asking Mom to help control Dad's drinking so the teen's party would not be spoiled, only to be criticized or punished for saying such a thing. So the child stopped trying.

The denial of children can be successfully challenged only with the help of an important "other" who validates the child's perception or helps the child to come to recognize the reality. Until recently, most important figures such as extended families, teachers, ministers, and physicians have failed to see the reality themselves either because the drinking is too well hidden or they don't want to see it or deal with it. Much of society would rather not see it and, therefore, tacitly colludes with the parents' point of view.

Many adults recall exceptions which are critically important to understanding the child's adjustment and later difficulties experienced as an adult. Many can recall a close or even distant figure— older sibling, aunt, teacher—who *knew* the reality and knew the child needed help. Even if this knowledge took no active form, the child knew and felt an unconscious bond with another version of reality. This knowledge may have provided an important means to cope with and survive the constant distortions in the home.

A nonalcoholic parent may acknowledge the alcoholism of the spouse, thereby validating perceptual reality for the child. But that parent may not be able to alter any other behavior or beliefs. Therefore, all family members are caught in the painful bind of knowing that a parent is alcoholic but continuing to behave in a reactive, codependent manner that is self-defeating and self-destructive. As a child explained:

> Even though we all knew my mother drank, we couldn't go to
> Alateen because that would be too much of an embarrass-
> ment. When I finally did go, I felt terribly isolated and lonely
> because the rest of the family didn't really support me.

The young child requires the *active* help of an adult to move into the process of recovery. And if that adult is *not* the parent, it remains an extremely difficult task for the child to step out of the family's homeostatic balance of behavior and beliefs that continue to support denial and maintain attachments.

The young child can move into recovery with the help of a close adult whose own denial is broken and who can alter behavior and beliefs and does. A codependent parent can serve this function for many children, but usually only after many years of active, destructive codependency, based on maintaining denial. However, the codependent, when ready, can facilitate and support the break in denial, subsequent treatment, and recovery for children. Still, the cost is perceived as high. Many codependents or significant others delay or choose not to intervene because of the danger of the split it will cause in the family. What will happen to my marriage, to me, or the children if I give up my denial? Most partners feel that the result will be abandonment and loss, just like the child or adult child feels: "I have to see things the same way as the alcoholic in order to preserve the relationship."

Prevention

There is now a major national emphasis on prevention of drug abuse and alcoholism in children. Efforts at "prevention" are primarily educational with books, films, and recovering speakers presenting the realities of alcoholism through their own reconstructed stories. There seems to be general agreement that education will lead to altered behavior and decision making relative to alcohol and drugs. More of these educational prevention programs include acknowledgment of parental alcoholism and important advice to children about how to get help. Certainly, the seeds are planted for children to challenge their own denial through the reinforcement of the message that they are correct in their perceptions and that they are not alone.

Missing in the conceptualization of "prevention" is an understanding of the dynamic processes involved in the familial transmission—drinking is the link to attachment and identification.

Drinking is *the* way I become an adult like my parents.

The strongest educational message may interfere with the solidity of denial, causing anxiety. Children may know, sooner rather than later, that their home is not like others, and that their parents aren't "normal." But they may not be able to do anything with this information to either alter their own behavior in the present or the future. They may learn that the parent isn't normal and intuitively *know* that they aren't normal either.

> I was 16 years old and I had not yet taken a drink of alcohol. But it didn't matter. I knew deeply that I was out of control just like my father and that I was going to be an alcoholic just like him.

But the education is critically important. Increasing knowledge and/or anxiety may make young people visible to outside helpers who will intervene, or they will be able to try again themselves to talk with someone.

Agencies designed specifically to help kids with educational information and treatment have been established for some time. *Children Are People* in Minneapolis, *Student Assistance Programs,* and *Kids Are Special* in California offer the education about parental alcoholism that will support the child's deepest recognition of reality.

Intervention

What is the role of intervention of those outside the family—teachers, doctors, ministers? First, to recognize parental alcoholism when they see it, or when the signs are present in the children. Next, to carefully consider what *active* intervention might follow: Is there room for intervention with the parent or the child? There is great danger in moving too quickly to validate the reality of parental drinking with a child who has everything invested in denying it. There may be great danger in moving too quickly to confront parents who may respond with anger, removing the child from treatment (for another diagnosed problem as the case in Chapter 3 illustrated) or from school. Careful assessment is required to determine the next appropriate step that will enhance receptivity rather than frighten and thereby strengthen defensiveness.

The family doctor—the parents' or the child's—holds the most accessible and authoritative position for challenge of denial. The medical profession as a whole must see as its responsibility the early assessment and diagnosis of alcoholism or codependence in a patient or patient's parent.

There are young children who are able to break denial and move into a process of recovery. These are generally children whose parents are also in treatment. With the parents' break in denial, a new family story is constructed that includes the reality of parental alcoholism. With their subsequent movement into recovery, the parents model new behaviors and beliefs that structure and support new identities for everyone in the family. If the child is in treatment, he or she will be learning about the realities of parental alcoholism and most important, that the child did not cause it. Children will also learn what to do and how to get help from the recovering parent or from someone else if either parent should relapse or "change their minds." The child will be encouraged and supported in maintaining the new view of reality and the new identity as the child of an alcoholic regardless of whether the parents continue in their own recovery. Still, it is difficult and most important for the nonalcoholic parent (if there is one) to sustain his or her own movement in recovery so the child can maintain an attachment to a figure who represents and supports the new beliefs and behaviors.

THE ADULT CHILD

What It Is Like

Adult children of alcoholics still bound by denial may be experiencing a wide range of recognized problems or they may be unaware of any difficulties at all. The latter are not likely to break denial or seek treatment until they do experience problems. Both groups, however, are bound by the central organizing principle of alcohol and the need for denial. They will be guided by patterns of behavior and relationship established and modeled in their first families. Congruent with these behaviors is a cognitive view of the world colored and bound by the centrality of parental alcoholism, the degree of denial and the story of the family adopted by all. Depending on the particular family, the cognitive and behavioral frame or equilibrium may be very narrow, with much energy required to actively sustain denial.

As noted earlier, the ACA may also be tightly constrained by the unconscious fear of "becoming an adult" which equals repeating the parents' pathology—becoming alcoholic or identified with the beliefs and behavior of a pathologically codependent parent.

Many ACAs with no conscious awareness of parental alcoholism or problems of their own will proceed into their adult lives, repeating behaviorally and cognitively the parents' patterns. Thus one sees generations of children becoming alcoholic like the admired grandfather or generations of children marrying alcoholics to repeat the patterns of codependence. The fear of repetition or the reality of repetition is often the trigger that begins the process of breaking denial.

Breaking Denial

Unlike the child, the break in denial of parental alcoholism for the adult is possible independent of the family's active drinking behavior, their own denial, and the beliefs that support it. But still, it is difficult.

Adult children will break denial when they can no longer maintain the status quo; when they recognize, often unconsciously, that they will be worse off themselves by maintaining it. Often, they are experiencing severe problems in their adult lives with no improvement through their own will or psychotherapeutic intervention. They may be drinking themselves and concerned about it, drinking themselves and someone else is concerned about it, frightened of their attitudes or behavior with their children, recognizing similarities between themselves and their parents, or frightened of having children because they will automatically reenact the destructive behaviors they experienced. Adulthood has become a holding on:

> My day-to-day life is nothing but tension—the tension of watching myself and holding myself together so I don't become my parent.

This awareness is often not recognized nor expressed directly. Individuals may be experiencing severe interpersonal problems with symptoms of anxiety and depression. With a suggestion by the therapist, they may be able to acknowledge a strong need for control in order to permit any relationship. Interpersonal difficulties may also be occurring in their work.

Often, the break in denial is preceded by their own "hitting bottom," the profound recognition they cannot will themselves to be different. In essence, it is a recognition of loss of control. No matter how hard they try, no matter what the strategy, they cannot make it better for themselves. This acknowledgment of loss of control often leads to a request for help.

They may or may not yet recognize parental alcoholism. If not, they will over time with the aid of a skilled helper. If they do, they may choose to enter treatment in a program designed for ACAs. Such a decision is filled with anxiety.

The Unidentified ACA

Many individuals seeking outpatient psychotherapy from a traditionally trained psychiatrist, psychologist, social worker, or marriage and family counselor will need help in the recognition of parental alcoholism and in unraveling its role in their own difficulties. They may present with a wide range of valid complaints including anxiety, depression, sleep disorders, eating disorders, problems with close relationships, marital or sexual problems, suicide attempts, or psychosis.

In giving a history, they may deny, avoid, or minimize parental drinking. An uninformed therapist will likely miss the diagnosis, providing one more significant adult that colluded with denial or simply did not know enough to press further.

An informed therapist will take the stance of "ruling out" parental alcoholism with every patient. In essence, the therapist must actively seek information about parental drinking to ascertain the absence of alcoholism. With such an active stance, therapists will find that unintentionally they have become specialists in working with ACAs simply by diagnosing their own case loads referred to them through traditional nonalcohol labeled or oriented sources. As one therapist indicated:

> Since reading about children of alcoholics, I've discovered that at least 60% of my patients had an alcoholic parent. I'm pretty sure it's always been that percentage or higher—I just didn't know it.

The therapist who is informed and able to make a diagnosis of parental alcoholism may find a patient who is not yet ready to hear. The threat is simply too great. The therapist may gently prod at the patient's denial or explanations that support it, in the same manner that one would challenge the logic and the behavior of the alcoholic. The therapist might also provide the patient with pamphlets and suggestions for books to read as a way to become more comfortable with the idea. A therapist might also suggest that the patient attend an Al-Anon group or 12-step group for ACAs as a way to gather information and to "try on" the label ACA. How does it feel to hear others talk or to think of yourself as ACA? What would it mean to you to think of yourself as an ACA? The answer to this question is often at the core of resistance to breaking denial.

Many patients are not strongly resistant to breaking denial. But they do need the therapist's validation or diagnosis in order to do so. Once acknowledged, these people may quickly seek a treatment identified specifically for ACAs. Therapists knowledgeable in alcoholism facilitate this process, referring patients to an alcohol clinic or therapist for treatment or consultation. Alternatively, the therapist may continue to work individually with the patient, referring the individual to ACA 12-step, Al-Anon, or another group for ACAs.

For most patients who can accept the label, a self-help group and/or an ACA therapy group is extremely beneficial, providing a new "attachment" that carries with it new beliefs and the therapeutic power of the shared experience. Both provide reinforcement for the new identity, the process of construction and reconstruction and the changes in behavior and cognition that will follow in recovery. The importance of a new attachment is as critical for the ACA as for the alcoholic. The break in denial signifies a loss of the parental bond. Individuals require a safe, stable, and readily available "substitute" for gratifying the strong dependency needs of transition and early recovery that accompany the perceived loss of the parental object. A single therapist may be hard pressed to be as available or as responsive as the patient may require.

BEHAVIORAL, COGNITIVE, AND DYNAMIC INTERVENTIONS

The break in denial involves the challenge of behavior and cognitive patterns and an exploration of underlying dynamics that contribute to maintaining the maladaptive and destructive beliefs. The inclusion of a psychodynamic framework in the drinking phase is of critical importance because of the relationship of parental alcoholism and its denial to attachment. Even if parental alcoholism has not been denied, the behaviors and beliefs must still be challenged with particularly negative adaptations explored. As Bonnie noted:

> My father's alcoholism was never denied by anybody. It was so obvious. So was my mother's hostility which *was* denied. It was OK to acknowledge his drinking but not OK to feel anything about it, especially anything negative.

In the process of Bonnie's early therapy, she looked at her own behavior and beliefs, centered on total denial of negative affect. With dynamic exploration, she began to realize that she pleased her mother and thereby maintained a bond to her by agreeing to feel only positive emotion. For Bonnie, the break in denial centered on her recognition that she did feel very negatively about her father's drinking and about her mother's rules for dealing with it.

The break in denial of parental alcoholism also involves dynamic exploration. For many, the label ACA is seen as a challenge and a betrayal of the parents. The idea of labeling oneself an ACA feels like breaking a rule, telling the family secret. Individuals often express a deep fear of abandonment. If they break denial, their parents will finally reject them. This is often a realistic fear. The break in denial signifies the beginning move to tell a different story about oneself and the family. Many feel guilt and a deep sense of loss at this recognition. To tell a different story is an aggressive act on their part. No wonder parents will react with anger, dismay, or disbelief.

Also important, the break in denial signifies the shattering of illusion—the challenge to beliefs and defenses that sustain a false sense of security, attachment, or family unity. Often the deepest fear underneath denial is the discovery that the child was not really loved, recognition of the reality of parental pathology, immaturity, and inadequate parenting. The chronic anxiety and frequent terror experienced as an adult and through the long process of uncovering psychotherapy is often a reflection of this unconscious recognition.

The key question for the person struggling with the break in denial is "what does it mean if I think of my parent as an alcoholic or a codependent?" Further, what does it say about me? About my childhood?

> Will such acknowledgment destroy my lifetime image of a good childhood? I liked my family and always believed we were normal.

Will acknowledgment validate underlying perceptions and deep feelings of being bad?

> I really knew my Mom was alcoholic but it was so hard to tolerate. If she was alcoholic, it had to be because of me. Whenever I accept the reality I feel worse about myself.

Are other realities strongly denied?

> If I say my parent is alcoholic, I have to say I am too. It's too much to deal with.

A recovering alcoholic echoed this dilemma as he struggled in therapy to determine whether his parents were alcoholic.

> I have accepted my own alcoholism as an adult and "rewrote" my story to include my drinking. But what does it mean if I accept my parents as alcoholic too? I don't want to believe that alcohol was so central to my whole life. Can't it be just a little detail? If I recognize my parents' alcoholism, I will have to rewrite the story of my whole life, and if I take away the alcohol, there will be nothing there. I'm afraid to look beneath the alcohol that bound us all.

As he explored further, the same theme continued:

> I've considered going to an ACA Al-Anon meeting but never quite manage it. I just can't stand the thought of spending the next decade unraveling my parents' alcoholism. Still, I know alcohol is central—it was like an anchor. It was my context, my reality.

Over the course of therapy, he vacillated between developing his own identity as an alcoholic and his own story with the need to include his parents' alcoholism. He had to challenge his denial of his parents' drinking in order to reconstruct the *real* story of his own. He found he could not limit his own story to his own drinking and his own adult life. Ultimately, he expressed his fear of challenging denial and beginning a "family reconstruction."

I am terrified if I look backward that I will lose my new view of reality. My parents' view of the world was so strong, so air tight. I'm not sure I could challenge it. I'm afraid I will find myself back in the same house so to speak—with the same logic that made it all seem perfectly reasonable. I don't know if I can trust myself to know what I know. Will I return to lying and lose it all?

Carl reassured himself and sought reassurance from other people in AA that going back was OK. He began to attend ACA meetings and deepened his exploration and challenge of the family denial.

I've started to write out my memories and to talk about my parents' drinking at meetings. It feels like the ultimate betrayal to me. I tried to talk about these things at 14 but nobody listened. I was chronically depressed and knew something was wrong but I couldn't get it out. Earlier than that I tried to say the problem was alcohol but got smashed down—"you can't say that!" The rule about not talking drove me nuts.

Over the weeks and months, Carl opened up his family history, challenging the logic and the story he had grown up with. But he felt lost, guilty, and alone. Finally, he wondered sadly:

What is more important, the photo of the party or the party itself? The picture is a reliable source of pleasure. The picture made my history and proved I was happy. How can I look closer at the party and challenge the photo?

Betsy further illustrated the anticipated sense of loss and loneliness that comes with the break in denial.

I went to an ACA meeting and was shocked by the instability of my own perceptions. My knowledge of the "facts" of my childhood would vanish if I went home now. I can remember feeling that I was about to betray my mother. She was always afraid I would be brainwashed. She must have been afraid that her drinking would be discovered.

You know, I never believed that people lie. Now I know they do. I wonder what else isn't true? If I go down this ACA road any further, it's going to take me away from feelings of closeness to my family. I wonder if I'm not making up feelings and perceptions about my parents?

The Decision to Seek Treatment

Adults seeking treatment recognize that they are bound to the family of origin. Many know intuitively that they learned an "abnormal form of reality" and are not able to function as adults in the world outside their home. Or, they recognize deficits in their development—holes covered by defensive adaptation or simply the family's "story." Most speak of role reversal, problems with identity formation and an inability to separate. A feeling of emotional unrest, a failure to "become an adult," protects against acting out the pathological identification. Indeed, the ACA is stuck. As one person put it:

The label "adult child" really fits—I'm stuck at 14.

TRANSITION

Transition: The Child

The young child breaking denial of parental alcoholism must have a figure of attachment who supports the new view of reality. Nothing else may change. The child cannot alter defensive patterns, beliefs, and behaviors without causing a constant threat to the self and the "integrity" of the family. The more significant adult figures who support the break in denial, the more permission given to the child, although issues of attachment and identity formation will still be critical. If one parent breaks denial, many children will feel terribly threatened by the decision of the parent to "change" the view of reality. Like children of divorced parents, they feel caught in the middle of two opposing views of the family and the world—this time centered around alcohol.

Children experience an all-or-none dilemma. By choosing one view of reality and one parent, they automatically betray and reject the other. Children in treatment who are asked to confront parents about their behavior often feel trapped. Denial is better than having to take a side.

Children who move through a process of recovery have parents who are in treatment and moving in a process of recovery themselves. The parents are changing their view of reality and now instruct the children to do the same. Even so, the young are leery. One parent may be very resistant, giving the underlying message to the children not to join the other parent, the new version of reality or the new beliefs and behaviors that support it. There may be underlying pressure by all to return to the status quo.

Adolescents, already struggling with separation and forming views of their own, may resist any pressure to join the family in its move into recovery. The adolescent may feel this "progression" as a severe "regression," fighting any pull to join. Adolescents also have great trouble with issues of control and great resistance to any new idea based on relinquishing it—in reality or as an abstract concept. Adolescents may also be preparing to become "like the parent," to identify and act out the identification. That may include becoming alcoholic or more actively codependent. A sudden shift by the family is felt as very threatening, an erosion of the youth's foundation of identification. The family cannot change its whole view of itself and reality *now!*

These dynamic issues of attachment and identity formation are tempered by the emphasis in treatment centers on the disease concept of alcoholism. The disease concept removes the central issue of alcoholism from the personal sphere. Individuals are instructed to explain erratic behavior and beliefs as part of a disease process. This conception is extremely useful for all concerned as it reduces guilt and somewhat tempers feelings of responsibility and control. Still, there is much resistance to accepting the disease concept. In fact, it is a major issue in ongoing treatment of adult children. Accepting the disease concept seems to require children and adults to give up their anger and their longing far before they are ready or able.

Transition: The Adult

The transition phase involves a focus on alcohol and a beginning look at its *meaning* as an organizing principle for the individual. Books, articles, and support groups provide cognitive and behavioral reinforcement for the new reality and substitute attachments as well. The individual must substitute objects that represent the new view and offer a sense of security.

In the transition phase, the individual tries on the new identity as an ACA, assesses its "fit," relinquishes it, and tries it on again till it begins to feel like "truth."

Treatment that focuses on education and support such as lectures, short-term groups, books, ACA 12-step and ACA Al-Anon groups and the National Association for Children of Alcoholics (NACOA) offer an introduction to "what it was like" and "what it means" with the implicit backing of validation for the uncovering of reality, the new "truths."

Services for individuals in transition offer behavioral and cognitive guidelines about how to hold onto the new point of view. Self-help groups and many therapy groups offer guidelines and support in detachment and disengagement. The emergence of affect may be strong or absent, depending primarily on defenses. For most, the break in denial is central and the focus narrow: on alcohol as a central organizing principle in development. What does it mean and what does it say about me?

Cognitive and affective range and equilibrium are narrow. A break in denial and movement into recovery by any member of the family will disrupt the pathological homeostasis of the family. Family members must find a way to include the "rebel" or extrude the individual with the new point of view.

The Task

The task for the adult child in transition is to move from denial of parental alcoholism to acceptance of its reality. The individual accepts that a parent is (or was) alcoholic and implicitly (if not explicitly) identifies as the adult child of an alcoholic. Acceptance of loss of control may or may not occur with the change in identity. Often, the recognition of parental alcoholism solidifies the person's belief in his or her responsibility to do something about it.

> I could never acknowledge that my parents were alcoholic because then I would have had to get involved. If I acknowledge it now, I'm afraid I'll have to confront them and try to convince them to change.

Few individuals in the transition phase realize that acceptance of loss of control is a part of the change in core identity. Acceptance of loss of control carries with it the recognition that the individual ACA is powerless to manage, control, or change the alcoholic or nonalcoholic parent.

While many people can and do break denial, it is more difficult and a much more central part of the task of recovery to recognize loss of control and alter one's beliefs and behaviors to match.

Focus on the Self

Central to this process is the ability to see oneself as the "identified patient (IP)." The core of the codependent position involves a central focus on the other with a denial of self, or self constructed only in reaction or response to another. Becoming the IP—the object of the focus in treatment and recovery—is often impossible. Assuming the label ACA is for many the first suggestion of a self independent from the needs or the centrality of the parents.

Individuals seeking treatment may accept the label ACA but not the IP status. They seek treatment with the hope of finally finding the "right" approach to "fix" the parent. Recognition of IP status often carries with it a tremendous threat.

Individuals involved in ACA 12-step or ACA Al-Anon groups learn quickly that the process of recovery involves not only accepting the reality of parental alcoholism, but actively altering one's established patterns of behavior in response to it. Individuals learn that the core of transition and early recovery involves detachment and disengagement; stepping outside of the beliefs and behaviors that organized the family's relationships and the construction of personal identities within.

Individuals learn that detachment involves a reorganization of actions, cognitions, and affects to match the new recognized reality of parental alcoholism in the past and the construction of a new personal identity in the present. After attending Al-Anon for sometime, Carl reported:

> I realized I have not changed anything. I need to stop nagging my wife about her drinking and put the focus on myself. I realized just how controlling I've been of everyone around me. It's so hard to see clearly when you're in the middle of it. I feel different now, on the "outside" and afraid. This way of being requires new behaviors and new responses. Things don't feel "normal."

For many the process of detachment, reconstruction, and new construction involves a threat to the very core of self. To recognize parental alcoholism and begin a process of detachment (separation) involves recognition of early and continuing loss, acknowledgment of developmental deficits, and the constant threat of loss of attachment. Individuals can often recognize the critical significance of maintaining shared beliefs.

> If I change the way I see the family and stop behaving in my usual way, I'll lose my place. What will I have to come home to?

Yet individuals also recognize, often intuitively, that they are stuck in their own lives because of the very failure to separate emotionally. They recognize that they are bound to their first family and need help with the process of disengagement and the concurrent construction of an independent sense of self.

Thus the break in denial is only the beginning. In the transition phase, individuals may go through a process of "fits and starts" like the alcoholic, accepting the reality of parental alcoholism and then retreating to denial once again. Exploring the resistance to the break in denial is often the key task of this phase.

Resistance

Resistance to accepting the reality of parental alcoholism, the loss of control, the status of IP, *and* the task of disengagement is often centered on the pull of attachment. Each new insight, each challenge of beliefs, and each successful shift in behavior threatens the core of attachment to parental figures. Indeed, patients often express a feeling of having orphaned themselves by breaking denial (Brown & Beletsis, 1986). The threat of loss of attachment often triggers a pull back into the beliefs and behaviors of the drinking phase—those beliefs and behaviors that supported and solidified the active, codependent position. Individuals "lose" their new identities, their new perception of the past and the present, and the new behaviors that support them and revert to old patterns that validate the parents' view of reality.

> Sometimes I struggle so much with this new reality. I feel so lonely. I know I must detach and hold onto my new way of seeing things but sometimes I just can't. I long for the sense of closeness or just contact, no matter how temporary, that comes with giving up my new beliefs.

Resistance to breaking denial, accepting loss of control and IP status are related to loss of attachment and to the very basic issue: Who am I? Dynamic probing and exploration in the process of psychotherapy helps determine the relationship of attachment and identity formation to the strength of the need to maintain denial. The therapist and patient ask the question: What would it mean to think of my parents as alcoholic? To think of my parent as codependent? No matter what the answer, individuals recognize intuitively that accepting the reality of parental alcoholism automatically says something about them as well.

> I can't afford to see alcohol as so central in my life because it interferes with my denial about my boyfriend's drinking. I know I'm a co-alcoholic, but I'm not willing to really accept that yet. I have to give up my boyfriend if I do.

Months later she continued, thinking about her father's alcoholism and her present relationship with her boyfriend.

> I said it publicly to someone else—my boyfriend is an alcoholic. I'm practicing saying it, hearing myself say it. Mostly it feels awful. To think of men as alcoholic equals being a dead, lost, wounded and hurt animal. How can they save and support me if they're alcoholic?

A few weeks later, she continued:

> I don't want to be an alcoholic and I don't want to be a codependent but that's who I am. I grew up in my parents' shoes and I walk in them now.

The early breakdown of denial, uncovering issues of attachment and identification, takes place with the primary defenses intact. In fact, denial is the only piece being challenged. The other defenses—control, all-or-none thinking, and a sense of responsibility—still provide the structure of the self that will contain the unraveling. But these defenses also limit exploration of core issues. The challenge of denial and core beliefs is framed by the all-or-none alternative: "I believe or there is nothing. I am responsible or there is nothing."

A recovering alcoholic, now examining her parents' alcoholism and the beliefs that bound them together, explores this dilemma.

> There are two worlds and no bridge. If I believe in a higher power then I must give up a belief in my own control and myself as the "manager." I need to give up being the director but then I open myself to being controlled or hurt by someone else's management. My mother modeled a value of

control. She was furious at my father for failing to control his drinking. She believed everybody could control themselves. She was constantly mad at everyone for being alcoholic. If I really look at my parents, I will have to choose between them. I can be alcoholic like my father, or controlling and angry like my mother.

The all-or-none dilemma framed her uncovering work for many months. She was able to explore herself as a child of an alcoholic in relation to her father, while maintaining her view of her mother as nonalcoholic. Throughout her work in recovery she returned to raise the question of whether her mother was also alcoholic. Denial of her mother's alcoholism was central to the whole family and formed the core of their beliefs. Ultimately, she expressed the following:

This is a denial that captures people. My mother's comfort depended on everyone being alcoholic so she could keep on being alcoholic herself.

In the long-term process of reconstructing her story, the defensive functions of denial, all-or-none thinking, control, and responsibility emerged.

I remember watching my parents "drift away." My mother went to sleep and my father passed out. Their "drifting away" is so fundamental to my sense of self and feelings of loss.

I felt I had to protect my mother. I did so by denying her alcoholism. I also felt closest to her when we drank together. I feel angry and hurt at my mother for her view of the world. My life evolved around trying to get her to change her view. It still does. My mother can't see herself or anybody else as alcoholic. The more I do, the greater the gulf between us.

In providing a framework for uncovering, the defensive structure also provides containment for affect. Defenses provide not only a structure for surviving a chaotic out of control family, but an alternative view of the world that gives an illusion of safety. Denial says it is not so. The belief in one's ability to manage and contain oneself and others bolsters denial and directs the course of interpretation of self and other and action in the world. The goal is control.

Further, it is an all-or-none world. There is a right and a wrong. You are in control or you are not.

> Being responsible for controlling others or fixing them gives
> my life meaning and says we all exist.

These defenses ward off feelings or helplessness, neediness, loneliness, isolation, and fear. These defenses ward off memories of parents who have "drifted away" and the affect that belongs with those memories. In transition, the defenses remain intact and, for the most part, the affect in its direct form, is unavailable.

BEHAVIORAL, COGNITIVE, AND DYNAMIC INTEGRATION

The therapeutic tasks of the transition phase involve an integration of behavioral, cognitive, and dynamic therapeutic approaches. The individual shifts identity (cognitive), accepts the label ACA and begins to change behavior in a way that is congruent with the new identity and the recognition of loss of control. The new behaviors are those that support "detachment" and "disengagement."

> I realize I must no longer run over to my parents' house or
> call them periodically through the day to make sure they're
> OK. I realize I cannot save them and I must stop trying. Still,
> it is hard. Often I can say these words and I'm still on my
> way over there. Relinquishment of behavior is so hard. I feel
> so guilty not taking care of them.

Often the individual struggles so much with fits and starts or with altering behavior that dynamic uncovering psychotherapy is required. Individuals explore their resistance to changing their beliefs or behavior. The dynamics vary tremendously between individuals but often center on issues of attachment, role in the family and identity formation. The individual just quoted explored her sense of guilt.

> If I am my mother's mother, how can I refuse to come when
> called?

Months later, this same individual added:

> I think I understand my difficulties detaching and changing my behavior a little bit better. Feeling responsible for my parents and going over to check on them gives *me* a sense of contact. I think I really long for them to check on me, or at least ask me how I am or show some *real* interest or concern. I often feel very empty when I'm there and sad when I leave. The only thing that makes me feel good is the sense I've been a good daughter.

Focus on Alcohol

The shift in identity, the beginning changes in behavior and the threat of object loss implicit in the transition phase result in a very narrow cognitive and affective equilibrium. The shift requires a central focus on alcohol—the realities of parental alcoholism in the past and present—to solidify the change in identity and behavior. The focus on alcohol provides the new schema for incorporating the realities of the past and ordering the processes of reconstruction and new construction in the present. The focus on alcohol and the new identity as the adult child of an alcoholic structure the reorganization of attitudes, beliefs, behaviors, and feelings.

The threat of the loss of attachment implicit in changing one's identity and beliefs requires substitute objects or, in Winnicott's terminology (1953), a "transitional object." Like the alcoholic, impulses to "act"—to return to old behavior—are often very strong and require an immediate replacement, a replacement that reduces anxiety and satisfies the impulse as well.

Like the alcoholic, ACAs in self-help programs are instructed to act on their impulses by going to meetings and reading literature that supports their new identity and instructs them in behavior change. They listen to the experience and advice of others which reinforces the new identity, the acceptance of loss of control, the need for detachment and the sense of self as the IP. The strongest pull at this point is to shift the focus off the self back onto the parent with the codependent logic reactivated:

> If only I could find the right way, or be a better son, I know my parents would stop drinking.

Another recovering ACA may gently remind this individual to put the focus back on the self.

The only person you can change is you. It's hard to give up the idea that you really can find the solution that will make it all right for you and everyone else. Recovery is all about just that: giving up the idea and getting on with your own life.

Individuals who belong to self help groups will learn the new language of Al-Anon or 12-step recovery programs that provides a framework for constructing the new identity and strengthens it at the same time. "Transitional objects" representing and reinforcing the new behaviors and language provide the substitute attachment that allows individuals to begin to relinquish the bond to parents, including shared beliefs and behaviors. Self-help meetings, literature, and people, as well as the therapist and ACA therapy group, provide the substitute parents and family for the one abandoned. As one patient said after a few weeks in group:

> You just can't change your whole view of your life overnight. It's like jumping off a cliff or jumping into a vacuum. You've got to have a net to catch you.

Another person added:

> You also need new parents to model everything you missed learning.

Chapter 9

Early Recovery

THE CHILD

The task of early recovery is to solidify the new behaviors and identity as the child of alcoholic and/or codependent parents. The child in treatment may still be receiving education about the disease of alcoholism including guidelines about how to cope with still drinking or now-recovering parents. Older children may be attending Alateen where they share experiences with other teens and learn to develop a program of recovery of their own; that is, to identify as children of alcoholics and put the focus on themselves.

For the most part, children who progress successfully into early recovery have parents who are recovering and who now model new behaviors and ways of thinking. Members of the family may all remain in treatment during the first year of sobriety which is a difficult period of adjustment for all. The adults are so often anxious and preoccupied with developing their *own* programs of recovery that the child may feel that nothing has changed. Indeed, the adult partner often feels the same. All members of the family may be relieved that the alcoholic is now abstinent, but uncomfortable with the disequilibrium of so much change and uncertainty about what the new "normality" will be. Will parents be more available? Will reality continue to change? Will home be safe?

The idea of "recovery" for children is so new that there is little research yet to outline what constitutes "recovery" or what the "process" includes. Our experiences in working with families at the Stanford Alcohol and Drug Treatment Center confirmed a view of recovery for the alcoholic and the family as one of reconstruction of the family's "story" and new construction in the present. In essence, children and parents continue to challenge the denial that characterized the family during drinking, developing a new family and individual portrait that incorporates the

236

realities of parental alcoholism—the essence of what was previously denied.

The family may be just as chaotic, upset, or traumatized by the process of change as it was during the drinking and an atmosphere of tension and uncertainty about the future may prevail. Children may require additional support to deal with the continuing or increasing instability of parents who are themselves coping with early recovery. Children may feel more anxious, even more terrified than before, and resist invitations to be involved in treatment.

THE ADULT

The Task

The task of early recovery for the ACA is to strengthen the new identity as an adult child of an alcoholic and new behaviors congruent with it. The task is similar to the transition phase in its continuing emphasis on breaking denial. The main difference is a feeling of greater distance and less need to act on impulse—the impulse to behave or think in "old ways." This can be misleading however. While the ACA may, indeed, feel and behave in a more detached way from parents, the individual may still be struggling with long-standing, severe problems or psychopathology that now become the work of recovery. Like the alcoholic and codependent parent, the ACA may "look" more disturbed when denial is removed.

In fact, early recovery is often quite similar to the transition phase in its focus on "fits and starts." While the alcoholic relinquishes the substance alcohol, codependents may not relinquish disturbed relationships entirely. The process of recovery, of detachment, thus involves giving up the pathological patterns of relationship, the disturbed dependency on the other, while not necessarily relinquishing the person or the relationship. Thus the lines of "abstinence" are far less clear cut. Individuals in stable early and ongoing recovery continue to challenge their denial, perhaps questioning whether the parent is *really* alcoholic and begin to question other long held perceptions and beliefs as well.

Thus the task of early recovery involves a mix of challenge of denial, change in behaviors to facilitate detachment, and beginning uncovering of core beliefs about the self and others that maintain denial and disturbed attachments. In the therapy group, these tasks are facilitated through the sharing of experience and advice, and support for opening up exploration of the past. The process of bonding, based on the shared identity as ACAs, provides a sense of new "family," a substitute attachment.

Focus on Alcohol

The focus in early recovery remains on alcohol as the individual settles into the process of behavior change, reconstruction, and construction of a new personal identity as an ACA. Cognitive and affective equilibrium—range and flexibility of perception and affect—will begin a process of expansion as the individual incorporates more realities from the past and the present. As the threat of uncovering old memories and new insights grows, cognitive and affective ranges may narrow as well. Individuals become confused, uncertain about reality, and move back to denial. Still, the process is one of expansion.

The process of reconstruction involves "making real the past," reconstructing a family and individual history as it really was. For many, this will be a long process, opening holes and blanks in one's childhood history and filling them in with facts.

Lagging far behind for most is the integration of affect that matches the recalled realities. Initially, individuals cannot recognize feelings at all because the emotional range congruent with their self-image and their defensive structure is severely limited. They are obsessed with control, so actively ward off experiencing feelings that accompany the experience in its early form. Much of early recovery involves a cognitive process of reconstruction from the vantage point of an *adult*. Regression, experiencing one's self as the child, is felt as a terrifying loss of control and warded off. Ironically, many individuals actively seek a group for adult *children* because they want permission to open the closed history and feel what couldn't be felt as a child. The desire and the danger go hand in hand.

The focus on alcohol, the supportive therapeutic environment and the strength of the individual's defenses provide a structure for affect tolerance. A too-early retreat into the past with deep emotions surfaced can feel overwhelming and out of control to all. For the most part, members' defenses provide the brakes. So, too, does the transference and the roles assigned to members.

A new member joined an ongoing group and felt continually anxious about the level of exploration and affective expression in the group. Ted viewed the therapist as facilitating the uncovering process and felt wary of her interventions. Ted felt safe in the presence of another member whom he saw as more supportive and nurturant and, therefore, available to step in quickly to change the subject or lift the group to a more defended, abstract level of interaction. Ted called Brent the "host," a positive role. Others, in the group for a longer period, also referred to Brent as the "host," but saw his supportive behavior as restrictive and problematic, holding them back from movement to deeper feelings.

The process of construction and reconstruction is a constant threat to the security of one's attachments to parental figures (and one's adult partners as well) and sense of core identity. The process often feels like a loss and is accompanied by depression, resistance and anxiety. What is lost is the attachment or the illusion of attachment that was structured and bound by the very beliefs now challenged.

BEHAVIORAL, COGNITIVE, AND DYNAMIC INTEGRATION

Frequently early recovery and ongoing recovery are characterized by a split. Parental alcoholism is no longer denied. But the beliefs about the self and others and the defenses adapted to sustain those beliefs and cope in the early environment are highly resistant to change.

The work of early recovery involves a focus on behavior change, altering routine patterns of behavior that facilitate detachment. Early recovery also involves cognitive intervention, focusing on the challenge of denial and facilitating the beginning reconstruction process with a new identity as an adult child of an alcoholic. Dynamically, the core of early recovery involves a process of establishing a new bond of attachment, a new "family" with new and different beliefs from which to reconstruct a portrait of one's real family and one's personal identity as a child and now adult within that family. The new attachment forms the base from which to uncover core beliefs and behaviors that maintain unhealthy, self-destructive attachments to parents and other adult figures. The new attachment is based on the congruence of behavior, cognition, and affect that validates the reality of parental alcoholism and one's identity as the adult child of alcoholic parents. Through the process of reconstruction and new construction of one's identity, regression within the transference to facilitate a corrective experience, renegotiating developmental tasks from this perspective, ultimate separation, and adult autonomy occur.

The Process of Treatment

In developing a specialized treatment program for ACAs, we have emphasized the therapeutic benefits of the long-term interactional group (Yalom, 1978). While many people require individual psychotherapy instead, or individual psychotherapy in addition, the benefits of group as a treatment of choice are many. The ACA group provides a setting for the beginning work of early recovery. Most critically, the group provides the substitute attachment, the therapist or the group as a whole, to replace the family being abandoned by breaking denial. The label ACA signifies the change in identity and implicitly outlines the tasks of reconstruction and new construction of one's identity and beliefs as the core of the group's long-term work.

In the early phase, the focus is on attachment to the group that represents the new identity and beliefs, bonding by the acquisition of the label ACA, identification through the sharing of experiences particularly related to alcohol and the continuing breakdown of denial. Members establish a working culture that includes a mix of advice and suggestions for real-life issues such as visits home to sober or drinking alcoholic parents, mutual support for the breakdown of denial, and exploration of transference phenomena occurring in the group.

The significance of the early environment—the "what it was like"—is highlighted in early recovery. Attachment, bonding, and the breakdown of denial are accomplished through the beginning process of reconstruction: "making real the past." Members begin to say what really happened, describing in detail for themselves and others the family atmosphere or "tone," feelings, and events. The sharing of experiences and the validation of the reality of one's original perceptions and feelings allows members to continue the process, incorporating the painful realities of the past into their new identities as adult children of alcoholics in the present.

Group members will also receive advice from others about how to alter behavior in a way that will facilitate detachment and disengagement. There is often great resistance to these changes because change signifies loss of attachment. Members often seek treatment with the hope of *finally* finding the answer or the right approach to successfully "fix" the parent.

Accepting the truth of the label ACA underscores the need to identify as a primary patient and to focus on the self. For many, there is no developed self, independent from the pathological attachment to parents. Or, the self is the "false self" represented by the defenses constructed to adapt to the disturbed family patterns of behavior, thinking, and relationship. Thus the status of IP is often difficult to assume because it challenges defenses too quickly.

Initially, the processes of new attachment, bonding, and reconstruction through the sharing of experiences occur within the framework of the defensive structure intact. Individuals often focus on issues of trust, experiencing anxiety about the safety of the group. They also demonstrate the core defensive adaptations which may constitute the most serious pathology and which will be the focus of long-term work.

Central to the long-term process of linking the past with the present is the development and exploration of transference: attributing to others, in the present, the qualities, beliefs or feelings that belonged to people from the past. Transference in the ACA group occurs before members join as individuals anticipate abandoning their families by breaking denial. Members often see and experience the group as family immediately.

THE PROCESS OF THE GROUP: FAMILY TRANSFERENCE

In recognizing the strong immediate tendency of patients to see the group as family, we developed the notion of "family transference" (Brown & Beletsis, 1986). Individuals will, over time, begin to behave in the group in the same way they behaved in their original families. In addition, they will imbue the therapist and other members with the qualities of those same first families. The process of the group involves close exploration of how the individual's beliefs, perceptions, and behaviors which were developed in the past affect the present. Deeper exploration of the transference involves reenacting the core beliefs, perceptions, and behaviors in relation to self and others *and* challenging their validity in the present.

We have marveled at how quickly the transference develops and how quickly the group develops into a close, working unit. Frequently, the initial transference is positive or idealized. Individuals attribute to the therapist(s) and other group members the qualities of an ideal family which will replace the one abandoned. This positive, idealized transference is helpful in rapidly developing the group into a cohesive working unit.

Initially, members do not understand the concept of transference and may expect the group to actually provide the active care and nurturing, missing in their first families. Certain groups and other patients may attempt to provide what was missed, usually with many problems resulting. The recognition that the long-term group (other patients and therapists) does not *become* the parent or family is often painful and disappointing. It is hard for members to understand the value of placing themselves in the role of child, opening up feelings from the past—especially deep feelings of need—and not have them gratified in their early form. The feelings of need and the wish to be a child, actively cared for and protected, is persistent.

Resistance to establishing a bond or an idealized transference with the group is often expressed in an angry, defensive posture toward others, a hostile, negative transference toward therapists or a more neutral refusal to accept any transference or transference interpretations. Many individuals experience no feelings at all, positive or negative.

The feelings of anger about the past and present are pervasive and help ward off deep feelings of need and helplessness associated with the reality of the past. Frequently, openly angry individuals have difficulty developing an attachment and working relationship with the group. They may have difficulty bonding at all, seeing the group instantly as a replication of the unsafe, attacking, out-of-control family. They may view the route to health, or survival, as escape or rejection and may leave the group prematurely. For many, departure is felt as a victory. They could not leave their families as children, but they can leave now. Unfortunately, they have not challenged behavior or beliefs and continue to view others as dangerous and untrustworthy, thereby replicating maladaptive behavior and beliefs. The process of recovery requires uncovering the past and challenging core beliefs and patterns of behavior in the present.

In early recovery, or at the start of a group, members bring the generalized transference, positive or negative, and establish a working alliance within this frame. Often, it is not explored or labeled. Indeed, deep exploration or transference phenomena does not become the major focus of the group's work until the group is advanced or individuals are in long-term recovery. The tasks of early recovery occur in the group through the supportive exchange of experiences, opening up of memories from the past and the giving of advice. In building a cohesive working unit, group members will begin to exploie thcir beliefs and perceptions toward others in the present in the "process" of the group, which is called the "here and now." Members learn the importance of reflecting on their feelings and perceptions in the present, often a strong contradiction to the environment of silence, secrecy, and denial in their childhood homes.

CORE ISSUES ARISING IN EARLY RECOVERY

The "Pull of Attachment"

In challenging denial, changing behavior and reconstructing one's story, the key issues outlined in the first two parts of the book emerge repeatedly as central themes. Individuals recall "what it was like," reconstructing the reality of the environment—what really happened and what it was like to be in the family. Individuals may determine what role or roles they played and recognize similar patterns in their adult relationships.

Central to the process of reconstruction are dynamic issues of attachment and identity formation as well. The challenge of defense still focuses only on denial although recognition of the need for control, all-or-none thinking and a sense of responsibility may occur. The uncovering process unfolds with these defenses intact and ordering the new construction.

As noted earlier, the issues of early recovery often center on what it means to break denial, what it means to identify oneself as an ACA. Issues in treatment often focus on belonging—do I belong here, do I qualify—or is my parent *really* alcoholic, was my childhood bad enough? And if I *do* belong, what does *that* mean?

Individuals may be struggling with holding onto the new identity and behaviors. The issue of belonging, feelings of need, and discussions of "family" may activate old "impulses." Visits home to parents often activate childhood memories and feelings, especially the longing for a parent who "cared." At the concrete level, visits home stimulate denial again and old behavior patterns that reinforced it. The "impulse" is to give up new beliefs in the service of activating the illusion of attachment or at least the hope. Individuals often experience the pull toward old beliefs and behaviors as a craving—a craving for something missed. They speak of it as a pull toward an old attachment that looks positive but is actually harmful. It is like the pull of the bottle. Individuals speak of the loneliness and isolation of their new beliefs and the lure of getting "sucked back into the vacuum," the "vacuum" of the family with attachments bound by the pathology of denial and defense.

The "old environment" and the pull of "home" symbolize the old beliefs and behaviors and the "promise" of reunion. It is a strong pull as individuals struggle with feelings of abandonment, emptiness, loneliness, and fear in the present. The pull of "home" also symbolizes the continuation of disturbed patterns of thinking and behavior that maintain attachments in the present. As one member early in recovery stated:

> I will give up my new beliefs if it means losing my wife. I would rather see things her way.

Another member, a recovering alcoholic, anticipating a visit home spoke about his fear:

> I am terrified of acknowledging my own alcoholism because it will embarrass my parents. They won't want me to go to AA because somebody might know them. My parents don't want me to be an alcoholic and don't want to be alcoholic themselves. I have altered my beliefs about myself and about them and everyone is frightened. I don't know if we have any neutral ground. What scares me the most is that I'll lose my awareness. Being home and listening to them will convince me I've got it wrong. It's hard to hold onto my new views and not get pulled back in.

After the trip, he thought about the schism he believed he had created:

> By choosing sobriety for myself, I've created an unbridgeable gulf between me and my family. I've got to let go of the idea that they will join me in sobriety. I can't argue them out of their thinking which is now so different from mine. When

I try, I get confused about what is real. The power of their logic is so strong. Several times I longed for a drink. I knew it would let me reconnect and have a family again.

In support, another member spoke about a recent visit:

I spent the holidays watching my family and was mad at myself because I couldn't be different in my behavior at a faster pace. It was like a time warp. I could picture myself behaving differently but couldn't do it. A day or two more in that environment and I would have lost my new reality entirely. Nobody seemed the least bit bothered by their own crazy logic and behavior. Pretty soon I was wondering again what was wrong with me.

The discussion of visits home awakens many other feelings and issues in addition to the fear of loss of new beliefs—the loss, in essence, of the core of one's new identity or sense of self, separate from the family's bonds. Issues of role reversal, deep need, and inability to trust are also reawakened. Before a visit home, a member casually reported her difficulties making travel arrangements.

My parents insist they want to pick me up at the airport which seems, on the surface, so caring. But I can't get a flight early enough to get me there before they start drinking. Isn't this the way the world works? You have to take into consideration your parents' drinking before you can let them take care of you.

Other group members laughed and shared examples of how they have to "arrange" visits or contact to make sure their parents will be sober enough to "parent" them.

I have a simple rule—call home before 10:00 A.M. Usually, they're still sober and might remember the conversation.

Linked closely to the focus on new beliefs is the issue of perception: what is real. A new member accented these themes as she spoke about her growing awareness:

I'm angry at my recognition of the depths that I've been influenced by my family's drinking. Everyone of us is alcoholic. I heard in AA that recovery means you have to stop drinking and change your whole way of seeing the world. It's like turning everything inside out and starting over.

My parents didn't know anything about alcoholism, especially that they had it. So they sat there, watching us march forth and do it too. How can a parent watch a child become an alcoholic?

I'm so afraid to trust my perceptions now. I have always given responsibility to others to keep track of reality and give it meaning for me. How can I trust myself to do it now? How can I know what it is I don't know?

I spent long years in therapy believing I wasn't alcoholic and that nobody in my family was either. I looked at my whole life through the filter of denying my alcoholism. How do I know this version of reality is any more real or honest?

For much of her early work in the group, Martha insisted that this therapy would be merely a process of "fine tuning":

I am terrified of having to reconstruct my whole life around the acceptance of my parents' alcoholism and the fact that their reality included denial of alcoholism. I'm going to have to choose between my new preferred view and that of my family. It's too painful. There are two worlds, each with a well developed fabric of logic. Yet these worlds are completely contradictory and I can't have them both. But they are equally compelling. It makes me sad. I want to be loved by my mother but I can't afford the cost of joining her version of reality.

The Threat of Loss

Linked closely to the longing for attachment is the issue of loss. In early recovery, it is often a constant, tied to the break in denial and the construction of new beliefs. What is lost is the attachment to first family, an attachment that secured a sense of belonging or illusion of belonging but that also guaranteed the repetition of destructive behavior and interpersonal patterns of relationship.

Tied by primitive, unfulfilled dependency needs, the parental responsibility defined by role reversal and a fear of identifying with disturbed parental models, the ACA views separation and maturation as a threatened loss of self rather than a path to healthy adult autonomy. Each break in denial awakens feelings of loss and a strong pull to reclaim the bond, no matter how destructive.

Visits home awaken both the intense longing and the threat of loss. Members often deal with the conflict by reverting to the hope that they can change the parent. This belief, which is counter to acceptance of loss of control, allows individuals to maintain their forward momentum, fueled by new beliefs, and maintain the sense of parental attachment at the same time. Often these individuals are mystified and hurt when parents resist pressure from the adult child to break their own denial and are not supportive of the ACA's new way of seeing things.

> I keep hoping that my parents will give up the idea that our family life was so great. I need my parents to change their ideas so I can feel close to them. I need my parents to think like me now. Otherwise I can't be around them. Their thinking is crazy and it's my old way. I'm still not allowed to take care of myself in their presence so I'm very vulnerable to being pulled back in.

In the group, conflicts centered on unfulfilled dependency needs are experienced within the transference. The group becomes the replacement family in which early conflicts are reenacted.

> You and this group have become my new interpreter of reality since I am giving up my parents' viewpoint. I hope to use this group and this version of reality to combat the weight of my mother's denial. Maybe I can still have a relationship with her.

> Sometimes the group feels too much like growing up. I feel small and helpless and want to curl up in someone's lap. Often that longing is connected to a strong desire to drink so I can really be close to my mother. Then I want to push you all away—turn my chair around or not come for a while. I get scared because how will I know what reality is?

In the group and in her adult life outside, this woman experienced repeated problems in establishing and maintaining intimate relationships.

> I keep searching for a parent to keep me grounded but reject finding any because they might have a different view of the world. Sometimes the longing is unbearable.

The Issue of Trust

The issue of trust is closely related to the longing for attachment. It appears early in the group's work and continues as a barometer of resistance and danger. The depth and power of painful past experiences is so great that lack of trust remains a constant theme and a defense against opening up the painful feelings of need and the memories attached to the longing.

Issues of trust are typically related to themes of early attachment and primitive need. In the group they may be reflected interpersonally as a refusal to "join," speak or become vulnerable. Or, lack of trust is defensive, a constant factor in regulating intimacy.

> Growing up I was constantly vigilant, watchful. There was no such thing as trust. What for? It was all survival.

In the group he maintained a vigilant stance and expressed his suspicion of the motives of others. For many months, he watched.

Another member considered the link between attachment and trust:

> I never wanted to drink but I couldn't let myself be a nondrinker. It just wasn't an option. I had to become an alcoholic first in order to become a nondrinker. Now I am obsessed with images of being helpless, injured and left behind. I've orphaned myself by no longer drinking but I can't trust anybody or anything to show me a different way. If you can't trust your family to teach you, why would you trust anybody else?

> I feel helpless because I can't even trust myself. For all those years I believed, just like my family, that I wasn't an alcoholic. There must be other beliefs that are just as wrong still lurking.

Role Reversal

In early recovery, role-reversal, a theme related to attachment, also emerges. It is also a defense, highly resistant to exploration or change. Members of the group quickly felt responsible for others, assumed the "therapist's" role, and supported others in the service of covering feelings or denying them. Feeling responsible or parental provided an illusion of control. It was the main antidote for feelings of helplessness or deep need. One member recalls:

> I was always an advisor for my mother. By age three I was supposed to *do* something to make it better for her. I would try to rescue her from my father's rage or comfort her when she cried. I felt good about this. But then she made up with him and did it all over again. I couldn't fix her or him or anything.

In the group, Jeff was quick to comfort others and express outrage on someone else's behalf. Then he would feel repeatedly disappointed and betrayed when others repaired their relationships and felt positively toward one another again. With careful exploration, Jeff realized he expected a promise, a bond of loyalty for protecting or supporting another.

In another group, members explored the same dynamic, first as a theme in their close relationships, and then as a defense with one another.

Several group members discussed their tendency to take "needy" partners and to feel responsible for taking care of them. At first they labeled the problem as one of choice.

> What's the matter with me that I keep choosing the wrong people? If I could just figure it out, I'd be able to pick a good partner—one who wouldn't be needy and then I could get my needs taken care of.

Others challenged this reasoning:

> That's just like alcoholic thinking. The problem is out there. What about you? Can you behave any other way? You need to have someone to take care of. That's what you look for in the world. If there's somebody to take care of, you can feel in control, useful and even important. And you don't have to feel needy yourself.

This discussion wove back to perception.

> It's better to be the helper than the helpee. It's much less vulnerable even if it's a cover. If you give up the responsibility and care taking, you open up to being vulnerable to others. It's all or none of course. What others say then becomes the truth. It's their reality and their operational mode. If I allow myself to be helped, I will buy that reality too. Reality is what you expect to see and how you construct it.

Another member, a helping professional in her career and a helper in the group, mused sadly:

> I mothered my mother, myself and now others in the group. It's all I know. As much as I long to be mothered, I can't allow it. To let anyone teach me anything is to identify with self destruction. Knowing it all is my only protection.

Other group members eventually saw this individual's need to take care of others as an obstacle to the deepening uncovering work of others.

> You want to take the pain away and make it all better, but that's not what I need. Yes, it feels bad, but it's time to feel it.

Over the course of treatment, she was able to shift the focus off of taking care of others and onto herself. But only with great difficulty.

> I'm constantly wondering what the difference is between taking care of myself and self centeredness. What's the difference between acceptance and compliance, between acceptance and taking shit?

Identity Formation

Questions of identity arise immediately in early recovery and form the core of long term work as well. Issues of identity—who am I—are related closely to attachment, beliefs about the family and the self and the significance of alcohol. Breaking denial and identifying oneself as the child of an alcoholic raises all issues together as Rick illustrated:

> I remember visiting my grandparents as a kid and watching my Dad talking and drinking with them late at night after the kids were in bed. I remember trying to get in, trying to join. I had the strong feeling that something important was happening and I didn't like feeling left out. Kids don't like to be told to shut up or go away. They want to feel like they're right there, a part of everything.
>
> Many years later, I remember sitting around talking with my father late at night. One time he offered me a drink. I knew right then I would be an alcoholic if I accepted. I would join

my Dad. I said no and have said no since then but I also feel
an acute sense of loneliness and something missed.

Not long after this recall, Rick mused about "being alcoholic."

At 18–19 years of age, many of my friends are already alcoholic. It's amazing. Maybe it has something to do with identity. You know, wanting to be just like your father. Mine is
committing slow suicide with alcohol. What can I do? I can't
throw out his bottle—that's behavior for an eight-year-old.
But I sure hate to watch.

Another patient, thinking about identity, reflected:

Alcohol was *the* central theme in my family but nobody
would agree with that. Being the alcoholic was more fun than
co-alcoholic or the child of. To be the child of was pretty
crappy—confusion, fear and disorder. There's less of a right
to be in treatment too.

Whether I think of myself as alcoholic frequently depends
on whether I think my parents are. What if there was no AA?
No treatment? Without it, I would not be an alcoholic because I would discard the identity.

Another member agreed:

I am always afraid I will give up my new knowledge of
myself as an alcoholic. I have such a need to have my parents
accept my being alcoholic but they can't because it challenges their beliefs. If my parents don't agree with me, then I
can't hold onto what I know. They define reality. Why does
alcoholism have to be such a big identity thing? Alcoholism
is a master status issue with the rest of the world revolving
around it.

For many others, identity formation is not enacted by becoming actively alcoholic, although being alcoholic is still a central
issue. Reconstruction of one's "story" illuminated the centrality.

The more I think about my life growing up, the more I see
that alcohol was the central metaphor for everything, even
problems in identity. Nothing was exempt. When I think
about my relationships with boys, they all involved drinking
and sex did too. I've always been attracted to drinking men

and the drinking life style even though I don't like it much myself. But I can identify. I've always had problems with food.

Another member struggling with his fear of being like his mother noted:

You know, I see more and more how much I'm like my mother. I've always been extremely guarded and vigilant with myself so I wouldn't be like her—critical, arrogant and arbitrary. But the vigilance doesn't seem to matter. Those qualities are there anyway.

In the group, members experience the danger of relinquishing new beliefs in order to return to old ones that signify attachment or safety. A group member struggled for months to challenge her consistently angry, bitter view toward the world. She would not give it up or consider even a chip in it because she would be vulnerable to abuse by someone. She resisted Al-Anon for months but finally agreed to try it. After several meetings, she experienced a turnaround. She felt calm, less angry and guarded, and less susceptible to the influence of others. In the group, she spoke about her new sense of herself and her fear of losing it.

I think of myself as the old Gretchen and the new Gretchen. They're so close I can feel them both as very real. It's wonderful not to feel so bitter and hateful, but I'm constantly afraid I'll lose it. The new Gretchen, with new beliefs and attitudes, will just slip away and I'll be back to the safety of my anger and isolation.

Identity concerns are also related to issues of "normality." A group member had long thought of himself as destructive, the bad apple of any bunch. In his early months in the group, he demonstrated the strength of this self-view, establishing himself as the "problem" in the group. He and others were able to recognize and label his developing role as the scapegoat of the group and all agreed they wanted to intervene, interrupting the stabilization of this role if possible. It was difficult for all. Members reported having to watch themselves actively because negative responses toward Jason had become automatic. Jason, too, had to actively alter behavior patterns that were part of his "normal" sense of himself.

After a number of months with changed behavior patterns, the group congratulated itself on its progress, and especially Jason. He reflected:

> It's so strange not to feel defensive, on guard against attack or criticism from all of you. I have to be constantly watchful still or I'll revert to old impulses. I have to remind myself that it's important to come and to come on time or else I set it up to be criticized. I'm not used to this new "normality."

Another member spoke of a similar need for vigilance:

> I realize I expect you to be unreliable and uncommitted and am looking for signs of it. I have to remind myself to stay open to feel in a different way rather than automatically criticize you and shut you out.

The theme of new beliefs versus old beliefs reappears continually through the work of the group. In early recovery, the new identity is still "shaky" and frightening. Resistance and the pull to return to old beliefs remains a constant threat. Often members feel caught, or even "stuck" because the pull backward is so strong.

> I'm biding my time. The "old frame" is just too powerful right now. I need to focus on holding onto the new knowledge of myself and not try to change too much else right now.

Separation

As members first join a group, beginning the process of breaking denial and constructing a new personal and family story, the issue of "separation" is often at the forefront. It is central to why people join. ACAs realize they are still emotionally attached to their families of origin in self-destructive ways. They are bound by denial and by the beliefs about the family and themselves constructed to preserve these bonds. To change as adults, they must challenge the premises on which their core sense of identity has been constructed. Implicit in the entire process of recovery is ultimate emotional separation from parents, whether alive or dead. Members seek treatment because they recognize intuitively that they cannot decree such a separation or step out of the self-destructive patterns of behavior acquired through parental attachment and development.

In early recovery, members explore the wish for separation often focused on issues of autonomy. The idea is usually accompanied by great anxiety.

The ground for separation is neither firm nor healthy. Individuals sense they have no choices and are threatened by the prospect of becoming an adult. They are guided and defined by maladaptive, defensive processes which they will transfer to new relationships.

Separation entails "becoming like the parent," acting out the unconscious identification already well formed. For many, this involves becoming actively alcoholic. For others, it involves a codependent stance: identifying with a reactive, helpless, dependent nonalcoholic parent and following suit. Many people enter treatment having become just like the parent despite having vowed not to.

A colleague (Bihary, work in progress) spells out this dilemma in her novel:

> A mentor is someone who shows you the ropes by which you hang yourself.

Others seek treatment because they are stuck. Development stopped short of emotional separation to ward off becoming like the parent. These individuals often live very restricted lives to insure control or they move into adulthood with adolescent identifications and behaviors locked in place.

For ACAs in treatment, the continuing attachment is harmful but separation looms as more so. Life is on hold.

> I didn't leave my home. I joined it. I went through the motions of rebellion but had actually adopted the self destructive behavior of my parents. I loved being with my family after I started drinking with them. It seemed so comfortable and familiar. I knew I'd never leave. Everyone was rotting, but it felt warm and good.

Another individual reflected the painful tension she experienced between attachment and separation in regard to marriage and children.

> I want so much to have a good marriage, a good relationship, and to have children. But I know deeply I am not equipped to do this. I feel chronically angry at the world and want

nothing to do with most people. I can imagine what a good mother would be like but it's not me. I am sure I would harm my children no matter how much I want it to be otherwise.

In another group, members had spent several weeks exploring the "tie" to their parents. Ultimately they shared feelings of despair and depression as they recognized the internal dominance of their parents.

Coming to group is not a Mrs. Fields' cookie. It's emotionally draining and hard work. I feel like I'm dragging my parents around with me here and everywhere. I live my life as if my parents are still in charge.

In this chapter, we have looked at the tasks of early recovery and the core themes and issues that emerge as individuals progress in treatment. They still struggle continually with the meanings attached to the new identity as the adult child of an alcoholic parent(s) as they begin the process of reconstruction of the past and new construction of a new personal identity in the present. The "pull" of attachment remains strong—the longing to give up the new beliefs to reclaim an illusion of attachment with the first family. Issues of abandonment, loneliness and difficulties with trust, feelings of responsibility and developmental issues of attachment, identity formation, and separation-individuation are central. In Chapter 10 we will follow ACAs into ongoing recovery, accenting the structural changes that become possible with the new foundation of early recovery established.

Chapter 10

Ongoing Recovery

THE CHILD

The process of ongoing recovery for the child is an unknown because of a lack of research and long-term experience with treatment and follow up. Implicit to the process of recovery is acknowledgment of parental alcoholism and incorporation of the realities, past and present, into one's identity as an individual and as a child within the family. Also implicit is the ability of the child to make this shift. As indicated earlier, it is extremely difficult, if not impossible, for children to break denial and shift their perceptions and view of reality if the parents continue their denial. Thus children who are moving in a process of recovery have parents who are also involved in recovery, or they have one parent or important adult figure(s) who confirms the new view of reality and actively supports the child's changing view. The altered view of reality must be represented by an individual who can or does serve as a key figure of attachment. Only then can the child proceed with the appropriate tasks of development.

Still, a child's attempt to shift attachment or adopt the point of view of one parent over the other is fraught with conflict. When a child is forced externally or internally to choose between parents or significant adults, critical aspects of development will be affected. Children will either have to split off their identification with parents into good and bad or stall identification with either in order to preserve the illusion of holding onto both.

The degree to which the normal, appropriate tasks of development—attachment, autonomy, identity formation, separation—did occur or can now occur depends on many variables: the child's age at onset of alcoholism and onset of recovery, which parent(s) is alcoholic, which parent breaks denial, whether the family is intact, the new family story in early recovery and how it unfolds and changes in ongoing recovery, the immediate concerns in early recovery. Other questions include, from the child's and the parent's view, has anything changed or has nothing changed? What are the long-range concerns for the child in ongoing recovery? What is the family environment now like? What is the relationship with parents like? Is there a new stable base of parental behavior, belief, and affect to which the child can attach and safely begin a process of repair? Or, is the trauma of the past enduring so that issues of trust and safety remain at the forefront?

For the child, all of these variables and questions are critical. Whether the child begins a process of repair and reconstruction, or whether key developmental tasks remain, depends on the child's age and the realities of what the child experienced during the active alcoholism and what the child experienced during the parent's recovery.

We still know little about the impact of recovery on children of any age and what happens to the course of normal development. Depending on age, the child's core development may still be in process and recovery may not be construed as primarily a process of reconstruction and repair as it is for adults.

These are critical questions which await investigation. At this point, we can only speculate broadly that the ongoing process of recovery involves reconstructing one's core identity, reexperiencing critical developmental tasks or experiencing for the first time developmental tasks from the basis of the new identity and new beliefs.

Certainly the significance of early environmental trauma—the depth and degree—will influence the entire process. The experience of several adult patients whose parents are in recovery suggests that the danger persists despite an altered environment and altered view of self and world by the parents. The remnants of trauma experienced with the drinking parent prevail, with defensive adaptation still dominant and geared to the potential of impending violence, abuse, emotional unavailability, or chronic trauma. Still, the individual's experience is of foremost importance in understanding the course of development, the damage, and the process of recovery.

THE ADULT

The Task

The task of ongoing recovery involves solidifying the identity as an ACA and the new behaviors congruent with it. The individual becomes more comfortable and adept at detachment and disengagement and is able to put the focus on the self as the identified patient instead of the "other" as the problem. The tendency to lose the focus on self is a constant that is tied to the codependent position and the difficulties accepting loss of control. Throughout the process of recovery, individuals are seduced over and over by the power of their belief in their ability to control others. The belief in control is enduring, serving as a structuring theme and a strong defense which must be challenged repeatedly.

The ongoing process of reconstruction and new construction of one's core identity proceeds on the base of new behaviors and beliefs. The core of long-term work involves the incorporation of the realities of the past into one's new view of self and an expanding, progressive awareness of one's feelings, attitudes, beliefs, and behaviors in the present. Both processes occur within the context of a new attachment or new "family environment" that provides the structure and support for the new beliefs and the reconstruction process. This attachment may be to an individual therapist, therapy group, or self-help group.

The new attachment to the therapy group and the new beliefs and identities represented by them also forms the structure and the base from which change occurs.

> Tammi announced that she had decided to leave her husband. It was clear to her that she could only tolerate the conflicting, intense emotions because of her strong attachment to the group. She realized up to this point that part of the terror involved in the idea of separating was her belief that she could not survive emotionally on her own. It was as if her sense of self was tied to her husband and she would lose it entirely if she left him. The group now provided the attachment and structure that would allow her to preserve her sense of self in the face of separation.

In another group, a member experienced a similar shift.

> Throughout her early months in group, Sandra insisted that she would alter her beliefs rather than challenge those of her husband.

It was his view of the world that bound their relationship and structured her view of herself.

With several years in the group, Sandra reported challenging her job supervisor's authoritative position. Sandra stood her ground, insisting that her view was legitimate. She told the group that she was terrified and shaking throughout the exchange but that she stuck to her view. She had decided that she would rather lose her job than alter her view to fit the supervisor's position which she knew was inaccurate and inappropriate to the current situation.

Several week's later she reported challenging her husband. She had come to the decision that her new beliefs about herself and him were more important to her than maintaining their relationship built on denial and false premises. She felt frightened about the potential for loss but was ready to risk it.

On reflecting over the next few months, she recognized that her ability to stand firm in her new beliefs was due to the strength of her attachment to the group and the support for developing her autonomy that she experienced. Almost incidentally, she commented on the sense of broader opportunity she felt awaited her now that she did not have to force her perceptions and feelings to match those of her husband.

Focus on Alcohol

The focus on alcohol continues throughout ongoing recovery as the core determinant and organizer of the new identity and new behaviors. The focus on alcohol—the realities of parental alcoholism in the past and present—orders the uncovering and new construction processes that are the central tasks of ongoing recovery. In transition and early recovery, the alcohol focus is frequently concrete as individuals must carefully structure their behavior and environment to strengthen their new identities as adult children of alcoholics. The pull of attachment is so strong that individuals must have a firm base of behavior and cognitive support to sustain detachment.

The alcohol focus in ongoing recovery may be more symbolic than concrete, now serving as the anchor and governing principle for the individual's emerging and developing sense of self through the process of reconstruction and new construction of one's personal identity. The alcohol focus, that is, the new identity as an ACA, forms the foundation and the structure for the main processes of ongoing recovery: (1) the challenge of deep beliefs and

(2) the challenge of defenses, which facilitate (3) structural expansion in cognitive and affective range and equilibrium.

The major developmental themes noted in the previous section remain central issues throughout treatment. In ongoing recovery, they are related closely to the expansion of one's sense of self *and* relationships with others. In fact, much of the most serious problems individuals face as adults are related to interpersonal attachment and close relationships. The heart of the long-term therapy group involves a challenge of one's beliefs, attitudes, defenses, and characteristic patterns of relationship within the transferential context of the here-and-now interactional therapy group. Significant differences between individuals muted in early recovery are now examined and challenged.

While early recovery is supportive, strengthening the new attachment, the new identity, and new beliefs, ongoing recovery is characterized by structural change, uncovering deep beliefs and challenging the defenses that maintain them. This chapter demonstrates structural change within the context of the interpersonal group focus.

Equilibrium

The process of ongoing recovery involves a continuing progressive expansion in cognitive and affective range and equilibrium ordered by the base of new behavior, identity, and the process of uncovering unconscious memories and beliefs developed originally to deny reality and preserve early attachments. This process of what patients call "incremental risk" is titrated by the defensive structure that must ultimately be challenged as a central problem.

In the early period of uncovering work, cognitive expansion predominates within the limits of the current cognitive structure and defenses. Affective experience or reexperience follows much later. Individuals can tolerate remembering events and stating them as reality long before they can tolerate and incorporate the affect that accompanies them.

Initially both cognitive and affective memory may be absent. Frequently the unfolding and expansion process begins by empathizing with another. Individuals can hear, incorporate, and tolerate the reality of another's experience and feel deeply on that person's behalf while maintaining memory and affective block themselves. Thus the sharing of experiences—what it was like—is extremely important in breaking through denial of one's own past.

The sharing of experiences from the past is also important to the validation of perception—that what I say happened really did occur, or that what I felt was real and appropriate. The sharing of experience and validation of perception help individuals build a story that "pulls" away from family. Yet the threat of loss and the predominance of defenses also insure that movement and expansion will be fraught with conflict, fear, and guilt. The key issues of role reversal and attachment surface repeatedly. The greater the "pull" away from the family, the stronger the fear of loss of attachment and the sense of guilt for abandoning the parent. Ultimately the pull of attachment and separation guilt are examined as defensive themselves, warding off movement toward individuation that would solidify a pathological identification with self-destructive, out-of-control parents and equally destructive interpersonal patterns of relationship.

The process of expansion ultimately includes the integration of what was warded off, whether memory, affect, belief, or major developmental tasks such as active identification with an out-of-control parent. But integration of what was warded off cannot occur fully without a challenge to the defensive structure. It is that challenge in concert with expanding equilibrium and the challenge of core beliefs which provides the focus of ongoing work. That challenge—of denial, of one's belief in control, the all-or-none view and the exaggerated sense of responsibility for others—takes place predominantly in the present, in the here and now of the group experience.

The building of one's new story—or identity—as the child of an alcoholic is a central aspect of early and ongoing recovery. It involves behavior change, cognitive and affective expansion related to the past and present. Individuals uncover core beliefs developed in the past that affect their behavior, attitudes, beliefs, and attachments in the present. The development of transference within the therapy group facilitates examination of one's behavior and beliefs in the present and their relationship to the past. Thus ongoing recovery involves a concurrent cognitive and affective uncovering and expansion of past and present.

Behavioral, Cognitive, and Dynamic Integration

Ongoing recovery shifts away from the dominant focus in early recovery on behavior change and new identity formation to the inclusion of and focus on dynamic uncovering exploration. But this shift is far less pronounced than for the alcoholic or chemically dependent person who must actively focus on behavior change to deal with strong impulses to use a substance. As indicated, the emphasis on behavior—responding to the pull of attachment and old behavior patterns emphasizing reactive codependent responses—continues throughout recovery as individuals struggle with underlying issues central to their development. Alcohol as the symbol of attachment and alcohol, or the denial of alcoholism as the reality, serves as a governing agent in their development. The "old" behaviors that symbolized attachment remain as a potential threat in relationships with parents and as a real problem in adult relationships with others. The behavior, attitudes, and beliefs adopted as the codependent child become the behaviors, attitudes, and beliefs causing severe problems in adulthood.

The belief in control and the rejection of loss of control continue as core difficulties. In ongoing recovery, some individuals are able to incorporate a belief in their inability to control or change the parent but they cannot transfer the concept to their relationships with others. Two group members illustrated this dilemma:

> I know you cannot tolerate my style and I know as soon as I speak you will attack, belittling me and calling me weak. But I keep trying. I just can't give up the idea that somehow I can get you to see me differently, like me, or at least have a dialogue. I can't believe I really can't change your view of me.

The individual speaking had great difficulty with the notion of powerlessness and his inability to control others. The person he couldn't control struggled with his need for control as well, but the focus was different. The latter could not relinquish or alter his all-or-none view of the world. There were good guys and bad, winners and losers, and strong and weak. The goal in life is to be able to separate the good from the bad, the strong from the weak; to identify with the winners and reject categorically the losers.

In the group, the two repeated their patterns of relationship without resolution although both were intellectually able to understand the dilemma. But cognitive awareness preceeded affective integration and change. Eventually Harvey could see that his persistent belief in his ability to get Ted to like him was just like his efforts with his father. Ultimately Ted could see that his categorical view of the world protected him against recognition of deep feelings of need and rage and a fear of becoming the bad, weak loser if he stopped warding it off.

In ongoing recovery, group members more firmly create a new identity as an ACA with the processes of reconstruction and new construction underway. Individuals can now begin to explore the deeper, unknown meaning of being the child of an alcoholic as well as other unconscious beliefs, attitudes and values. Individuals involved in self-help and 12-step recovery programs acquire a new language of recovery that structures behavior change and cognitive and affective expansion (Brown, 1985; Lewis, 1977; Santostefano, 1980). A language of recovery, including the term codependence, provides a sense of order and consensual validation. There is now a vocabulary to describe and validate what was previously denied.

Many find within the 12-step programs of ACA, Al-Anon, and AA a structure for focusing exploration and attribution on the self. Through the relinquishment of control, individuals learn repeatedly that the only persons they can control are themselves and that that control is paradoxical. The belief in control over self is also relinquished with control "turned over" to a higher power. Central to the work of ongoing recovery for individuals involved in 12-step programs is the construction and maturation of a personal philosophy or belief in and relationship with a higher power.

THE PROCESS OF TREATMENT

From the viewpoint of the integration of behavioral, cognitive, and dynamic therapies with systems and developmental theories, core issues and problems in the past and the present emerge as themes in the group and within the transference. Themes arising in early recovery—attachment, loss, trust, perception, autonomy, identity formation, separation—reappear. In the context of a developing "family transference," deep beliefs structured early in development and the behaviors and defenses utilized to maintain and support them are challenged.

This uncovering and reenactment occurs within the frame of a deepening and expanding cognitive and affective awareness. The core defenses still frame and order the deepening process. These defenses must be challenged in the deepening process and particularly in the process of integrating what was denied or warded off cognitively and affectively. In the advanced group, this work takes place within the thematic framework of relationships and with exploration of transference relationships in the here-and-now.

Thus the process of recovery in the long-term therapy group involves the establishment of a transference relationship which provides the structure for the reenactment and exploration of core beliefs and behavior patterns, the expansion of cognition and affect, and the challenge of defenses. The three processes reciprocally reinforce each other (Bandura, 1985). In this chapter, we will examine these tasks from two perspectives: first, within the framework and process of behavioral, cognitive, and affective expansion, and second, within the context of the interactional focus of the group.

The Process of Expansion: The Loosening of Controls

As noted, a core feature of the process of ongoing recovery is behavioral, cognitive, and affective expansion achieved by incorporating the realities of the past and present into one's view of self and challenging core beliefs about the self as well. The process of expansion is a part of all human growth. For ACAs this is difficult because it requires a loosening of controls in order to be able to expand one's frame to incorporate a wider range and flexibility of both perception and affect. Defenses are intensified because the perceived danger from the outside and the inside heightens the need for control. This highlights the significance of the interaction of the system and the individual—the early environment, the what it was like—to the process of treatment. External danger from the environment and the need for safety are constants. Thus the tension of the expansion and uncovering process is severe and the emphasis on control a constant.

These processes reciprocally influence one another (Bandura, 1985; Mahoney, 1977). Cognitive and affective expansion both facilitate and are facilitated by the uncovering and challenging of core beliefs (Rosen, 1985; Guidano & Liotti, 1983). Thus the break in denial and the reconstruction of the realities of one's past are a necessary foundation for new construction and healthy maturation in the present.

Behavioral Expansion

The process of expansion occurs on many levels from concrete behavioral change to shifts in unconscious perception and core belief. Both the structure and the process of the group reflect these changes. Once attachment to the group is secured, members can begin to challenge and expand their behavioral, cognitive and affective range. The following is an example of expansion at the behavioral level:

> Betsy realized she had taken Carl's regular seat and offered to change places. Carl accepted, stating again how important it was to him to have the stability of the point of view represented by this same seat as he explored new ideas and feelings. Carl described his life-long attempts to be different from his father in order to define a separate identity and "base" in his family. He was good in science and math—subjects in which his father did not excel—as another way of defining his differences. A constant place in the group gives him a similar kind of defined difference, safety and predictability. The one chair gives Carl a certain point of view which he has grown to like. The risk of changing seats carries with it the imagined threat of losing his new found ability to feel and express himself.

Several months later Carl chose another seat. To everyone's surprise, he noted:

> I feel like it's time to take a look at things from a different perspective.

Another group member, Paul, experimented with a new behavior that was inconsistent with his beliefs about commitment.

> Paul suffered great distress as Tony got up and walked out of the meeting. Paul maintained that Tony had broken the ground rules. Members were to give the group high importance, show up and not leave. Tony's departure and the therapist's refusal to run after him jolted Paul.

Paul could imagine only two alternatives to disagreeing—violence or leaving the group forever. Tony was gone and he would not be back. It reminded him of his father who abruptly blew up and stormed out of the house. Nothing could ever be talked about or resolved.

At the next meeting the therapist reported to the group that Paul had called to say he would be absent because of a "conflicting appointment." Group members joked that Paul was putting something else ahead of the group. Paul returned and, over the next few weeks, explored the impact of his decision to miss a group.

I was certain I would never be back if I once decided not to come. Commitment is forever. It's all or none. But that's not what happened. I still felt like a member of the group and I had no trouble coming back.

Experimenting with a new behavior and challenging his belief facilitated his deepening exploration of issues of attachment and autonomy. He longed for a close, committed relationship but felt that having one meant losing himself. Being able to choose to miss a group meeting opened up the possibility of a wider range of interactions within a relationship that would still signify commitment.

A final example of behavior change related to expansion involves the issue of dress. Ken often came to group in a suit and tie which others saw as a statement that he was closed, arrogant, and superior. Will, however, longed to be able to don a suit and tie— the symbol to him of becoming a man—and not lose sight of his feelings. One day he arrived at group wearing a suit, tie, and tennis shoes. He decided to "try it on" to see what it felt like. For much of the meeting he was guarded, still and wary. He explained that he was quite anxious and uncomfortable because he was afraid he would lose his "feeling side." He needed to monitor himself constantly to make sure he wasn't closing down. Losing his "feeling side" was not the only threat. Wearing a suit and tie equaled becoming a man which equaled becoming drunk, violent, and emotionally inaccessible. At the end of the meeting, he sighed, pleased that he had survived. He noted that the tennis shoes were a concrete reminder that he does have feelings (just in case he forgot).

Cognitive and Affective Expansion

Dreams play an important role for members individually in expanding their cognitive and affective awareness. They also play an important role within the process of the group, often indicating a loosening of controls.

After many weeks of difficult interactions in the group with members feeling stuck and unequal in the "pace" of their uncovering work, several reported dreams.

In Brent's dream, he was being pushed and challenged by the group about his "surface" responses and his denial of any feelings. He finally told others to shut up and leave him alone. To his amazement, they did and he began to cry. He was astounded that he could defend himself and that others would listen to him.

After Brent related the dream, he told others how relieved he was to know that deep down he does feel. The content of his dreams—the criticism of others and his ability to protect himself—illuminated the source of his fears in the group. He felt defenseless in the face of hostility and criticism from others. Following this dream, he began a more open exploration of his memories and his transference interactions with others in the group which centered on his constant sense of danger.

The themes of belonging and safety are also related to expansion and the loosening of controls. Following weeks of struggle in the group, several members reported dreams:

WENDY: I was huddled up in a corner freezing in the snow. Then it slowly changed to mud.

PAULA: I've been afraid to read the summary these last few weeks because I was afraid it would be full of negative judgments. I did read it and saw it was neutral. Then I dreamed I wrote my own summary and reported it to the group. I was amazed that I could write my own view of what happened here.

A NEWER MEMBER CHUCKLED: I'm not there yet. I dreamed I was swallowed up in a tornado the night before the group.

Frank never dreamed and never felt and was frequently amazed at the others' capacity for emotion. After many months in group, Frank said he had a dream and everyone cheered.

I saw my father as helpless, embraced him and cried. It was at an earlier time in my life. I woke up and had all the feelings I must have felt back then. I felt like I belonged to the group finally and that there really is a depth of feeling I have absolutely no conscious access to.

Dreams are also a gauge of progress defined individually. In group interactions, Katie frequently focused on her feelings of powerlessness and helplessness in the face of others' dominance and control. To be involved with others, especially to allow oneself to rely on others, was equal to insuring destruction. After several years in group, Katie reported the following dreams:

> I was riding in a car with my mother driving. She was drunk and missed a turn. I yelled at her to pull over so I could take over. This was a sign to me that I have more control than I think and I can take care of myself when I'm involved with others.

> In another dream, my husband is drinking and wants my attention. I simply told him I was busy and would pay attention when I was ready. Can you imagine? I really am improving in my ability not to get caught up in taking care of others.

Another example of the loosening of controls and the significance of dreams is related in the following. For several weeks members talked about anger abstractly, accenting their fear of it in others and themselves. Matthew then related a dream:

> I was participating in a boxing match that was restricted by a screen between the fighters with only a small opening through which the hands could go.

Group members chuckled at the image and the external conditions of control necessary in order to experiment with greater feeling. Later on in the group, Matthew gingerly challenged another member. He and others recognized he was trying out his "boxing" in the group.

Feelings

The processes of expansion of cognition and affect, including the challenge of belief and defense, are also reflected around issues of feelings. The following example focused around themes of attachment, boundaries, and autonomy.

When he first joined, Dan struggled with a sense that any "feeling" would be equal to the loss of himself. But it was a desire to feel and to connect the split-off parts of himself that brought him to treatment. In his early months, Dan couldn't recognize or label a feeling. Later he could, but confined his expression to intellectual description. After several years, Dan surprised himself and others by violating his own code of less expressive behavior. With the announced departure of a "soul-mate" in group, Dan reached out to hold her hand for a brief period. Later he realized that he could spontaneously go ahead and express his feelings without "fusing" himself to her or the rest of the group. He could feel and maintain a sense of his independent self.

A few weeks later, the whole group spoke about the pain involved in changing. They had envied Dan and felt embarrassed at the same time watching him. They now spoke about the process of change:

> Progress in this group feels like going backwards. I can intellectually see that growth requires expanding the range of what I feel but it also feels horribly out of control and awful.

The notion of "splits" was raised in another group in similar fashion. Rick is two separate personalities which he believes should be split. One is the person in the grey suit whom he presents to the world. The other is the person in group who has feelings which he allows himself and others to see. Rick is frightened that the two might be one and the same. He acts as if feelings might slip out on any occasion if he is not in careful control.

Gary marvels at the notion of splits. His emotions are a constant part of him, not separate at all. In fact, his emotions get him into trouble. He would value a middle ground—less guarded, suspicious, and volatile but it means altering his basic view of the world and letting others in.

Members recognized in retrospect that there was an unusual feel to the meeting that day. They were exploring new territory, revealing new information and testing the impact. In this gingerly, tentative process of revelation, members glimpsed a middle ground they could only imagine previously. A few weeks later, Will reported that he had done an amazing thing:

> I empathized with a colleague. It felt good to me and phoney, like I see Gary doing. But it was very effective in opening our discussion. Soon I began to worry about whether I could control the degree of intimacy. Would I be able to stop the other person from talking too much or revealing too much?

Bonnie, long frightened about revealing herself, sighed:

> Good for you Will. But I don't know. The act of talking seems out of control. I found myself very open with dinner guests and wondered why I was revealing so much. I watched myself in amazement because it felt so out of control.

Ken, a member whose absence of affect was a source of chronic irritation to others noted:

> I always thought my feelings were in my head and that's
> what I describe. Now I know my sweaty palms and the
> numbing in my stomach are pertinent to what I'm feeling.

Still, the issue of his lack of affect and lack of empathy was a
continuing theme. Members were upset because he was too vague
and always just slightly tipped to the side of uninvolvement. As
the group deepened its feelings, Ken was more likely to wonder
"what's the big deal?" Ken was actually disturbed but didn't
know how to show it differently.

> This is the story of my life. I was always cut-off from friends.
> There are huge unknown, unexplained parts of myself. I
> have trouble here in group simply because I can't remember
> what it was like. I do feel a pretty chronic sense of loss. But I
> don't have the memories to be more concrete.

Group members actively challenged Ken about his guardedness in group hoping he could begin to allow himself a greater
variety of feeling and experience in the present. They also hoped
to feed him "mental pictures" so he could identify and start
remembering.

While Ken felt he was making progress, the group stayed focused on his under-reaction and minimal range of response. Ken
noted that he was afraid of being like his mother who was manipulative, wearing different "faces" to achieve her ends and frequently
"out of control." His narrow range of affect and lack of responsiveness to others reflected his protection against the threat of manip-
ulation and of being manipulative and out of control himself.

In another group which was deepening the level and intensity
of its cognitive and affective exploration, a member's refusal to
empathize became a serious issue for others. One spoke on the
group's behalf:

> It's difficult for us to continue to dig when you refuse to feel at
> all and deny that you could feel any pain at all. Why are you
> here? The experience of being in group has been painful. I've
> reopened memories and feelings from childhood—things I
> couldn't feel then growing up in a disturbed family. I was so
> controlled and responsible for everyone else my emotions
> were unavailable. It's OK with me if you can't empathize with
> what I'm feeling but it's not OK that you feel superior because
> of it. I grew up with that. I don't need it here.

Another group, together for a longer period of time, explored the threat of expansion in relation to boundaries, control, and the threat of a middle ground. After several weeks of opening up without moving back to a defensive stance, two members waved to one another after the meeting. Sally waved a second time but Matt did not return it. The following week they explored the meaning of these actions:

> Matt explained that he felt scared when Sally waved a second time. It was OK to wave once because that was in the "boundaries" of the group. But it was not OK to wave a second time because that was outside the "boundary." Matt realized he had felt open and vulnerable with Sally in the group that day. On leaving, he carried the same feelings. He realized that the openness of feeling equalled sexuality. It was OK in the group because the limits are prescribed. But it's not safe outside. He also recognized that he expects the other person to set the limits. But Sally did not. Her second wave meant a loss of control for Matt if he returned it. It would be equal to sexual expression and their open relationship in the group would be destroyed. With further exploration, Matt realized he felt exactly the same about anger. He cannot express any or it will lead to violence. Matt realized he has little sense of small steps. The thought is equal to the act and he is always potentially out of control. Now he questioned: "does any feeling automatically have sex or violence attached?"

Roles and Structure

Expansion in cognitive and affective range, the challenge of belief and the challenge of defense also occur in relation to changes in role or structure inside the group and out.

Bonnie had always achieved a strong sense of identity, well-being, and purpose as a helping professional. But she also found herself more and more limited in making autonomous decisions and in career advancement. After much deliberation and anxiety, she decided to give up her profession.

> I need lots of attention today and "good mothering" from the group. My profession has given me a positive structure and a sense of well being that I am also giving up. In letting go of this security, I am opening myself to unknown feelings and a new sense of myself. I want to stop feeling responsible for others and taking care of others. I want to take energy for myself. I feel like it's time to be a "clumsy

adolescent" exploring myself and the world within the safety of a supportive family.

Not long after this decision, Bonnie reported that she was now reading about ACAs and considering going to Al-Anon.

> I couldn't read before or listen to others in meetings because the more I learned the more I felt responsible for everyone.

Over several months in the group, she struggled to hold onto her new, more vulnerable, sense of herself as an adolescent. But it was hard.

> I feel hurt to see Paula be insightful because that was my role in here for so long. But as the group observer, I paid a price because I never felt like I was taking care of my own needs. I'm now more involved with my own feelings and the parts of myself I don't like. I also feel more confused and inarticulate so it's hard to see Paula praised for these qualities. I have to remind myself that these changes are important for me and that I'm making progress because it feels like I've lost a great deal.

Bonnie joined the group because she was terribly concerned about her inability to tolerate an intimate, committed relationship with a man. She had achieved a sense of stability by constructing a narrow environment which she could also always control. She longed for more but always became anxious and depressed at the possibility of a closer relationship. Bonnie became aware of her need for control and the limits of the narrow world she constructed when she joined a singles group.

> It is wonderful and awful. I have lost my "mooring" and my identity by getting out of my usual structure. I am attracted to a man and have let myself feel dependent on him, even though I am constantly scared to death. This is an amazing experience. I realize I want to let myself be more dependent and give up control with a man but I fear I'll be hurt. I am opening up many feelings I haven't had in my adult life because I've so carefully constructed my environment. I have to get away from my careful control to realize how frightened I am. I've been having a lot of nightmares as well and recognize I was terrified as a child, something I am never aware of as an adult.

Several years later, Bonnie, now living with someone, reflected on the changes she had made.

> It's incredible that I could tolerate living with someone, much less learn to deal with his unpredictability, mood changes, wishes and needs. I feel naked, establishing a new identity for myself. I've changed the way I look and am coming to a completely different view of myself. It's like I've opened up the half of me I always had to deny. The world seems bigger and richer though still scary. But I can share my own experiences more fully and those of friends without having to feel responsible for anyone.

The relinquishment of a "structure" that has provided security and identity was also experienced by a member who decided to move. As soon as the decision was made, she became frightened, anxious, and sad.

> I am moving out of the structure by which I have defined myself. The house allows me to stay attached to my family and is a mediator at the same time. I have built that house and nurtured it to parent me back which it does. I feel comfortable and safe in that home like I've never felt before.

Members now spoke more abstractly about the false structure of defenses which also provided definition but severely limited them as well. At the top of the list was control.

Control

The issue of control is a constant through the entire process of recovery. It is a theme, a defensive structure and, indeed, the hub of the wheel around which developmental issues are examined or reexperienced. Thus the focus on control is often a central factor in the process of expansion.

The threat of loss of control and the threat of expansion are linked to the issue of spontaneity of feelings and range of behavior. Brad reported with amazement a deep, ongoing sense of fear on behalf of his cat.

> I am constantly watching to make sure my cat doesn't get out of the house. I'm certain something terrible will happen if she wanders out.

Prodded by others, Brad drew a parallel to his own sense of fear in the group.

> I guess it is a metaphor because I am really frightened in here. I'm afraid to let my feelings out "baldly", just as they are, without first having a conceptual framework to explain them. I can't risk experiencing an unknown feeling because something bad will happen.

Brad and others could see that the fear of spontaneity and loss of control were related to a recent "calamity" in the group. An unpredictable disagreement occurred in which people had hurt feelings. Exploration revealed basic differences that could not be resolved. Initially members agreed that it is better to stay shut down and "in control." Vulnerability, spontaneity, and open exploration will result in disaster.

The need for a "conceptual frame" is a common theme throughout the work of the group. It is often expressed as a wish for rules or a map which will chart the course for uncovering. The "rules" or "map" provide a false reassurance that nothing surprising or out-of-control will emerge. This illusion of security quickly vanishes as the group deepens its uncovering process and members experience anxiety. The lack of a rule or an explanation alerts members to the reality of unknown feelings and memories yet to be recalled.

> There's a dark pit down there that seems bottomless. I know I have to look but I resist. For the time being I need to stay on top and scan it with a flashlight.

The prospect of opening the "pit," the hole or the "sack of shit" is recognized by many as the core of their work in group. Yet they unconsciously and automatically invoke the safety of "incremental risk" to reassure themselves of their ultimate control. Despite the strength of defenses developed to cope, the slightest hint of feeling or chip in the "pit" feels like total loss of control.

Ben could stand only so much building of emotion in the group before he began to joke. Others knew by now that Ben was feeling overwhelmed and asked him directly what was distressing him.

> I can hardly sit still when Bob cries in here because he looks just like my father when he was drunk and slobbering. I do value the feelings in here and I want them for myself but I can only take a certain amount.

The process of change as one of "incremental risk" was demonstrated by a group member who spoke of her spontaneous decision to "set aside a preconceived idea."

> I found out a party I attended was a birthday celebration and I had not brought a gift. At first I was very upset but decided to enjoy myself anyway. Simple but amazing. Before I would have continued to feel awful and shrunk from social contact the whole night.

Continuing, she shifted levels:

> You know, I wish deeply to change but to do so radically is to betray others or be too aggressive. I stopped drinking but it was too radical so I started again. Alcohol is a buffer. I want to feel more but to do so is painful and out of control. Alcohol moderates uncontrollable feelings.

The possibility of loss of control over the uncovering process is often expressed in discussions of "pace" in the here-and-now of the group.

> The pace of things has been too intense in here over the last several weeks. It feels spontaneous, frightening and out of control. Suddenly the group reminds me of my family and I am overwhelmed by a sense that something could go wrong at any moment.

The process of cognitive and affective expansion is, for most people, carefully titrated by their own defenses although members have difficulty recognizing or trusting these mechanisms. On the other side is the dawning awareness that defenses may reappear to interfere with the consolidation of insights or feelings into one's new view of self. Polly explored her continuing guardedness from this vantage point:

> I am afraid of slipping back into my angry, distorted attitudes and perceptions. I feel like my guard is in the service of allowing myself to stay open and attentive to others. I don't want to lose the new ground I've worked so hard to grasp.

Following a period of great expansion and change in attitude, Marci felt herself losing ground but could not explain it. Another member offered this observation:

> Ever since you started going out with your new boyfriend you've been adjusting your life to fit what you believe is necessary for him. That's the old codependent position. You've stopped going to Al-Anon and lost your new identity and foundation of recovery. You're back to shaping your behavior according to what you think will please him. I can see it in group too. You've gotten more defensive again and shifted the focus of exploration off yourself.

In addition to expanding one's own range of cognition and affect, individuals also expand their range of reaction and response to others which is often just as difficult and anxiety provoking. The group setting and the here-and-now provide a framework for altering interpersonal patterns of attention and response.

Several members spoke about feeling very depressed and bad about themselves today. Joe asked others not to try to "fix" him in case anyone had an urge to jump in.

> I realize that I need to feel rotten today and the group needs to let me without getting into a dispute or attempting to convince me that I'm really a good person.

Others refrained from challenging Joe and the group "hung" in an atmosphere of depression. Jack spoke about his difficulty resisting the pull to cheer everyone up:

> It's hard to sit still. I run the risk of feeling just as bad and depressed as everyone else because I identify and understand so readily. It reminds me of being around my depressed, drunken mother. If I couldn't fix it up, I was always in danger of getting dragged in.

EXPANSION AND CHALLENGE WITHIN THE INTERACTIONAL FOCUS OF THE TRANSFERENCE

Transference and the Value of Group

In our earlier papers (Cermak & Brown, 1982; Brown & Beletsis, 1986), we looked at key themes within the context of group therapy. We also focused on the value of group therapy for the supportive work of early recovery and the uncovering work of ongoing recovery. The support involves bonding through acquisition of the label ACA, the sharing of experiences past and present related to parental drinking, the validation of perception, and the giving of advice, often centering on ways to approach a drinking parent or a problematic relationship in the present.

Uncovering involves the process of expanding one's behavior, perception, and affect, and challenging beliefs and defenses as I have just outlined. It also involves a re-creation of early interpersonal experiences through the development of what we have called a "family transference." With time and stability of membership in the group, individuals will begin to behave and to view others in a manner similar to their behavior, perceptions, and beliefs in their first families. The long-term interactional ACA group provides the setting to uncover and discover these behaviors and beliefs from the past and ultimately challenge their validity in the present.

Exploration of the transference involves linking the past with the present to illuminate and clarify the maladaptive beliefs and coping strategies that helped individuals survive in a traumatic environment. These beliefs, behaviors, defenses, and coping strategies were also the bricks and mortar of attachment and identity formation as outlined earlier.

The codependent position is implicitly one of reaction and response *to another*. It is thus inherently and fundamentally interpersonal. So too are attachment, the development of self and identity formation conceived in relation to primary others. As I have spelled out, one's definition of self is heavily influenced by the predominance of parental alcoholism as an organizing principle and by the dictates of the environment and the individuals within required to cope with it.

Because of the dominance of the interpersonal adaptations and focus, group therapy is a powerful means to re-create the early environment and focus the work of therapy on interpersonal uncovery and exploration. I have used clinical material from the long-term groups throughout the book and will now focus particularly on the interactional nature of the transference and its role in the long-term process of change and recovery. The same core issues—defenses and developmental themes—that structured the work of the group throughout treatment reappear. Wendy illustrated with the issue of denial.

The Challenge of Defense within the Transference

Wendy identified with how much energy it takes to deny. Last week in group, she heard what she was really thinking and feeling for the first time as the words came tumbling out of her mouth. She also was frightened, feeling suddenly out of control. This break-through followed months of defensive, angry insistence that group members were trying to control her. She had insisted that the group would accept only certain aspects of her, that they wanted no part of her anger, sadness, or needs. She had always felt con-trolled by others' fear of her. In the group, Wendy "arranged" a situation to prove this assumption.

> She expressed her anger outright at several members who resisted and then became angry in return. Wendy increased her control and rigidity telling others that they had just verified how really unacceptable she is by getting angry at her in return.

> Members quickly challenged her, suggesting that she made it hap-pen and that she is really afraid of herself. Wendy then recalled scribbling on the wall of her room as a child, bitter and angry. She used to dissociate entirely from her action, denying to her parents that she had done it. Wendy now speculated that she is afraid she is really just like her parents deep down—violent and destructive. Her emotions are so close to the surface she must be constantly on guard and even brittle, lest they all spill out.

In this example, Wendy illustrated the dominance of her de-fensive adjustment, her projection or "transference" of motive or intention onto others, the challenge by the group and the opening of the past that had been warded off.

Louise offered another example around the issue of interaction and control.

> Louise feels ill and upset today. She feels repeatedly frustrated in her efforts to be a part of the group. She doesn't seem to "get it" and is challenged when she participates. Interaction is perceived as a denial of her needs. Interaction means she must become pas-sive and attentive to the others. So she provides no invitation for feedback or exchange with others. Feedback in the present equals criticism: She is not doing something right.

After long exploration of her difficulty interacting, Louise rec-ognized that she approaches people with a belief that she is not worthy of their attention and therefore it is extremely risky to hear what others have to say. It is safe to help others. So she lets her own feelings build, solves her problems herself and then periodically reports to the group. She gets nothing back but has no concept that she is missing anything.

> A state of "interaction" involves a lessening of control and is very threatening. When I'm involved with other people, I automatically feel helpless and criticized and respond from that framework.

As the weeks passed, Louise experimented with greater inter-action, loosening her control and "reporting" approach. With the shift came feelings of confusion, disorientation, and anxiety.

The individual in the next example also reached a point at which he could explore his interactions within the group, again centered first on the dominance of his defense.

> Gary is always wary, automatically assessing his environment. He must be careful not to get trapped by anyone so that he makes a mistake, breaks a rule, or humiliates himself. Thus, in any interaction, he always precedes a direct response with a defensive explanation so he does not get caught.

It took many months in group for Gary to realize that there was anything problematic about his world view. In the group, he recognized that he approached everyone with suspicion and an expectation that he will be betrayed. Gary began to trace his interactions with others and ultimately could see how he generated hostility by his own defensive stance. People respond to him with fear, suspicion, and their own defensiveness.

As Gary deepened his exploration he found a core belief:

> I have always distrusted everyone of high social status. It is not new, just a part of how I see the world. It's funny though, when I first came to group, I decided that everyone here was upper class. Obviously that belief affected everything I saw and thought about the group.

Cory illustrated her use of the group to uncover a deep belief and interaction patterns that stem from it.

> Cory finally sees that her patterns with the new member, Sally, are very similar to her interactions with her parents. Cory applies the

same level of importance and intensity she experiences with her family to all people regardless of the relationship. A stranger thus has the same level of importance and power to reject her. Cory realizes she never developed close relationships with anybody outside of her family so she never developed a sense of any "in between." There is only the close family level. Now, in group, she is stunned as she recognizes how intensely she feels about someone she doesn't know.

I have referred several times throughout the book to the "arrival of a new member," an incident in the life of the group that is always important, typically difficult, and frequently a source of great anxiety for the old group members as much as the new. In the stable advanced group, a new person may be welcomed with little regression or defensiveness demonstrated by old members. Such ease of entry is infrequent because the advanced group has challenged its members' defenses and individuals now function with characteristic openness and vulnerability. The new member, still well defended, is seen as a strong threat.

The following examples illustrate the power of the new member, like the power of an alcoholic parent, to be viewed as dominant, a source of danger and control, and to set in motion a defensive response. In the examples, members react to the newcomer's actual behavior. But, in fact, power and dominance are often attributed to the new person and a defensive posture invoked *before* the individual joins the group. The unknown new person is seen as dominate, dangerous, controlling, needy, manipulative, and out of control.

The new member feels there is nothing she can do to gain approval but she keeps trying to gain admittance. The group says "no" in various ways.

After several weeks, the therapist wondered why the group was not asking itself what was going on. Members were engaged in a process of excluding Debbie no matter what she said or did. Debbie perceived the group as actively hostile towards her although members maintained they were simply protecting themselves. Ultimately the group began to explore the subtleties of the patterns of their interactions. Mitch spoke:

> Debbie needs to be the "driver." I try to maintain the open level we've established and she asks questions about rules. I feel cut-off and the whole level of feeling shifts. Debbie reminds me of what I was like when I joined and I don't want to fall back into that pattern.

Paul spoke with emotion:

> As a result of this group, I have come to understand that things can develop slowly and that I might just be capable of a close relationship. But it's important for us not to determine a particular course for the group or for our relationships in here ahead of time. Debbie, your behavior pulls for this: jump in, organize and set up the rules. Then you can't see what's underneath or what might be possible by letting things be.

The group then discussed the issue of control. Debbie wondered who would invite her in or if she would have to nudge her way. Members agreed that they felt controlled by her so they were unwilling to extend her a direct invitation. Their hostile rejection seemed a necessary protection.

The group continued their defensive interactions for weeks. The impasse was loosened in a ritual of interaction that occurred before each meeting.

Members gathered together on a bench before each meeting. Debbie always arrived slightly later and chose a seat on another bench, separate from the others. Group members had thought about going to sit with her but realized such a move would be equal to deserting their membership in the group and their new beliefs. One day Debbie decided to follow Paul to the other bench. In the group, she became quieter and was able to hear that her aggressive, controlling style was not valued and, in fact, members were trying very hard *not* to be that way. Ultimately Debbie examined her refusal to perceive the group norms while she had continued to insist that she was being rejected.

During the course of these events, members stayed in the present, focusing on their interactions and responses to Debbie in the "here-and-now." But they also spoke about the familiarity of their feelings and later explored the transference aspects of their reaction to her. As Paul noted:

> It was all I could do to sit still and shut you out. You reminded me so much of my mother who was always running every thing and covering everything up as well. She was always "driving."

The focus on control, the all-or-none cognitive frame and the sense of responsibility are enduring defenses that ultimately must be challenged in the course of the advanced group's work. Ultimately, these defenses are at the heart of members' continuing difficulties with interpersonal relationships. Without challenging these defenses in the here-and-now, members can only speculate about loosening control, developing a middle ground or neutrality in relationships. Members must experiment with these concepts in reality to actively alter the dominant structural function of the defenses. The entry of a new member into an advanced group once again highlights these issues:

> The central theme today, as it has been for weeks, was the issue of control. Throughout the meeting, there was a chronic sense of hostile tension and taut emotions. Angie spelled out her dilemma:
>
>> Whoever has the floor has all the control and everyone else must actively resist or get sucked in. I tried to welcome Gina but she wouldn't respond with the same level of vulnerability and openness. I know she's just come and is all defended but I felt cut-off and unheard by her. Why should I stay open and accessible to her only to be misunderstood?

Gina felt more and more rejected and increased her attempts to "get it right" by talking more. Others pointed out her obvious need for control and her lack of insight. Gina grew more anxious:

> I feel like a bull in a china shop. I keep knocking things over and can do nothing right.

The group constantly focused on control with members feeling the issue in all-or-none terms. Gina is seen as "in charge" when she is speaking and others must continue to withdraw. Angie needs to see her as "wrong" in order to stay outside of any interaction with her. Quickly the group was paralyzed. There was an enemy, a new person, who kept taking control. Older members, now less well defended, felt greatly endangered, very much like children who have no control over parents. The only choices are passive and active aggression, rejection, or withdrawal. There is a right and wrong, a good and bad, and nothing in between. Any empathy opens the possibility for total loss of self to the other's point of view.

Following the intensity, paralysis, and struggle, group members shifted to an abstract level. They wondered whether it is possible to experience greater vulnerability and deeper feeling if others do not come along. Are relationships all or nothing? Can you move closer? Can you control the distance? Can you tolerate such difference and variability? How can you ever trust?

Finding a middle ground remains a major focus of the group's work throughout ongoing recovery as the following example illustrated.

The group discussed several themes today: boundaries, limits, seeking and developing intimate relationships while not being intrusive or rejected. Members were searching among themselves for cues and clues as to how to find the middle ground. Carrie said she wants people to be responsive and sensitive to her needs at the particular time. Sometimes she wants a hug and sometimes she doesn't. Others in the group laughed noting how difficult it is to read Carrie. Most members agreed that they are too worried about making a mistake with her—misreading the cues—so refrain from extending themselves at all.

The group continued its discussion. Carrie said she operates on the basic belief that she comes from a "bad" family which means she has no idea what normal behavior is or what constitutes intimacy so she is always guessing herself. Whenever she is uncomfortable she automatically assumes she must be behaving inappropriately.

Some defenses seem minor and therefore are by-passed or neglected in explanations of events and reactions. In fact, "minor" defenses often cover major problems or central issues. Rick illustrated with tardiness:

For the first time in months Rick came early and joined other members outside just before the meeting. In the group he asked members to explain their well established perception of him as having one foot out the door. This notion had never made sense to Rick and he had never been able to appreciate the significance of his tardiness to others. Rick believed that coming late was important only for the first five minutes of the group while others insisted that it affected his entire participation. He always was behind, having to catch up or explain himself so he was never seen or felt to be a key member, initiator or "starter."

Rick began to come on time and experienced great anxiety. Soon he realized that coming just a few minutes late protected him from having to initiate, an action he felt as too competitive and aggressive. Action also signified an identification with his violent, loud and out of control father. Coming late was a protection of himself and others.

When Defenses Hold

Over the course of the long-term group, members come to agree that a key feature of their work involves challenging the defenses that have served so well. Yet such challenge is fraught with fear. Members have reached a point at which they can recognize the limitations in their defensive style and indeed, understand that many of their most enduring intrapersonal and interpersonal problems stem from their defenses. But they cannot yet step out of the frame that has provided a limited sense of safety, a feeling of belonging and, for many, the only sense of self possible.

The course of recovery is often stalled or ultimately halted entirely by the threat of defensive challenge. It may be quite possible to comprehend abstractly the deep beliefs or attachments protected by the defenses, while it is not feasible to challenge or alter them. In such a case, the group becomes bound by the defensive struggles of one member or the defensive block of the group as a whole. Will, a group member for several years, continued to feel constricted by his narrow range of affect, spontaneity, and perception. He was dominated in group and in his closest relationships by a preoccupation with control and an unrelenting perception of others as dangerous and potentially intruding on his autonomy.

As the group moved deeper and deeper into challenging their defenses, Will became increasingly anxious and stalled. He was tardy, absent, and withdrawn from group. Ultimately he decided to leave, but not before examining his decision to maintain his defenses.

> Will spoke today in terms of "promises" and "forevers" which fits snuggly into his all or none view. He and the group looked closely at that frame, or sense of structure, that literally gives meaning to his life and to him. It is the all-or-none frame of battle with another. There's going to be a winner and a loser. The other person is out to get Will, to mess with his mind, or impose an agenda. Life, and his sense of being, is tied to the battle. He feels very threatened and anxious if there is a conclusion, if someone wins or loses.

> Will realizes that if he stayed in group, he would have to look at his drinking which he is still not ready to do and to his relationship with the therapist, both dominated by his categorical all or none frame. Will noted:

> I "wrote my mother off" long ago, clearly an all-or-none decision. It worked well to reduce my anxiety but I've also begun to feel it reduces the range of my opportunities.

Will now spoke about his concern that he is deceiving himself. He has always relied only on his own input and decision making and has missed important benefits and choices by doing so. He views the world in a way that always fits with his own perspective. Thus he never has to challenge his own premises or his own denial.

Will continued to speak about his defenses, recognizing that he is bound by them as much as they protect him. It is a core dilemma. He has little room for flexibility or range in perception or emotion. Everything is interpreted through the filter of battle, of win or lose. Suddenly it feels terrifying. If he were to stay, his entire framework of defenses would be blown away.

He noted again that his "facade," or what he has come to think of as his defense, really is the only "self" he feels.

> I am a "house of cards." I've been able to tolerate pokes and nudges, pulling out a card here and there over time. But suddenly I feel overwhelmed and the threat of all the cards tumbling out at once is very real.

But Will is beginning to think that he might miss something really important about himself.

> I feel like a stubborn kid who is digging my heels in. I'm going to miss taking the leap that would actually provide me with so much more.

Group members commented about how hard it is for children of alcoholics to struggle with issues of control or to ask anybody for help. They always had to solve problems on their own as kids so why should they ask for help as adults.

In working with recovering alcoholics, we (Brown & Yalom, 1977) characterized the process of uncovering as one of "cyclotherapy," a process of "fits and starts" with greater or more abrupt retreat a part of the normal flow. I characterized the work of ongoing recovery for alcoholics in a similar fashion (Brown, 1977), with cognitive and affective expansion regulated by the strength of the new identity as an alcoholic. New insights are often preceded by a brief return to familiar defenses. This phenomenon of cyclical growth has long been recognized as a part of the normal process of psychotherapy and, indeed, of any process of change itself (Whitaker, 1953; Watzlawick et al., 1974).

Because of the dominance of defenses within the family and the resultant dominance of defenses in development of the self, the dominance of defenses often characterizes the process of group as well. A cohesive, deepening group finds itself stalled periodically as members consolidate new gains and strengthen the ground for further exploration. Such a defensive balance often re-creates the atmosphere of the original family with one or more members as the dominant "alcoholic"—angry, hostile, aggressive, controlling. Group members feel caught in an all-or-none struggle for control. Either they relinquish their view, beliefs, sense of control, and autonomy or they continue to defend, maintaining the group in a defensive cold war.

The group as a whole cannot resolve the dilemma nor can members continue in an opening, uncovering mode. The group goes on hold with members angry and defensive. In essence, the group has replicated the very essence of the family's struggle. They may recognize it and speak about it but they cannot break through it or by-pass it. Ironically, group members demonstrate to one another the survival function of their defenses within their first families. The preservation of autonomy required a defensive cover of the self. A hostile, mistrusting, defensive posture toward others was the only means of self preservation. A group that had experienced cohesion through the process of early recovery became stalled for many months as the prospect of deeper uncovering work loomed large. Members began to focus on their differences and find them intolerable. As expected, and indeed desired within the interactional model of group therapy, they transferred onto one another the same negative perceptions and beliefs that guided them in their relationships outside the group. However, the negative transference and the defenses held. Members could not step outside of the categorical frame of their self and world view to examine the bind. The cold war prevailed instead until members began to leave the group one by one.

Several group members remained, forming the base of a new group that did not replicate the angry defensive patterns of relationship. Months later they spoke about the differences:

> In the first group I reaffirmed my belief that empathy will just cause me problems and I needed to maintain the distance I

thought was a problem when I entered. Now I can see that group had become just like my family but none of us could see it. I adjusted to the unsafe, angry atmosphere that was pervasive for so long. I adjusted so much that it seemed normal and I couldn't pinpoint my anxiety as stemming from the lack of safety in here. It's only because this group is so different that I can see how locked in I was before.

Over the next few months, she explored the "transference" that she could not examine previously.

I realize that the environment and the feeling of being endangered are very significant to me. I wish it could be different but the reality is I'm very much affected by my sense of others' moods, behavior or potential anger. I have an ever present sense that if I speak or comment on what I see or feel, I'll be cut to the core. Then I would feel "not OK." The tension in here really was like my family. My mother used to explode in rages because of what I said.

As members reconstructed the reality of the group's long defensive struggle, they also spoke about the critical significance of having one's feelings and perceptions validated. Shirley concluded:

You know, I was virtually silent in here. I was completely dominated by my fear of speaking because of criticism from others. How did we hold it together for so long and why did we all keep coming?

Katie provides a final example of the power of defenses and their impact on interactions.

Katie was upset that Stephanie forgot to mention in the summary that she was late which she had done on purpose with great difficulty. Stephanie failed to note it reinforcing Katie's belief that she is not noticed by others or is even ignored.

Stephanie then examined why she had left it out. She is always aware of Katie's fear of intrusion. As a result, she unconsciously omitted a reference to Katie in the interest of not drawing attention to her which Katie might have felt as intrusive.

Others then examined how much protection they feel Katie needs. As a whole, members agreed that they consciously refrain from asking her questions or actively seeking her involvement so as not to intrude. Katie realized that she had quite successfully guaranteed her "autonomy" and "control" but also isolation and feelings of unimportance.

IN SUMMARY

In this chapter, we have examined the challenge of defense and the expansion in behavioral, cognitive, and affective range and experience that results. Through exploration of the transference in the interpersonal context of long-term interactional group psychotherapy, individuals examine distortions in perception, belief, affect, and behavior that were adaptive in their childhood families but now restrict them severely as adults.

In the final chapter, we will look at the whole from the vantage point of the individual ACA in treatment: What is progress?

Chapter 11

What Is Progress: Growing Up, Growing Out, and Coming Home

In this book, I have developed a theoretical and applied framework for viewing the development of psychopathology through childhood and the subsequent treatment for adults who grew up with an alcoholic parent. I emphasized the critical significance of integrating a systems point of view with developmental theory. I have relied heavily on the recent integrated formulations of cognitive-dynamic and developmental theories (Bowlby, 1980; Bowlby, 1985; Guidano & Liotti, 1983; Rosen, 1985) to develop a theory based on recognition of parental alcoholism as a central organizing principle in the family and the child's development of self. In Part One, I described the impact of the environment and the overwhelming dominance of defensive adjustment required in the family. Next, I examined the impact of the environment and the organizing principle of parental alcoholism on individual development accenting themes of attachment and identity formation. As Bowlby and Guidano and Liotti have suggested, psychopathology can be understood as a function of attachment and the demands of the individual and the system to maintain it. Thus I developed the core hypothesis of this book:

Attachment — early and ongoing — is based on denial of perception which results in denial of affect which together result in developmental arrests or difficulties. The core beliefs and patterns of behavior formed to sustain attachment and denial within the family then structure subsequent development of the self including cognitive, affective, and social development.

In the final part, I outlined a process of recovery, also strongly grounded in cognitive and developmental theory.

In lay terms, recovery is conceptualized as the process of "making real the past." It is a process of new knowledge construction, ordered again by the centrality of parental alcoholism, but this time to promote healthy maturation. It involves breaking denial and challenging beliefs and defenses—the very denial, beliefs, and defenses on which key attachments were formed.

The break in denial and the acquisition of the identity ACA are often experienced as a "second-order change" (Watzlawick et al., 1974). The new information and new identity bring a shift or transformation in the basic premises that structure knowledge about the self. Subsequent exploration and uncovery occur within the framework of a new set of beliefs or ordering schemas—in this case, the reality of parental alcoholism.

During the periods of transition and early recovery, much "progress" takes place as individuals uncover and reconstruct a past that now makes logical sense. There is relief and, for many, a heightened anxiety as well. Individuals recognize that ongoing progress and recovery involve a continuing "break" with the beliefs and interpersonal patterns of relationship that bound core attachments within the family. "Progress" in ongoing recovery involves challenging one's core *structure* of beliefs and defenses while still maintaining an attachment. Often members wonder how this can be possible. "Progress" involves reconstruction and new construction of a personal identity grounded in acceptance of the reality of parental alcoholism and it involves corresponding structural challenge and re-ordering.

In this final chapter, I will illustrate these theoretical concepts from group members' own discussions and assessment of what constitutes "progress."

WHAT IS PROGRESS

Prior to treatment and many times during treatment, individuals wonder what it is all about, what kinds of changes are possible, and how they will know when they are finished. Initially, members enter treatment with an idealized sense of what they want for themselves and from others. These early expectations reflect the impact of the environmental trauma present within the early family—the predominance of defensive adjustment necessary to cope in the family and the developmental difficulties experienced within the context of the pathological system, all organized around the centrality of parental alcoholism. Individuals conceive of change in a dichotomous fashion equating progress in treatment with reversal. Individuals hope to feel safe instead of frightened, anxious, and unsafe, good instead of bad, to be able to have needs instead of taking care of others' needs, to have a close, loving relationship with another who is responsive to those needs, to feel in control, to have feelings that are comprehensible and manageable, to make order out of chaos, and in essence, to live happily ever after. It takes hard work and time in treatment to recognize and comprehend the depth and complexity of the reconstruction and new construction processes that form the foundation for significant change that is far more than reversal. Indeed, members begin to *really* understand a concept of personal responsibility and the notion of "incremental risk" as they realize that expansion, challenge of beliefs and defenses, and changes in behavior come from within and that such changes are not possible without a safe context that reinforces the validity of the new identity as an ACA, the reconstructed reality of the past, and the intrapsychic and interpersonal experiences in the present.

Deep changes usually do not occur in a vacuum. They do not come as a "fix" from someone else and they are not the result of finding the right formula, manual or how-to guide. Deep change comes from within. For ACAs, the most significant change begins with the acquisition of the identity ACA. It proceeds with the reconstruction process of "making real the past" and the development of an autonomous sense of self from this new base.

Individuals are bound by the attachments, beliefs, and defenses constructed to maintain and survive a pathological family system. The process of recovery is a developmental one of challenge and separation from these pathological bonds. Initially, the promise of reconstruction, developmental repair, and ultimately emotional separation is experienced much more as a threat because it too is all-or-none. Growth is experienced from a lens of isolation and loneliness. The challenge of belief and defense and the expansion of cognitive and affective range initially carry a corresponding fear of abandonment. To step out of the family system, to challenge one's view of what happened then and now is equal to losing the attachment entirely.

Only with the long-term process of recovery do individuals begin to incorporate experientially, as well as abstractly, the possibility of "grey," the idea of a middle ground. This concept represents advances in cognitive and affective development with higher order defenses now accessible. Experiencing "grey" within the group and incorporating it as a part of the self constitutes "progress" as the following examples illustrate:

> Charlie tells the group that he feels overwhelmed by their discussion of loss, making peace, feelings about one's parents, and the effects of parental alcoholism on children. He must drop out emotionally. But others are supportive, pointing out that his ability to tell them his feelings is much different from his total lack of tolerance when he joined the group. At that time, he had to stay away from group entirely in order to be able to deal with his feelings.

A group with several "old" members and several "new" members illustrated the notion of "grey":

> Today the group was working at two levels. The new members are inquiring about rules, noting how anxious they feel without a structure and a sense of knowing what is the right behavior in group. The newcomers feel the group is frightening and out of control. Old members explain that this lack of structure is a structure in itself and they now feel safe with it. The new members have not yet discovered this.

The new members continued to focus on rules until several weeks later an "old" member spoke about change.

> Dan described how change for him has been a slow gradual process. He becomes aware of something in the group and at another time, realizes he can make a small change in his behavior or his way of looking at things. Gradually these small changes grow into bigger changes. Dan then adjusts his new self image to fit the changes. Dan points out to the newcomers that it's difficult to understand how this occurs when you are standing at the threshold or you are caught in all of the patterns that you want to change but can't.

The wish to find a middle ground and the reality of beginning to incorporate a middle ground are further illustrated:

> Initially Carla spoke as if she were doing something wrong because she is feeling badly. Group members emphasized that she is not doing anything wrong and there are no steps to take to change anything. She is experiencing the complexity and "grey" which she has long desired and the reality that bad feelings and good feelings often go hand in hand.

The uncovering of core beliefs is also recognized as part of "progress." Sara demonstrated the notion of a threshold of change as she described herself poised between two different views of herself:

> Sara said she had an important dream which helped her make sense of her current feeling of being very split—it is as if she is holding onto two different self images at the same time. In her dream, two perfect people fall in love. Sara is on the "outside," observing and feeling badly that she can't be perfect herself and therefore will never have a love relationship. In group, Sara discussed her basic identity as someone alone. She needed to see herself this way to survive and she cannot alter the view now to be able to perceive herself in relation to someone else. Sara survived by dissociating herself from her family. She could decide that she did not belong and be an outsider by virtue of that decision. "Belonging" always meant the loss of herself. Would she ever be able to have a relationship where these truths would no longer hold?

In the advanced group, members struggle with integrating complexities. They struggle with relinquishing the idealized hope of a magical "cure" or a new family that will be perfect. They come, instead, to experiment with a broader range of feelings, beliefs, and behaviors that include the ability to tolerate uncertainty, ambiguity, and even inherent contradiction in one's relationship with oneself and in relationships with others. The notion of "interdependent" relationships becomes a viable concept.

After opening up the possibility of a concept of interdependence, a member relinquished temporarily her major defense—seeing herself as always in control and contemptuous of others close to her. In describing the episode to the group, she accented her vulnerability and what felt like a regression. It was hard to recognize or really feel good about this kind of "progress."

> Karen reported the painful, devastating experience of finding out that her boyfriend had become interested in another woman. Karen spoke about the pain of feeling rejected and the pain of having realized that she does care about him and does want to be committed to him. She and her boyfriend have been able to talk about their relationship and Karen was able to feel and behave quite differently than ever before, not getting defensive or guarded. She allowed herself to feel vulnerable even without being able to control the outcome. It is a position of vulnerability, openness and dependency

that she has carefully avoided all her life. At the beginning of her relationship, Karen told her boyfriend that she did not want him to see her as needy or clinging. This would be intolerable to her. Karen now recalled how much she needed from her parents as a small child and how unresponsive her parents were. She was often brushed aside or forgotten.

As Karen spoke about the past, she noted that she can recall the events vividly but still not the feelings that go with them. She noted that the feelings must be so terribly painful for her to have blocked them so thoroughly. She can feel the pain of allowing herself to be vulnerable in the present, which is a big step.

A similar openness and lack of defensiveness is noted by members who are saying goodbye to a long-term member. The group discussed among themselves and demonstrated the key question: What is progress?

When Charlie arrived, he said it was important to him to say goodbye to everybody in person. It was also extremely difficult. He noted that in the past, he would have decided to go and then left immediately, closing the door on all feelings and everything left behind. This time, because of what he's learned in the group, he decided to allow himself to feel whatever it was that came up. He would stay, say goodbye, and he would listen to what others had to say to him.

Paula noted that through the process of group, she is learning how to be in charge of her own well being which includes being able to listen to others' concerns about her and then to decide for herself what is right for her. Through the course of this meeting and for the time he's been in the group, Charlie has been moving toward making decisions that are his own, rather than in response to others, particularly within the early framework of what his mother's or father's wishes might have been for him.

The Use of the Summary

I have referred throughout the text to the use of the summary. It is an important tool for members and the therapist in the process of group. One of the most important uses is as a gauge of progress. Members will often refer back to earlier summaries, or reread the course of their work over the last year or more in an attempt to trace the development of a particular issue or determine how they have changed. The following summary is an example of a group working in ongoing recovery. On this occasion, members focused on the past, with minimal interactions between them.

The group then began what was to be a very close, opening up group, which everyone agreed at the end had the feel of the way it's supposed to be—a group that "gels"—the feeling of connection between members. There weren't any discussions about safety today—in fact members laughed about how long it seemed they have been stuck on the feeling of danger. The group started out today with a sense of safety and trust and members each opened up new feelings in the present and recalled episodes and feelings from the past as well. There were a number of important themes which members built on and piggybacked off one another.

Jackie began saying that she was amazed that her experience in group last week was so similar to what it had been like with her family. She now spoke about the unpredictability and uncertainty in dealing with both of her parents and how she had curled up inside herself to survive. She had not stood up or responded with anger, learning as a late adolescent that she could withstand the power of her mother's physical abuse and violence and not be hurt by it. Jackie was upset that she responded with anger last week in the group but she also saw it as a step in a new direction. It was difficult to tolerate the intensity of emotion that went along with it but she realized it would be a different kind of price to pay than what she had done as a child. In order not to be affected by her mother's emotion and violence, Jackie had to shut down.

The theme of the power of the parent, or the power of another to determine everything about the self was a core for everyone tonight. Karen spoke about her pattern of constantly seeking approval at work and elsewhere, feeling automatically that she is not doing something right. She asks her boss if that is correct and the boss says no. Karen then berates herself, feeling that her asking is probably felt as a pain. No matter what, Karen is repeatedly in the position of seeing herself as inadequate to the dominance, power, "correct" view of the "other."

Wendy and Diane now spoke about the power of identification. Wendy never knew what feelings were her own based on her own experiences and internal life. She was just intensely angry until she realized that those feelings of anger belonged to her mother. The realization is one thing, but giving them up is another and a very hard task to accomplish. Diane too recognizes that she has been closely identified with her mother. Certainly her need for insulation and isolation and her need to totally deny her feelings is in the service of not being like her mother, among other things. She is also frightened that if she expresses herself, people will seek revenge.

On the recent occasions she has expressed herself in the group, saying what she thinks and feels, she has been terrified to return, fully expecting anger and criticism from others.

Howard then spoke about his sense of himself as a small child, desperately needy, searching for the approval or affection of another, only to be rejected. Later on, he spoke about needing very much to please others and to jump in and take care of others. Jackie suggested that Howard's need to rescue others might be a reflection of his need as a child to be taken care of. She added that Howard often jumps in to "rescue" others by diverting attention so no one has to feel. Howard also saw that he was the parent to his parents. He was the "perfect child" and played a major role in the equilibrium that his parents could establish. It was as if Howard worked very hard to enable his parents to maintain those roles. Clearly Howard also assumed parental duties as well, certainly parental emotional duties. Howard described having to be emotionally supportive of his ailing, fragile father who looked to him for sustenance. Throughout the meeting, group members agreed that their parents' needs were so great that it wasn't possible for the children to need anything. They put their energy into surviving the physical abuse and/or taking care of their parents. Dan recalled several episodes of severe physical abuse, as an example of how "annhilated" he would be by his father for any attempts to have a self, to assert it or to challenge his parents' behavior or viewpoint.

This part of the discussion introduced the idea of a sense of self—a child that was separate from the parents—who had a self that was free to develop, to have opinions or needs and a sense of self as an adult. Dan wondered whether there weren't some positive benefits to be had from all of the pain he endured—that he did become a "strong" person. Yet everybody talked about their inability as adults to feel like adults. The "strengths" they developed through surviving parental abuse and neglect did not result in giving them feelings of a sense of self or autonomy. Instead, they still feel very fragile, frightened of anger, and childlike, looking for approval. Will said he is working very hard to have opinions of his own. Will said he still has trouble holding onto or even formulating views of his own. He will be swept up into the view of another as the correct view as soon as he hears it. In the group he is constantly changing his opinion as others elaborate their own views.

The subject of anger was also an important theme today. Jackie spoke about how difficult it is for her to tolerate anger and Karen agreed, with both giving examples of lack of tolerance for anger in their childhood families. Will, however, related a wonderful experience of expressing his anger, in contrast to the fear expressed by others. Will told his boss what he needed and how he felt and the boss listened. Will couldn't believe it. Here was an example of the positive benefits of knowing what one wants and standing up for it side by side with examples of how such self expression was not tolerated in the past. Group members looked at the reality that one can never predict the response but it is important to learn to have opinions and assert oneself anyway. Members agreed that it is not easy to do this if you don't have a strong enough sense of self to begin with. Karen introduced the question of feeling "empty" even with repeated approval. The meeting came to an end although it felt difficult to stop.

The next examples, portions of consecutive meetings, illustrate changes in behavior or point of view within the interactional focus of the "here-and-now." Members try out new behaviors, perceptions, and interactions with each other which do not yet feel like "progress."

Monday Group Meeting
November 10

The meeting opened with all members present. Pamela said she had a reaction to the summary. In reading it carefully, she realized that her parents really began to argue a lot and to have severe difficulties in their relationship when her mother went to school to upgrade her skills so she could support the family. Pamela's father became anxious and angry, with fantasies and accusations about the men Pamela's mother would be meeting in class. Pamela wondered whether she was seeing therapy in a similar light—as an intruder into her relationship with her family. She said several times how important last week's meeting was to her because she learned so much. The more she talked, the more it seemed that she was a big source of her worry and fear. She had accented the fact that her therapy was just for her—taking care of herself. Later on in the meeting, she spoke at length about "taking care of herself" as did others, touching on the very painful and anxiety provoking issue of "deep insatiable need."

Betsy also wanted to mention something about the summary which she said was difficult for her. In the summary of two weeks ago, Stephanie stated that all members were present when the meeting started. Betsy had been 20 minutes late and was upset that Stephanie had not reported this. She was also upset that Stephanie omitted an important interchange between Betsy and Ann. She was very angry at first and then hurt. Betsy felt that these are examples of how she was excluded and then felt she does not exist.

Hank then shared his own sense of being overlooked many times in the writing of the summary. Hank had felt over the years some sense of irritation because his comments and participation were minimized in the summary. He had taken the responsibility of that minimization onto himself, believing that he was more intellectual, more theoretical, and less "dramatic" or "emotional." Hank had a sense of blending into the woodwork and always felt much safer with ideas rather than emotion.

Ben was amazed at the importance now being given to the summary and how often and how people are mentioned by Stephanie. Ben said that he never realized that Stephanie had so much power.

Monday Group Meeting
November 17

The meeting opened with all members present except Betsy, Ann, and Ben who each arrived late. Hank said he thought a lot about Joyce during the week, wondering what action she would take. Joyce said she was very excited and it was obvious from her expression. Her parents had decided to come for the Holiday dinner and agreed to maintain the limit Joyce had set: no drinking. Ben said it was great to see somebody set a limit and have it work.

The issue of limits was pertinent for Betsy who said she was having a terrible time at work. She then outlined several major problems that fit together into a pattern by the end of the meeting. First, she was unable to recognize in many situations that she needed to set a limit and often felt overwhelmed or victimized. When she saw that she needed to set a limit, she could not do so or was terribly frightened. She then began to be confused about her perception and her version of reality—the problem that needed the limit—began to crumble. This was the essence of her developing sense of self and her own reality as a child and the essence of her relationships as an adult. Now, she outlined a problem very clearly that nobody else had any trouble advising her about. She was overwhelmed with responsibilities at work that did not belong to her.

Ben and Ann were clear about the kinds of assertive action Betsy needed to take in order to take care of herself, reduce their anxiety, and reduce the inappropriate work load. But Betsy continued to describe the horror of the problem, almost bypassing the clear assertions offered her. Stephanie quickly wondered how people were feeling and Betsy wondered if she was "yes butting." Ann said she was feeling frustrated. Stephanie said it sounded like Betsy was caught. She got to the point where she could recognize she needed to set a limit, but now she was unable to take the action. With some painful exploration, Betsy realized for her to take action would be very aggressive. It meant she would have to attack her boss.

Others pointed out how polarized Betsy's thinking was. Couldn't she "name the problem" without being hostile or attacking? To Betsy there was no such middle ground. Much of what she was talking about today related closely to Joyce's confrontation with her parents. What was important: Joyce *had* named the problem. She had gotten to a point where her parent's opinion and reaction did not matter. It was more important to her to set a limit and to say what Joyce's version of reality was regardless of the outcome. Betsy seemed very distressed to hear that she would have to reach such a state of letting go of the others' opinion or outcome.

The importance of the other became clearer as Betsy explored this issue going backward in her life. Suddenly she was filled with emotion as she realized that the opinion of the "other" had always been the most important, the right version of reality, and the leading force in her own view of herself and the world. Any view that she held would always "crumble" if it differed from someone else important to her. Betsy gave several examples of failing to set a limit with a friend and altering her view of reality when it conflicted with hers. She always ended up being wrong or bad. That was how it was growing up. She said she also found herself wondering this week why she was in a group of ACAs. She was the only person in her family who thought that anybody was alcoholic.

Amidst the pain of looking at these issues, Betsy and others were also noting progress. Betsy said that for a long time the other person's version of reality was the only sense of self that she had. If that other person and that version of reality were removed, there would have been no Betsy left. Now, she had a sense of herself separate from the "other," but it was still very difficult to hold onto a different version of reality.

Betsy's experience recently, in the past and in the group today, was "frustrating" for Ben and Ann. Stephanie suggested that it was hard for them to see Betsy so caught, unable to take an action. Both agreed that was true. Neither would ever allow someone else's opinion to so affect them as they stated. Each one maintained that they would fight to hold onto their version of reality. It was hard for Ben to understand how Betsy could so let go of her entire self to the needs or view of the other. It wasn't hard for Joyce to understand. She said she knew the reality of her parents' alcoholism for 20 years but only last week was she "ready" to say it out loud— when the consequences didn't matter anymore.

During this discussion, Ben turned to Joyce and spoke about Betsy. Betsy said she was uncomfortable and told him to talk to her directly. Joyce and Ben laughed, noting how aggressively Betsy had set a limit.

Then Betsy proceeded to point out to Ben and Ann how they had described exactly the same alteration of their perceptions in other situations. Betsy recalled that Ben wanted to pick his own art decorations as a way of establishing his own views and opinions. Betsy recalled that Ann felt cornered with a polarized position in terms of men. Remember when she said if a man wanted marriage, she would be out the door? Ann agreed. Ben also agreed, asking Betsy if she wanted an art catalog by way of confirmation. Everybody laughed. There was general agreement that Betsy was not confused in challenging people in the group today and that she had held her ground quite well.

Monday Group Meeting
November 24

The meeting opened with all members present. Stephanie said she was going to add a new person and wanted the group's feeling on whether that person should come next week or the following. Betsy and Pamela both wanted to draw out the addition of a new member as long as possible with both indicating they would rather keep the group as it was. Everybody shared the feeling that the new person would disturb the open, vulnerable, close working group that now existed. Several spoke about the threat of disruption, particularly if the new person were to be critical or judgmental. Hank expressed his concern that he could be very much influenced by somebody judgmental and he would not be able to counter that person's power. As it turned out, the issues of power, control, and limit setting were again the main theme of today's group. Now members wondered whether they would be able to hold onto the strength they now had developed or whether a new person would have the power to set them back. At the end of the meeting, Ann joked that the group could prepare to "dejell," an indication that a new person does indeed have a powerful impact in upsetting the cohesiveness.

Betsy said that last week's meeting was very helpful for her. She was concerned that she might have been too confrontational with Ann. Others said that she wasn't and gave her positive feedback about how clear and straightforward she had been—not helpless or indecisive or confused at all.

There was a brief pause and Ann said she wanted to raise an issue. She spoke about feeling caught at work, unable to find a middle ground that would permit her to express her dissatisfaction and even her anger in a modulated way. Ann felt she must either "shut down" or explode. This issue came up in relation to employees whom she must constantly confront about job performance. Later on it also came up in relation to her own bosses who did not complete their responsibilities, believing instead that Ann would pick up any slack. Ben defined this as a sense of over responsibility. But it also came up under the heading of "setting limits."

As Ann was describing her dilemma at work, Stephanie wondered whether she had ever felt that bind in the group. Ann "knew" she should have experienced it in the group if Stephanie was asking so she said "probably." She and others laughed but quickly saw that Ann had had this experience last week. As Ann thought about it, she recognized that she was very frustrated with Betsy and now turned to her to express that frustration directly. She said with great feeling that she had been terribly frustrated and upset last week. She was bothered by Betsy's sense of being incapacitated to do anything on her own behalf. She wanted her to get in there and "grab hold of the problem" which was what Ann did. As Ann spelled out her own difficulties, others pointed out the parallels and the irony involved: Ann was having the same difficulties setting limits that Betsy described last week. Ann maintained that it was not the same because she did not feel incapacitated. But Stephanie pushed, noting that "shutting down" reflects a sense of being helpless and incapacitated. Ann shut down last week rather than express an explosion toward Betsy.

Ann had a feeling that there was a middle ground—a way of expressing her anger and feelings without exploding that she just could not see yet. Ann learned to take 10 minutes out to calm herself down and assess the issue when she felt angry and frustrated. Hank pointed out that that sounded like a very positive middle ground that Ann already practiced. Ann said a big problem for her was the lag time in knowing what she felt. She was able to stop and think before acting when she knew that she was feeling angry. But last week she wasn't aware of feeling frustrated at all until Stephanie asked her this week.

THE PROCESS OF RECOVERY

In an earlier work (Brown & Beletsis, 1986), we outlined the process of recovery as one of "growing up, growing out, and coming home." This conception underscores the importance of linking the past with the present and integrating a systems point of view with developmental theory.

Growing Up

In undertaking the process of recovery in a therapy group, individual therapy, a self-help 12-step program, or all three, individuals begin a process of breaking denial, reconstructing a new family story based on the reality of parental alcoholism and separation from still very primitive attachments. The latter are bound by the shared beliefs, role reversal, and identity formation required to maintain the system. No wonder so many adults specify a desire to separate from the family of origin as a key reason for seeking treatment.

"Growing up" involves forming a new attachment to the therapy group, the therapist, the ACA or Al-Anon 12-step group, a sponsor, or the principles of ACA or Al-Anon. In the therapy group, it involves re-creating within the family transference the context or system in which early development took place. The process of uncovering, through the exploration of the transference, involves clarifying the degree to which the defensive needs of the system and attachments to individuals within it overshadowed opportunities for conflict-free development of individuals within. How central an organizing principle was parental alcoholism? And what was the impact on the child and adult?

In the "growing up" phase of transition and early recovery, issues of trust, safety, and dependency are often central. In ongoing recovery, particularly if individuals utilize 12-step programs, issues of basic trust and dependency may now be incorporated or explored within the realm of spirituality or the concept of a higher power.

Individuals who do not utilize 12-step programs often struggle with the issue of control around the notion of who or what to trust or depend on and frequently translate the idea and the need to another person as Len illustrated:

Len was quiet and withdrawn for several weeks. Finally he noted how upset and devastated he had been by an interaction with Jess a few weeks back.

Jess and I had a "special" conversation in the parking lot after the meeting. I felt honored and privileged by his confiding in me. But the next week Jess couldn't remember the details of the conversation and clearly did not have the same depth of involvement that I had. I was so disappointed because I thought it was really special. Jess' failure to remember reminded me so much of my alcoholic father. I was repeatedly disappointed in my hopes of what my father could give me or be for me.

Another group member noted his reaction:

I feel humiliated on your behalf, Len. You are trying so hard to get a reaction but nothing comes. Your behavior reminds me of the way I throw myself at people who can give me nothing.

A new member illustrated the issue of safety:

Josh always remained quiet until Sherry arrived, had spoken, or invited Josh to speak. It became clear to him that without Sherry, the group was dangerous and he could not participate. In examining this reality he noted:

I've always been an introvert, going through life in a brown paper wrapper. Now I feel it's possible for me to emerge, to be seen by myself and by others. But not unless Sherry is here.

For most, relinquishment of control signifies total dependence on another human being which is terrifying. Thus, the sense of personal control, of being "in charge" of oneself and one's life is often relentlessly grasped and defended. The crux of many severe interpersonal problems rests on this very issue. Individuals view the relinquishment or lessening of their need for control and the all-or-none view as a submission that will result in annihilation or harm to themselves.

The concept of an inanimate higher power to whom control is relinquished provides the means to move beyond the polar struggle centered on interpersonal control, the need and fear of dependence and the struggle for autonomy.

For most people, the idea of a higher power is considered religious—indeed, many members of 12-step programs refer to their higher power as God—so many balk, reaffirming their belief in their own control as opposed to the perceived need to adopt religious beliefs. It takes most people a long time in recovery to become comfortable with the concept and the language and to actively construct a higher power.

The concept of a higher power solves a number of interpersonal dilemmas. It interrupts the dichotomous framework for interpreting dependency relationships on the human level while elevating the all-or-none issues of trust and dependence to an abstract level. Individuals develop a submissive, deferent sense of self in relation *to* a power greater than self that is defined by the individual. Paradoxically, individuals maintain control of constructing their higher power while relinquishing control to it at the same time.

By constructing a power greater than self, individuals are frequently able to see themselves as equal to others and to detach from familiar pathological dependent or codependent relationships. The tendency to form destructive dependency relationships is always a threat as primitive longings re-emerge through the course of treatment and ongoing recovery after treatment. Vesting those needs in an inanimate higher power constructed by the individual provides the paradoxical resolution to an apparently unresolvable dichotomy.

> I am either alone, totally dependent on myself, or I am lost, swallowed up and ultimately destroyed by depending on another.

The concept of a higher power is more frequently invoked and incorporated in the work of therapy for individuals who utilize 12-step programs or who have a strong spiritual or religious life already developed. In the group, issues of spirituality and ideas of God are often discussed in relation to the themes of trust, attachment, or dependency as Shirley noted:

> I want to believe in a loving God but if I do I risk feeling bewildered and hurt like a picture of a Hiroshima child. I

would like to trust in God and think that God meant well for
me, that I could expect not to be hurt. But I always expect a
trick instead. I can't make sense of what happened to me as a
child and believe in a loving God at the same time.

A fundamentally inherent concept or experience of God is often
uncovered in treatment. Integrating the contradictory elements of
her experience with "God" was a central feature of recovery for
Ellen.

I remember way back—I must have been seven or eight—to
the horror of my family. I can see an image of fear, doom,
and despair as I waited for the next round of violence. Then
came the sexual abuse. I can remember "going away," simply
leaving that place and reassuring myself that God would
take care of me. I think that saved me. I really did believe
there was something bigger, kinder, and more well-meaning
than my family. I still believe that, or rather I want to believe
that, but I can't let go and really experience the safety I
know would come with trusting.

The broad realm of spirituality and the question of a higher
power are central to individuals involved in 12-step recovery programs. But what happens to people who do not believe in God?
What happens to those who reject membership in a self-help group
because they equate affiliation with a requirement to adopt religious beliefs? The central core that sustains the individual in ongoing recovery is relinquishment of a belief in self-power, the belief in
one's ability to control oneself *and* another. The belief in loss of
control is central to the individual's new identity as the child of an
alcoholic and as a recovering codependent individual. People who
have difficulty constructing a belief in a higher power may be ad-
vised, like the alcoholic in AA, to remove themselves from a self-
centered orientation; to do so they must acknowledge a power
greater than the self. For many, it is not as difficult to accept the
notion of universality, or a "higher order" to the universe that is,
indeed, outside of one's personal control or authority as it is to
adopt specific religious beliefs or language.

Individuals in AA and Al-Anon are encouraged to put their
trust in the power of the group and the established traditions of
the group's conscience (*not* individuals within the group) or the
doorknob if necessary. It is the function of relinquishment of
self-power and not the form that is important.

Ironically, the pull to believe in the power of self results in a return to a codependent position. The individual is caught between a reliance on self with a sense of superiority and the opposite, a feeling of need, inadequacy, and inferiority and a desperate search to find a "higher power," a caretaker, in another person. Constructing a belief in an abstract power greater than the self establishes equality between individuals. Dependency needs are legitimized and vested outside the self or others.

Growing Out

Implicit to the break in denial, acquisition of the label ACA, and beginning treatment is the task of separation—of growing up again and growing out—to establish adult autonomy and separation from the pathological bonds of the past. The core pathology in the early bonds of attachment within the family, including role reversal, made "growing out" a difficult or impossible task because the child perceived that autonomy would insure parental destruction. By assuming responsibility for whatever was occurring or not occurring in the home, children solidify pathological bonds and emotional ties to the family of origin. During the course of treatment and recovery, individuals must face repeatedly intense feelings of guilt for leaving the still sick family behind. Primitive ties to the family of origin are maintained long into adulthood, interfering with the establishment of new, mature primary families by a continuing hope of fixing the needy parent.

The primary tie is also maintained by a corresponding hope: If I can fix my parent, I can then get the parent *I* need. The fears of being a parent, or becoming a parent oneself may activate these conflicts, forcing the individual to seek help.

"Growing out" involves the development of a healthy autonomous sense of self. Issues of dependency and interdependence, boundaries, limits, modeling, and identity formation are central to the entire reconstruction and individuation process. Individuals recognize intuitively and later, quite concretely, that they indeed are arrested in their development. The arrest, or holding off of becoming an adult, is in the service of warding off self-destruction or harm to others that will accompany active identification with destructive parental figures.

The process of recovery includes breaking down the barriers to identification established in the service of survival. Individuals must begin to incorporate what was warded off, search for pockets of healthier parental behavior or belief, or reinterpret actual parental behavior and belief from a new perspective. Sue illustrated:

> Sue's parents are moving to a smaller home and have given many pieces of furniture to their children. Sue chose a special rocker she liked as a child but became anxious as she brought it home.
>
>> It's sitting in the middle of the floor in a "decontaminant" phase. There are so many painful memories attached that I'm not yet ready to incorporate the rocker as part of me in my home.

Carla registered her amazement:

> I don't see why you'd even want it! Get rid of it!

And Sue replied:

> I'm looking for ways to symbolically incorporate my family into my life in some kind of neutral way rather than categorically rejecting everything about them.

Another member, looking for "healthy pockets" illustrated:

> Alice notes that her new way of thinking magnifies her separateness from her family. Yet she is beginning to be able to feel the depth of her need for her mother.
>
>> I am looking for back roads to connect with her—for ways not to be different or separate.

Several other members illustrated progress in "growing out." Tony illustrated a change in perspective:

> My father believed that life is shit—it will all come out rotten. I didn't want that attitude but I became the family problem anyway. I realize now I can't change his attitude or view of life, but I can change my interpretation.

Drew illustrated progress over the course of several years in group. In early recovery, he recoiled from group discussions about maturity, success, and adult partnerships. He maintained his belief that being alone was the only path possible for safety and integrity even if the price was loneliness.

You know what success is? You know what relationships are all about? I can remember driving to the club in my father's brand new shiny Lincoln with my mother propped up beside him so she wouldn't pass out on the way. That's what being an adult is. They were like mannequins—propped up and smiling for the world.

Several years later Drew reported a different sense of being an adult.

Drew reported on his recent trip home. He was quite pleased because he was able to tolerate being with his parents without becoming overly anxious or getting hooked into old patterns and responses. He was even able to be in a restaurant and not feel humiliated on behalf of his father. He recognized for the first time that he is a different person and he is not behaving badly himself.

Recognizing and accepting the reality of parental alcoholism is also part of "growing out." Members illustrated strategies they have developed to cope with a family environment that does not change.

Members discussed the notion that contact with parents is all or none. Several said it is not possible to maintain one's independent identity and positive feelings about themselves and have any contact at all. Carla tried to remember and even reminds herself that she has a "difficult parent" and that's the way it is. This helped her remember that she would come out on the other side still intact. The loss of herself is always a great threat.

Jack chuckled, noting that he used to think of himself as a "visiting psychologist" when he came home to deal with his parents in order to get enough distance.

Group members agreed it is hard to feel good about themselves because it requires a let down in vigilance. They still need to be watchful and vigilant lest a parent intrude. Feeling positively requires a relinquishment of that vigil.

The issue of modeling is critically important to ultimate separation. Individuals recognize and express their deepest and clearest awareness that healthy, autonomous development does not take place in a vacuum. Many report having looked for models in teachers, ministers, the parents of friends, or in literature and films. Members need guidance in becoming an adult emotionally. They may have determined many times previously that they would not replicate the patterns of their parents, only to find they could not will themselves to be and do it differently.

Therapist modeling is an extremely important issue throughout the course of group. Several members, always very anxious about feeling or expressing anger, were able to begin to explore these feelings in themselves following the group's confrontation of the therapist.

> The whole time wc were challenging you I expected you would get angry and tell us our view was not correct. You would tell us that you know what is real and that it is not OK to disagree with you or even see things differently. I was so relieved when you were able to accept our criticism and not retaliate. You seemed to survive and not be diminished by accepting the reality of your error. I need to learn how to do that. And I need to learn how to be angry as well.

The process of growing out includes learning from others alternative ways of behavior and constructing reality and then experimenting with doing it differently. Karen illustrated:

> Karen spoke next on the subject of "successes." She too is marveling at the different sense of herself she has been having recently. She now has new options, ideas and even feelings open to her that before she just could not incorporate into her sense of herself. She gave an example. Her parents are having an anniversary party and expect her to be there. Up to now she would have felt that her only option was to go even though it is a very painful and unsatisfying experience for her. Or, she might have been able to stay away now, but only with an excuse. Now she simply feels that she has the option to choose not to go simply because she doesn't want to. It is utterly amazing to her to have this choice. She explained that she is getting a sense of separateness for herself that allows her to consider new options. This sense of being separate also applies to her feelings and her beliefs. She smiled as she said that a new "truth" is "creeping up on her." This truth is the reality of her parents' alcoholism and the fact that even though her father still denies that he is alcoholic, it is her truth that he was and is. She's beginning to feel that it can be her truth even though it isn't truth for him.

The group moved into a discussion of "what is progress?" and "what is different?" Diane summarized:

I can now meet my own needs rather than thinking that others always come first. I can speak up in the group and outside and take the time I need. I am able to hear the different opinions of others without closing down. I am able to tolerate my husband's withdrawal without going after him or interpreting the withdrawal as anger at me. I have made these changes first by recognizing what I'm doing, experimenting with a different behavior or a new idea in here and then transfering these new ways of thinking and being to the outside. It hasn't happened overnight and most changes are subtle. But actually it's like reversing figure and ground. Shift an old belief a little bit this way or even turn it over and there's a whole new perception on the other side.

Coming Home

Individuals actively involved in reconstructing the family history reach a point of readiness to identify and separate. It often includes a greater ability to incorporate complexities of the parents, to broaden a parental portrait to include much "grey." Parents are no longer all bad or all good any more than the ACA is.

"Coming home" may include a capacity and readiness for acceptance, forgiveness, and perhaps feelings of love for parents rekindled and now possible as part of an integrated, more complex, portrait. "Coming home" may include confrontation, actively breaking attachments, and patterns of behavior that bound the individual to the past. Individuals may "announce" their separation by advising parents about their membership in a group for ACAs. Sometimes such an announcement is the first time a parents' alcoholism has ever been acknowledged. Or, individuals refuse to participate in denial or the distorted logic of the system, going around or stepping back.

> For many years, Ellen survived by refusing to see herself as like her father in any way. There was nothing positive about him and she had closed the book on him long ago. With progress in her recovery, she became ready to open the book. She made a visit home and interviewed relatives. Returning to group, she felt a new sense of calm and a new, broader picture of her father.
>
> Ellen said she no longer feels chronically angry with men. She sees this change as part of a cycle of progress occuring over the course of many years of work. She has opened exploration of her father in an attempt to find a deeper portrait of him—beyond his alcoholism

and illness—that she can incorporate into her own sense of self. In talking with relatives, Ellen found that her father had many friends and was noted for his intelligence. Ellen smiled, now able to relate her own keen intellect directly back to him. "I finally have a healthy tie to my father, one I can be proud of."

For a few individuals "coming home" may involve a real return to parents who are now sober and engaged in recovery programs themselves. Such an outcome is rare. It is more commonly experienced within a new family, such as the group, or individual therapy or the support network of ACA 12-step or Al-Anon. The treatment "family" represents the new home, the new beliefs and behaviors that one can always come home to. Warren, in group for five years illustrated "coming home" to his real family. Both parents had been involved in AA and Al-Anon for years.

Warren spoke with joy, wonderment, deep relief, and even sorrow. His weekend with his family had been wonderful, beyond his hopes and dreams. His parents were able for the first time to talk about what really happened and what it was really like for all of them during the course of his mother's alcoholism. He and his family spent the whole visit remembering events, episodes and the general atmosphere of what it had been like. In essence, the family rewrote their history together, with everyone now incorporating the reality of his mother's alcoholism and what had happened to each of them as a result. Warren said the acknowledgment of the reality of what it was like was profoundly important to him because now he felt like he really had roots.

Another member who did not have a real recovering family to return to recognized her formal treatment was over as she mused in group:

Who will I tell my story to? Who will know what it was like and what happened to me?

She smiled and added:

I know and that's enough. It's my story now. I have made it real and I have made it mine by coming here. Now I'll take it with me.

References

Ablon, J. (1976). Family structure and behavior in alcoholism: A review of the literature. In B. Kissin and H. Begleiter (Eds.), *The biology of alcoholism: Social pathology: Vol. 4.* New York: Plenum Press.

Ablon, J. (1980). The significance of cultural patterning for the alcoholic family. *Family Process, 19,* 127–144.

Ackerman, N. W. (1956). Interlocking pathology in family relationships. *Changing concepts of psychoanalytic medicine.* p. 35, New York: Grune & Stratton.

Ackerman, N. W. (1958). Toward an integrative therapy of the family. *American Journal of Psychiatry, 114,* 727–733.

Aronson, H. S., & Gilbert, A. (1963). Preadolesent sons of male alcoholics. *Archives of general psychiatry, 8,* 235–241.

Bacon, S. (1945). Excessive drinking and the family. In *Alcohol, science and society.* New Haven: Quarterly Journal of Studies on Alcoholism.

Baker, S. M. (1945). Social case work with inebriates. In *Alcohol, science and society.* New Haven: Quarterly Journal of Studies on Alcoholism.

Bandura, A. (1985). Model of causality in social learning theory. In M. Mahoney and A. Freeman (Eds.), *Cognition and psychotherapy.* New York: Plenum Press.

Bateson, G., Jackson, D., Haley, J., & Weakland, J. (1956). Toward a theory of schizophrenia. *Behavioral Science, 1,* 251–264.

Beck, A., & Emery, G. (1985). *Anxiety disorders and phobias.* New York: Basic Books.

Beckman, L. (1975). Women alcoholics: A review of social and psychological studies. *Journal of Studies on Alcohol, 36,* 797–824.

Beletsis, S., & Brown, S. (1981). A developmental framework for understanding the adult children of alcoholics. *Focus on Women: Journal of the Addictions and Health, 2,* 187–203.

Bergmann, M. V. (1985). The effect of role reversal on delayed marriage and maternity. *Psychoanalytic study of the child, 40,* 197–219.

Bihary, S. (1986). (novel in progress). Stanford University: Institute for Research on Women and Gender.

Black, C. (1981). *It will never happen to me.* Denver: MAC.

Blane, H. T. (1968). *Personality of the alcoholic: Guises of dependency.* New York: Harper & Row.

Blos, P. (1962). *On adolescence: A psychoanalytic interpretation.* New York: Free Press.

Bosma, W. (1972). Children of alcoholics: A hidden tragedy. *Maryland State Medical Journal, 21,* 34–36.

Bowlby, J. (1980). *Attachment and loss: Vol. 3.* New York: Basic Books.

Bowlby, J. (1985). The role of childhood experience in cognitive disturbance. In M. Mahoney and A. Freeman (Eds.), *Cognition and psychotherapy.* New York: Plenum Press.

Bowen, M. (1974). Alcoholism as viewed through family systems theory and psychotherapy. *Annals of the New York Academy of Science, 233,* 115–122.

Bronfenbrenner, U. (1977). The ecology of human development in retrospect and prospect. In H. McGurk (Ed.), *Ecological factors in human development.* Amsterdam, The Netherlands: North Holland.

Brown, K. A., & Sunshine, J. (1982). Group treatment of children from alcoholic families. In *Social work with groups.* New York: Haworth Press.

Brown, S. (1974). *Personality characteristics of the teen-age daughters of male alcoholics.* Master's thesis, California State University, San Jose.

Brown, S. (1985). *Treating the alcoholic: A developmental model of recovery.* New York: John Wiley & Sons.

Brown, S. (1986). Children with an alcoholic parent. In N. J. Estes and M. E. Heinemann (Eds.), *Alcoholism: Development, consequences, and interventions.* St. Louis: C. V. Mosby.

Brown, S., & Beletsis, S. (1986, Winter). The development of family transference in groups for adult children of alcoholics. *International Journal of Group Psychotherapy,* 97–114.

Brown, S., & Yalom, I. D. (1977). Interactional group psychotherapy with alcoholics. *Journal of Studies on Alcohol, 38*(3), 426–456.

Burk, E. D. (1972). Some contemporary issues in child development and the children of alcoholic parents. *Annals of the New York Academy of Science, 197,* 189–195.

Cantwell, D. (1972). Psychiatric illness in families of hyperactive children. *Archives of General Psychiatry, 27*(3), 414–417.

Catanazaro, R. J. (Ed.) (1968). *Alcoholism: The total treatment approach.* Springfield, IL: Charles Thomas.

Cermak, T. (1984). Children of alcoholics and the case for a new diagnostic category of co-dependency. *Alcohol, Health and Research World, 8,* 38–42.

Cermak, T. (1986). *Diagnosing and treating co-dependence.* Minneapolis, MN: Johnson Institute Books.

Cermak, T., & Brown, S. (1982). Interactional group psychotherapy with the adult children of alcoholics. *International Journal of Group Psychotherapy, 32,* 375–389.

Chafetz, M. E., Blane, H. T., & Hill, M. J. (1971). Children of alcoholics. *Quarterly Journal of Studies on Alcohol, 32,* 687–698.

Chiles, J., Strauss, F., & Benjamin, L. (1980). Marital conflict and sexual dysfunction in alcoholic and non-alcoholic couples. *British Journal of Psychiatry, 137,* 266–273.

Cloninger, C. R. (1983). Genetic and environmental factors in the development of alcoholism. In S. Blume (Ed.), *Journal of psychiatric treatment evaluation,* [Special issue on alcoholism].

Cloninger, C. R., Bokman, M., & Sigvaardsson, S. (1981). Inheritance of alcohol abuse. *Archives of General Psychiatry, 38,* 861–868.

Coates, D., Vietze, P., & Gray, D. (1985). Methodological issues in studying children of disabled parents. In S. K. Thurman (Ed.), *Children of handicapped parents: Research and clinical perspectives* (pp. 155–178). Orlando: Academic Press.

Cork, M. (1969). *The forgotten children.* Toronto: Addiction Research Foundation.

Cotton, N. S. (1979). The familial incidence of alcoholism. *Journal of Studies on Alcohol, 40*(1), 89–116.

Craik, K. J. W. (1943). *The nature of explanation.* Cambridge, England: Cambridge University Press.

De La Mata, R. C., Gringras, C., & Wittkower, E. D. (1960). Impact of sudden severe disablement of the father upon the family. *Canadian Medical Association, 82,* 1015–1020.

DiCicco, L., Davis, R., Hogan, J., MacLean, A., & Orenstein, A. (1984). Group experience for children of alcoholics. *Alcohol, Health and Research World, 8*(4), 20–24.

Ekdahl, M. C., Rice, E. P., & Schmidt, W. M. (1962). Children of parents hospitalized for mental illness. *American Journal of Public Health, 52,* 428.

El-Guebaly, N., & Orford, D. R. (1979). On being the offspring of an alcoholic: An update. *Alcoholism: Clinical and Experimental Research, 3*(2), 148–157.

Ellwood, L. C. (1980). Effects of alcoholism as a family illness on child behavior and development. *Military Medicine,* March, 188–194.

Erikson, E. (1963). *Childhood and society.* New York: Norton.

Fairchild, D. M. J. (1964). Teenage children of alcoholic parents. *Fort Logan Mental Health Center, 2,* 71–75.

Fawzy, F. I., Coombs, R. H., & Guber, B. (1983). Generational continuity in the use of substances: The impact of parental substance use on adolescent substance use. *Addictive Behavior, 8,* 109–114.

Fine, E. W., Yudin, L. W., Holmes, J., & Heinemann, S. (1976). Behavioral disorders in children with parental alcoholism. *Annals of the New York Academy of Science, 273,* 507–517.

Fox, R. (1962). Children in an alcoholic family. In W. C. Bier (Ed.), *Problems in addiction: Alcoholism and narcotics.* New York: Fordham University Press.

Fox, R. (1963). The effect of alcoholism on children. In the *Proceedings of the 5th International Congress of Psychotherapy* held at Vienna, August, 1961, part 5, p. 57. Basel, Switzerland: S. Karger.

Futterman, S. (1953). Personality trends in wives of alcoholics. *Journal of Psychiatric Social Work, 23,* 37–41.

Glass, D. D. (1985). Onset of disability in a parent: Impact on child and family. In S. K. Thurman (Ed.), *Children of handicapped parents: Research and clinical perspectives* (pp. 145–153). Orlando: Academic, Press.

Goodwin, D. W. (1979). Alcoholism and heredity: A review and hypothesis. *Archives of General Psychiatry, 36,* 57–61.

Goodwin, D. W. (1971). Is alcoholism hereditary? *Archives of General Psychiatry, 25,* 545–549.

Goodwin, D. W. (1984). Studies of familial alcoholism: A review. *Journal of Clinical Psychiatry, 45*(2), 14–17.

Goodwin, D. W., Schulsinger, F., Hermansen, L., Guze, S. B., & Winokur, G. (1973). Alcohol problems in adoptees raised apart from alcoholic biologic parents. *Archives of General Psychiatry, 28,* 238–243.

Goodwin, D. W., Schulsinger, F., Knop, J., Mednick, W., & Guze, S. (1977). Alcoholism and depression in adopted-out daughters of alcoholics. *Archives of General Psychiatry, 34,* 751–755.

Gorad, S. L. (1971). Communication style and interaction of alcoholics and their wives. *Family Process, 10,* 475–489.

Gorman, J. M., & Rooney, J. F. (1979). Delay in seeking help and onset of crisis among Al-Anon wives. *American Journal of Drug and Alcohol Abuse, 6*(2), 223–233.

Gravitz, H., & Bowden, J. (1984). Therapeutic issues of adult children of alcoholics. *Alcohol, Health and Research World,* Summer, 25–29.

Gravitz, H., & Bowden, J. (1985). *Guide to recovery.* Holmes Beach, FL: Learning Publications.

Greenspan, S. I. (1979). *Intelligence and adaptation: An integration of psychoanalytic and Piagetian developmental psychology.* New York: International Universities Press.

Greenwald, R. (1986). *Shattered spirits.* Los Angeles: Robert Greenwald Productions.

Greer, B. (1985). Children of physically disabled parents: Some thoughts, facts and hypotheses. In S. K. Thurman (Ed.), *Children of handicapped parents: Research and clinical perspectives* (pp. 131–143). Orlando: Academic Press.

Guidano, V. F., & Liotti, G. (1983). *Cognitive processes and emotional disorders.* New York: Guilford Press.

Haberman, P. W. (1966). Childhood symptoms in children of alcoholics and comparison group parents. *Journal of Marriage and the Family, 28,* 152–154.

Hanson, K. J., & Estes, N. J. (1977). Dynamics of alcoholic families. In N. J. Estes and M. E. Heinemann (Eds.), *Alcoholism: Development, consequences and interventions.* St. Louis: C. V. Mosby.

Hawkins, H. N. (1950). *Some effects of alcoholism of the parents on children in the home.* St. Louis: Salvation Army Midland Division.

Hethrington, E. M. (1979). Divorce: A child's perspective. *American Psychologist, 34,* 851–858.

Hindman, M. (1976). Family therapy in alcoholism. *Alcohol, Health and Research World, 1,* 209.

Hindman, M. (1977). Child abuse and neglect: The alcohol connection. *Alcohol, Health and Research World, 1*(3), 2–6.

Hofmeister, R. J. (1985). Families with deaf parents: A functional perspective. In S. K. Thurman (Ed.), *Children of handicapped parents: Research and clinical perspectives* (pp. 111–130). Orlando: Academic Press.

Hong, K. M. (1978). The transitional phenomena: A theoretical integration. *Psychoanalytic Study of the Child, 33,* 47–79.

Hunter, G. (1963). Alcoholism and the family agency. *Quarterly Journal of Studies on Alcohol, 24,* 61–74.

Jackson, J. K. (1954). The adjustment of the family to the crisis of alcoholism. *Quarterly Journal of Studies on Alcohol, 15,* 562–586.

Jackson, J. K. (1962). Alcoholism and the family. In D. J. Pittman and C. R. Snyder (Eds.), *Society, culture and drinking patterns.* New York: John Wiley & Sons.

Jacob, T., Dunn, J. N., & Leonard, K. (1981). Patterns of alcohol abuse and family stability. *Alcoholism: Clinical and experimental research, 7,* 382–385.

318 **References**

Jacob, T., Favorini, A., Meisel, S. S., & Anderson, C. M. (1978). The alcoholic's spouse, children and family interactions: Substantive findings and methodogical issues. *Journal of Studies on Alcohol, 38,* 1231–1251.

Johnson, J. (1984). NIAAA Clinical center conducts family research. *Alcohol, Health and Research World, 8,* 6–9.

Jones, M. C. (1968). Personality correlates and antecedents of drinking patterns in adult males. *Journal of Counseling and Clinical Psychology, 32,* 2–12.

Kagan, J. (1984). *The nature of the child.* New York: Basic Books.

Kammeir, M. L. (1971). Adolescents from families with and without alcohol problems. *Quarterly Journal of Studies on Alcoholism, 32,* 364–372.

Kaufman, E. (1986). The family of the alcoholic patient. *Psychosomatics, 27*(5), 347–360.

Kaufman, E. (1985). *Substance abuse and family therapy.* Orlando: Grune & Stratton.

Kaufman, E., & Pattison, E. M. (1981). Differential methods of family therapy in the treatment of alcoholism. *Journal of Studies on Alcohol, 42,* 951–971.

Kearney, T. R., & Taylor, C. (1969). Emotionally disturbed adolescents with alcoholic parents. *Acta Paedopsychiat, 36,* 215–221. (Abstract: *Quarterly Journal of Studies of Alcoholism,* 1972, 33, p. 243.)

Kegan, R. (1982). *The evolving self.* Cambridge, MA: Harvard University Press.

Khan, M. M. R. (1963). The concept of cumulative trauma. *Psychoanalytic Study of the Child, 18,* 286–306.

Kornblum, H., & Anderson, B. (1985). Parents with insulin-dependent diabetes: Impact on child and family development. In S. K. Thurman (Ed.), *Children of handicapped parents: Research and clinical perspectives* (pp. 97–109). Orlando: Academic Press.

Krystal, H. (1978). Trauma and affects. *Psychoanalytic Study of the Child, 33,* 81–116.

Lane, R., & Schwartz, G. (1987, February). Levels of emotional awareness: A cognitive-developmental theory and its application to psychopathology. *American Journal of Psychiatry, 144*(2), 133–143.

Lemert, E. M. (1960). The occurrence and sequence of events in the adjustment of the family to alcoholism. *Quarterly Journal of Studies on Alcoholism, 21,* 679–697.

Lewis, M. (1977). Language, cognitive development and personality: A synthesis. *American Academy of Child Psychiatry, 16*(4), 646–661.

Lewis, M., & Feiring, C. (1979). The child's social network: Social object, social functions and their relationship. In M. Lewis and L. A.

Rosenblum (Eds.), *The child and its family.* New York: Plenum Press.

Lidz, T. (1973). *The origins and treatment of schizophrenic disorders.* New York: Basic Books.

Lidz, T., & Fleck, S. (1965). Family studies and a theory of schizophrenia. In *The American family in crisis.* Des Plaines, IL: Forest Hospital Publications.

Lindemann, E. (1944). Symptomatology and management of acute grief. *American Journal of Psychiatry, 101,* 141–148.

Lisansky, E. S. (1960). The etiology of alcoholism: The role of psychological predisposition. *Quarterly Journal of Studies on Alcohol, 21,* 314–341.

Loewald, H. W. (1960). On the therapeutic action of psychoanalysis. *Psychoanalytic Study of the Child, 11,* 54–88.

Mahler, M., Pine, F., & Bergman, H. (1975). *The psychological birth of the human infant.* New York: Basic Books.

Mahoney, M. (1977). Reflections on the cognitive learning trend in psychotherapy. *American Psychologist, 32*(1), 5–13.

Mayer, J., & Black, R. (1977). The relationship between alcoholism and child abuse and neglect. In F. Seixas (Ed.), *Currents in alcoholism: Vol 2.* New York: Grune & Stratton.

McCollum, A. T. (1981). *The chronically ill child.* New Haven: Yale University Press.

McCord, W., & McCord, J. (1960). *Origins of alcoholism.* Stanford: Stanford University Press.

MacDonald, D. (1956). Mental disorders in wives of alcoholics. *Quarterly Journal of Studies on Alcoholism, 17,* 282–287.

Miller, A. (1981). *The drama of the gifted child.* New York: Basic Books.

Miller, A. (1984). *Thou shalt not be aware.* New York: Farrar, Straus, Giroux.

Moos, R., Finney, J., & Gamble, W. (1982). The process of recovery from alcoholism: II. Comparing spouses of alcoholic patients and matched community controls. *Journal of Studies on Alcohol, 43,* 888–909.

Morehouse, E. (1979). Working in the schools with children of alcoholic parents. *Health Social Work, 4*(4), 144–162.

Morehouse, E. (1984, Summer). Perspectives. *Alcohol, Health and Research World, 8,* 35–36.

Morehouse, E., & Scola, C. (1986). *Children of alcoholics: Meeting the needs of the young COA in the school setting.* South Laguna, CA: National Association for Children of Alcoholics (NACOA).

Morris, P. (1958). Some disturbances of family functioning associated with psychiatric illness. *British Journal of Medical Psychology, 31,* 104.

Nardi, P. M. (1981). Children of alcoholics: A role-theoretical perspective. *Journal of Social Psychology, 115,* 237–245.

Newbrough, J. R. (1985). The handicapped parent in the community: A synthesis and commentary. In S. K. Thurman (Ed.), *Children of handicapped parents: Research and clinical perspectives* (pp. 181–193). Orlando: Academic Press.

Newell, N. (1950). Alcoholism and the father image. *Quarterly Journal of Studies on Alcoholism, 11,* 92–95.

Newsweek. (1979, May). p. 79.

Niven, R. (1984, Summer). Children of alcoholics: An interview with NIAAA director. *Alcohol, Health and Research World, 8,* 3–5.

Novey, S. (1968). *The second look.* Baltimore: John Hopkins University Press.

Nylander, I. (1960). Children of alcoholic fathers. *Acta Pediatr., 49*(1), 9–127.

Nylander, I. (1963). Children of alcoholic fathers. *Quarterly Journal of Studies on Alcoholism, 24,* 170–172.

O'Gorman, P. (1981). *Prevention issues involving children of alcoholics.* In U.S. Department of Health and Human Services: Services for children of alcoholics. (NIAAA Research Monograph No. 4) (ADM 81-0007). Washington, D.C.: U.S. Government Printing Office. (Publication No. (ADM) 81-0007)

Orford, J., Oppenheimer, E., Egert, S., Hendsman, C., & Guthrie, S. (1976). The cohesiveness of alcohol-complicated marriages and its inferences on treatment outcome. *British Journal of Psychiatry, 128,* 318–319.

Paolino, J., & McCrady, B. (1979). *The alcoholic marriage: Alternative perspectives* (pp. 357–365). New York: Grune & Stratton.

Parnitzke, K. H., & Prussing, O. (1966). Children of alcoholic parents. *Psychological Abstracts, 40*(6809).

Piaget, J. (1970). Piaget's theory. In P. Mussen (Ed.), *Carmichael's manual of child psychology* (3rd ed.), (pp. 703–332). New York: John Wiley & Sons.

Pollack, O. (1952). *Social science and psychotherapy for children.* New York.

Post, F. (1962). The social orbit of psychiatric patients. *Journal of Mental Science, 108,* 759.

Reiker, P. P., & Carmen, E. H. (1986, July). The victim-to-patient process: The disconfirmation and transformation of abuse. *American Journal of Orthopsychiatry, 56*(3), 360–370.

Roe, A., & Burks, B. (1945). Adult adjustment of foster children of alcoholics and psychotic parentage and the influence of the foster home. In *Memoirs of the section on alcoholism studies, No. 3.* New Haven University Press.

Rosen, H. (1985). *Piagetian dimensions of clinical relevance.* New York: Columbia University Press.

Rosett, H. (1976). Effects of maternal drinking on child development: An introductory review. *Annals of the New York Academy of Science, 273,* 115–117.

Russell, M., Henderson, C., & Blume, S. *Children of alcoholism: A review of the literature.* New York: Children of Alcoholics Foundation.

Rutter. M. (1966). *Children of sick parents.* London: Oxford University Press.

Sameroff, A. J. (1975). Early influences on development: Fact or fancy? *Merrill-Palmer Quarterly, 21,* 267–294.

Sameroff, A. J., & Chandler, M. J. (1975). Reproductive risk and the continuum of caretaking casuality. In F. D. Horowitz, M. Hethrington, S. Scarr-Salapetek, and G. Siegel (Eds.), *Review of child development research: (Vol. 4).* Chicago: University of Chicago Press.

Sameroff, A. J., & Seifer, R. (1983). Familial risk and child competence. *Child Development, 54,* 1254–1268.

Sameroff, A. J., Seifer, R., & Zax, M. (1985). Effects of parental emotional handicap on early child development. In S. K. Thurman (Ed.), *Children of handicapped parents: Research and clinical perspectives* (pp. 47–66). Orlando: Academic Press.

Sandler, J. (1967). Trauma, strain and development. In S. S. Furst (Ed.), *Psychic trauma* (pp. 154–174). New York: Basic Books.

Sandmeier, M. (1980). *The invisible women and alcohol abuse in America.* New York: McGraw-Hill.

Santostefano, S. (1980). Cognition in personality and the treatment process: A psychoanalytic view. *Psychoanalytic Study of the Child, 35,* 41–65.

Satir, V. (1964). *Conjoint family therapy.* Palo Alto: Science and Behavior Books.

Schaffer, J. B., & Tyler, J. D. (1979). Degree of sobriety in male alcoholics and coping styles used by their wives. *British Journal of Psychiatry, 135,* 431–437.

Schuckitt, M. A. (1983). A prospective study of genetic markers in alcoholism. In I. Hanin and E. Usden (Eds.), *Biological markers in psychiatry and neurology* (pp. 445–454). Oxford: Pergamon Press.

Schuckitt, M., Goodwin, D. W., & Winokur, G. (1972). A study of alcoholism in half-siblings. *American Journal of Psychiatry, 128,* 1132–1136.

Schuckitt, M. A., & Duby, J. (1982). Alcohol-related flushing and the risk for alcoholism in the sons of alcoholics. *Journal of Clinical Psychiatry, 43*(10), 415–518.

Searles, H. (1975). The patient as therapist to his therapist. In P. L. Giovacchini (Ed.), *Tactics and techniques in psychoanalytic therapy: Vol. 2: Countertransference* (pp. 95–151). New York: Jason Aronson.

Seixas, J. (1979). *Living with a parent who drinks too much.* New York: Greenwillow Books.

Sloboda, S. B. (1974). The children of alcoholics: A neglected problem. *Hospital Community Psychiatry, 25,* 605–606.

Spiegel, J. (1957). The resolution of role conflict within the family. *Psychiatry, 20,* 1–16.

Steinglass, P. (1980). A life history model of the alcoholic family. *Family Process, 19*(3), 211–226.

Steinglass, P. (1981a). The impact of alcoholism on the family. Relationship between degree of alcoholism and psychiatric symptomatology. *Journal of Studies on Alcohol, 42*(3), 288–303.

Steinglass, P. (1981b). The alcoholic family at home. Patterns of interaction in dry, wet and transitional stages of alcoholism. *Archives of General Psychiatry, 38*(5), 578–584.

Thune, C. (1977). Alcoholism and the archetypal past: A phenomenological perspective on alcoholics anonymous. *Journal of Studies on Alcohol, 38*(1), 75–88.

Thurman, S. K. (1985). Ecological congruence in the study of families of handicapped parents. In S. K. Thurman (Ed.), *Children of handicapped parents: Research and Clinical Perspectives* (pp. 35–43). Orlando: Academic Press.

Thurman, S. K., Whaley, A., & Weinraub, M. (1985). Studying families with handicapped parents: A rationale. In S. K. Thurman (Ed.), *Children of handicapped parents: Research and clinical perspectives* (pp. 1–8). Orlando: Academic Press.

Triplett, J. L., & Arneson, S. W. (1978). Children of alcoholic parents: A neglected issue. *Journal of School Health, 48,* 596–599.

Typpo, M., & Hastings, J. (1984). *An elephant in the living room.* Minneapolis, MN: Compcare Publications.

Vaillant, G. E., & Milofsky, E. S. (1982). Natural history of male alcoholism, IV. Paths to recovery. *Archives of General Psychiatry, 39*(2), 127–133.

Watzlawick, P., Weakland, J., & Fisch, R. (1974). *Change.* Palo Alto: Science and Behavior Books.

Wegsheider, S. (1978). *The family trap.* Crystal, MN: Nurturing Networks.

Wegsheider, S. (1981). *Another chance: Hope and health for the alcoholic family.* Palo Alto: Science and Behavior Books.

Whitfield, C. L. (1980). Children of alcoholics: Treatment issues. *Maryland State Medical Journal,* 86–91.

Whitaker, C., & Malone, T. (1953). *The roots of psychotherapy.* New York: Blackiston.

Williams, M. (1984, Summer). Research on children of alcoholics: Expanding the knowledge. *Alcohol, Health and Research World, 8*(4), 6–11.

Wilson, A. (1985, Spring). On silence and the holocaust: A contribution to clinical theory. *Psychoanalytic Inquiry,* 63–84.

Wilson, C., & Orford, J. (1978). Children of alcoholics: Report of a preliminary study and comments on the literature. *Journal of Studies on Alcohol, 39*(1), 121–142.

Winokur, G., Cadoret, F., Dorzab, J., & Baker, M. (1971). Depressive disease: A genetic study. *Archives of General Psychiatry, 24,* 135–144.

Winokur, G., & Clayton, P. (1968). Family history studies: IV, Comparison of male and female alcoholics. *Quarterly Journal of Studies on alcoholism, 29,* 885–891.

Winokur, G., Reich, T., Rimmer, J., & Pitts, F. (1970). Alcoholism: III, Diagnosis of familial psychiatric illness in 259 alcoholic probands. *Archives of General Psychiatry, 23,* 104–111.

Winnicott, D. W. (1953). Transitional objects and transitional phenomena. *International Journal of Psychoanalysis, 34,* 89–97.

Winnicott, D. W. (1960). The theory of the parent-infant relationship. *International Journal of Psychoanalysis, 41,* 585–595.

Wolin, S. J., Bennett, L. A. and Noonan D. L. Family rituals and the recurrence of alcoholism over generations. *American Journal of Psychiatry,* 1979, *136,* 589–593.

Wolin, S. J., Bennett, L. A., Noonan, D. L., & Teitelbaum, M. A. (1980). Disrupted family rituals. *Journal of Studies on Alcohol, 41*(3), 199–214.

Yalom, I. D. (1970). *The theory and practice of group psychotherapy* (1st ed.). New York: Basic Books.

Yalom, I. D., Brown, S., & Bloch, S. (1975). The written summary as a group therapy technique. *Archives of General Psychiatry, 32*(5), 605–619.

Index

Summary, written, x, 167, 294–302
Survivor (also hero, model child invulnerable), 20, 30, 181
Systems theory (see environmental view)

Tension, 54–57
Theory development, ix, xi, 4, 5, 9, 26, 138, 168, 205–214, 290–294
  integrated model, 4, 138, 168, 201
  model of interaction, 5
  model of recovery, 7, 201–203, 209–210
  stages of recovery, 202, 211–212
  summary of, 202–207, 211, 213–214, 290–294
  what is progress, 290–294
Therapy (see also group therapy), 206
  and attachment, 222
  dynamic, 261
  as holding environment, 206
Thinking disorder, 4, 33–36, 47, 63, 65, 72, 141, 184
  anxiety disorder, 98
Thurman, S.K., 66–68, 72, 141
Transference, 241, 261, 264, 276–288
  challenge of defense, 278
  and codependence, 277
  family, 241–243, 263, 277
Transition, stage of, 226–235
  the adult, 227–235
  the child, 226–227
  "fits and starts", 212, 230
  growing up, 302–306
  reality, 226
  resistance, 230
  task of, 228
  therapeutic integration, 233

Transmission of alcoholism, 14, 37, 78, 182
Trauma, 2, 29, 31, 79, 91, 92, 95–97, 98
  acute, 96
  affect storm, 97
  chronic, 96
  defensive exclusion, 96, 98
  effects of, 96–97
  life context, 96, 98
  mounting vulnerability, 96
  strain, 96
Traumatic environment, 2, 5, 6, 29, 79, 88, 91, 92
Treatment, process of (see also recovery, process of), 263–288
Triadic therapeutic partnership, ix
Trust, 154, 173, 248

Unpredictability, 50–51, 54–55, 57, 163

Variables, viii, 5, 9, 10, 26, 67, 69, 76, 88, 89, 90, 91, 257
  assessment, 80
  family diagram, 80–85
  severity, 10, 76, 79, 89
  time of onset, viii, 10, 76, 89
  which parent alcoholic, 10, 76, 79
Visits home, 114, 244–247

Wegsheider, S., 18, 19, 36, 53, 59, 64, 105, 205
Winnicott, D.W., 165, 205, 234
  holding environment, 165, 205, 212
  transitional object, 234–235